Phyllis Hartnoll

The Theatre
A Concise History

Fourth edition

Revised and extended by Enoch Brater

294 illustrations, 46 in colour

Thames & Hudson world of art

FRONTISPIECE Eugene O'Neill's *The Hairy Ape*
directed by Peter Stein for Schaubühne in Berlin

First published in the United Kingdom in 1968 as as *A Concise
History of the Theatre* by Thames & Hudson Ltd, 181A High Holborn,
London WC1V 7QX
www.thamesandhudson.com

Fourth edition 2012

British Library Cataloguing-in-Publication Data
A catalogue record for this book is available from the British Library

ISBN 978-0-500-20409-2

Printed and bound in China through Asia Pacific Offset Ltd

Contents

CHAPTER ONE

The Greek and Roman Theatre

The origins of the theatre go back far into the past, to the religious rites of the earliest communities. Throughout the history of mankind there can be found traces of songs and dances in honour of a god, performed by priests and worshippers dressed in animal skins, and of a portrayal of his birth, death and resurrection. Even now similar ceremonies can be discovered among primitive peoples. But for the theatre as we understand it today three things are necessary: actors speaking or singing independently of the original unison chorus; an element of conflict conveyed in dialogue; and an audience emotionally involved in the action but not taking part in it. Without these essential elements there may be religious or social ceremonies, but not theatre. It has been argued that the earliest extant Egyptian texts for funerals and coronations, some dating as far back as 3000 BC, are really plays. But an order of service for a coronation in which the king is crowned by the high priest is not a playscript. The event is firmly rooted in reality; and according to Aristotle a play is 'an imitation of an action, and not the action itself'. Even the famous Passion Play of Abydos, which recounts the death, burial and resurrection of the god Osiris, is really a directive for a corporate religious exercise. Before we can talk of theatre we must wait for something a little further removed from reality.

It follows therefore that the first great theatrical age in the history of Western civilization is that of Greece in the fifth century BC. It was there that tragedies and comedies, some of which still exist, were first performed by actors and not by priests, in special buildings or precincts which, though hallowed, were not temples. The ruins of some of these still stand, and provide us with archaeological evidence. There is also some documentation of both performances and buildings, and the influence of both can be traced in the European and American theatre up to the present day.

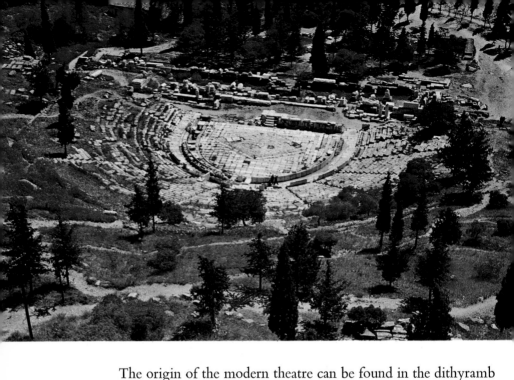

The origin of the modern theatre can be found in the dithyramb
(or unison hymn) sung round the altar of Dionysus, the wine-god
whose cult had spread to Greece from the Near East, by a chorus of
fifty men, five from each of the ten tribes of Attica. The process of
evolution from this simple act of worship to the full-scale Greek
tragedy as we find it in classical Athens must have been a slow one,
and it is not possible to pinpoint exactly the various stages. But in the
earliest plays we find again the fifty members of the chorus, and
Ill. 1 always in the centre of the stage is the altar of Dionysus. The lyric
form of the dithyramb accounts for the sung choruses in the play,
and its poetic content. Most important of all, the widening of the
scope of the dithyramb, which originally dealt only with the life and
worship of Dionysus, to include tales of demi-gods or heroes,
legendary ancestors of the Greeks and their associate peoples, is
reflected in the plays. The deeds of these heroes, good or bad, their
wars, feuds, marriages and adulteries, and the destinies of their
children, who so often suffered for the sins of their parents, are a
source of dramatic tension, and give rise to the essential element of

8

1 (*left*) The Theatre of Dionysus in Athens as it is today. During successive reconstructions it has lost the circular orchestra which survives at Epidaurus (*see Ill. 14*), but the base of the altar of Dionysus can still be seen in the centre of the semicircle

2 (*right*) Greek actor holding a tragic mask and wearing a short chiton and high boots (*cothurni*), from a vase-painting of the late fourth century B C. The mask is that of a strong, handsome hero in the prime of life, with fair hair and beard

conflict – between man and god, good and evil, child and parent, duty and inclination. This may lead to comprehension and reconciliation between the conflicting elements – since a Greek tragedy need not necessarily end unhappily – or to incomprehension and chaos. The plots of all Greek plays were already well known to the audience. They formed part of its religious and cultural heritage, for many of them dated from Homeric times. The interest for the spectator lay, therefore, not in the novelty of the story, but in seeing how the dramatist had chosen to deal with it, and, no doubt, in assessing the quality of the acting, and the work of the chorus, both in singing and dancing, about which unfortunately we know very little.

But Greek drama was not confined to tragedy. Even at its most reverent, the human spirit needs relaxation, and comedy crept in with the revels which took place in the villages when the harvest had been safely gathered in. They were enlivened by the antics of the satyrs – half men, half goats – who were the attendants of Dionysus. *Ill. 3* It was from their fooling, and from the rough horseplay of other village festivals, that the first true comedies of the theatre developed.

9

The dithyramb probably continued for some time to extend its scope without achieving any dramatic content. Something, some new element, was needed if worship was to become theatre. And since the natural human reaction to any form of communal activity, when the time comes to catalogue it, is to identify each phase with some recognizable person, it is not surprising that the honour of inaugurating the theatre should be ascribed to one man, Thespis, the leader of a dithyrambic chorus whose name has become synonymous with acting – the 'Thespian art' – just as 'robes of Thespis' means theatrical costume. Thespis is said to have travelled from Icaria, his birthplace, with his chorus, carrying his belongings on a cart whose *Ill. 3* floor and tailboard could form an improvised stage. In the course of his wanderings from one festival to another he eventually reached Athens, and there, as was only right and proper, he was the first to win a prize at the newly established dramatic festival, the City Dionysia.

The great innovation that Thespis made was to detach himself from the chorus and, in the person of the god or hero whose deeds were being celebrated, to engage in dialogue with it. He was thus the first actor as well as the first manager. The step he took was even more revolutionary than it seems to us, for he was the first unsanctified person who dared to assume the character of a god. This had hitherto been the prerogative of the priests or kings, who by virtue of their office were already partly deified. The way was now open for the independent development of the actor and of a building suited to his needs. The early theatres of Greece, like the one at Delphi, for *Ill. 4* instance, were always built near a temple. They continued to be the focal point of a corporate act of worship, but the interpretation of the plays acted in them was entrusted to men who were primarily actors, and only by tradition servants of Dionysus. The spectators too, among whom were some of the former actor-priests, changed. They were still conscious of the religious significance of the play, but they began to judge it as a work of art, and eventually as entertainment, and so became an audience rather than a congregation.

Of the three main festivals of Greece, the Rural Dionysia, held in mid-winter and laying stress on Dionysus as the god of fertility, gave

10

3 The Cart of Thespis, a reconstruction from an Attic vase-painting. Dionysus attended by satyrs is shown on his way to the City Dionysia

to the theatre the leader of the chorus, who was probably the head-man of the village, and also the word for tragedy (from *tragos*, a goat, either because a goat was sacrificed on the first day, or given as a prize on the last). The January festival, the Lenaea, was mainly devoted to merry-making, with elements which contributed to the later development of comedy (the word comes from *comos*, a revel or masquerade). But the festival for which all the extant Greek plays were written, as well as many others which are now lost, was the City Dionysia, celebrated at Athens in April, and attended not only by all able-bodied citizens, but also by official representatives of the federated and allied states. Arrangements began about ten months in advance. Poets who wished to compete had first to submit their works to the presiding officers, who chose three plays for perform-ance. To each poet was then assigned by lot a leading actor, and a patron, or *choregus*, a wealthy man who as part of his civic duties paid all the expenses of the production. The actors were paid by the state. The author of the play composed the music for it, and arranged the dances. Until specialists took over, he also trained the chorus. And until actors increased in numbers and importance he often played the chief part himself.

The first day of the City Dionysia was given over to the splendid procession which is depicted on the frieze of the Parthenon. The actors took part in it, wearing their stage clothes, but without masks. The next three days were devoted to tragedies, and the fourth to comedies, though later on the comedies were given in the evenings, after the tragedies, which began at dawn. Each writer of tragedy had to contribute three plays, either a trilogy on one theme, or three separate plays on a linked theme, and a satyr-play, about which little is known. It seems to have been a bawdy comic comment on the main theme of the tragedies, and was retained as a link with the early worship of Dionysus. Comic dramatists were limited to one play each. A prize was awarded to the best comedy and the best tragedy, to the best production (hence the importance of having a generous *choregus*) and later to the best tragic actor, who need not necessarily have appeared in the winning play.

Of the many poets who wrote for the City Dionysia, and whose names and play-titles we know from various catalogues compiled in ancient times, the earliest and perhaps the best was Aeschylus. Born in about 525 BC, he was known in his lifetime as a soldier and a citizen as well as a poet. He fought at Marathon and Salamis, and died in 456 BC, while on a visit to Syracuse. He is believed to have written about eighty or ninety plays, of which we have seven complete texts and numerous fragments. His *Oresteia* is the only example of a dramatic trilogy which has survived. In his plays we can follow the development of the Greek theatre. In the earliest the chorus still numbers fifty, as in the dithyramb, and there is only one

Ills. 5, 6

4 (*left*) The Theatre and Temple of Apollo at Delphi, fourth century BC

5 (*below*) Clytemnestra killing Cassandra, from a vase-painting of *c.* 430 BC. This episode from Aeschylus' *Oresteia* took place off-stage. The costumes probably depict those worn on-stage, both parts being played by men

actor. Later the chorus is reduced to twelve, and a second actor is introduced, followed eventually by a third. All Aeschylus' plays are powerful, majestic, and written in superb verse. After his death they were often revived, though normally only new plays were given at the festival, and they are still well-known and often acted in translation, particularly the first part of the *Oresteia*, which deals with the murder of Agamemnon by his wife Clytemnestra.

The next well-known dramatist of Athens was Sophocles, who was younger than Aeschylus and of a very different temperament. His most productive period of playwriting coincided with the finest phase of Athenian history, under Pericles. He too wrote about ninety plays, of which seven survive, and won eighteen prizes, always the first or second, never the third. His last play, *Oedipus at Colonus*, a sequel to the better known *Oedipus the King*, which has often been *Ill. 262* revived in the modern theatre, was written at the end of his long life – he was ninety when he died – and produced posthumously. Sophocles, who was of a serene and well-balanced disposition, handsome, successful and highly esteemed by his contemporaries, was a less powerful writer than Aeschylus, whose themes were cosmic, but more humane, more closely concerned with the complexities of human relationships as opposed to those of gods and men. His plots are more complex, his characterization, as in his *Antigone* and *Electra*, more subtle, his lyrics more flexible and harmonious. Greek tragedy, in his plays, is moving away from the simplicity and severity of its origins, and the chorus, which he increased from twelve to fifteen, probably for some technical reason connected with the pattern of the choral dances, is less closely integrated into the action.

The innovations of Sophocles were continued by his younger contemporary Euripides, the last great writer of Greek tragedy. Born in about 484 BC, he died in 406, the same year as Sophocles. He was a man of good family, something of a recluse, and more of an individualist than either of his predecessors. Among his plays, of which eighteen survive out of a possible ninety-two, is the *Cyclops*, the only complete satyr-play which we now have. Sceptical, modern in outlook, and as he got older, increasingly outspoken, Euripides was evidently less popular in his own day than Aeschylus and

14

6 Apollo protecting Orestes from the Furies, a scene from Aeschylus' *Oresteia*, shown in a vase-painting of *c.* 370

Sophocles, winning a prize only five times. His plays were more easily understood and appreciated by later generations, which may account for the number that have survived, and they are still popular today. They are unusually realistic, no longer pure tragedies, but tragi-comedies, even melodramas. Several of them are studies of abnormal states of mind, and he was interested in problems of feminine psychology. Among his innovations was the use of the prologue, in the modern sense of the word, to summarize the situation at the opening of the play. He also accelerated the process by which the chorus became less and less important. In some of his plays - the *Medea*, for instance, and the *Hippolytus* - which deal with the emotions of individuals rather than the great public events debated in earlier tragedies, he must have found the chorus an encumbrance, and his successors tended to dispense with it altogether, using a vestigial group of singers and dancers to break up the action with independent interludes.

15

While tragedy was developing in the hands of these three dramatists, the various forms of comedy fused to produce the plays of
Aristophanes, who was born in 448 BC and died in 380. He is the
only comic dramatist of Athens of whom we have complete plays;
of others we have only fragments. But, like Shakespeare, he seems to
embody in himself half a dozen writers. Much of his comedy is
ephemeral and closely related to the politics and social customs of his
own day. The best of it defies translation. Yet so strong is the
tradition of his genius that his name is used as a label for bawdy,
topical and sophisticated comedy in all countries. We have eleven of
the forty plays which he is known to have written, and many of
them take their titles from the disguises assumed by the chorus –
Ill. 7 *Knights, Wasps, Birds, Clouds, Frogs*. And it is mainly through the
chorus that the author's satire is conveyed. The basic idea in each play
is comic in itself, and is reinforced by a series of loosely-connected
incidents which give full scope to the inventiveness of both author
and actor, for here, as always in comedy, the actor contributed much
to the final effect. No modern writer could hope to get away with
the invective, social satire, personal criticism, buffoonery and
obscenity of the bulk of Aristophanes' work. In translation the wit
and savagery tend to evaporate. A modern audience knows too little
about the background to be able to appreciate the topical allusions.
All that can be done is to stress the universal as opposed to the contemporary aspects of the play, perhaps with discreet modernization
of some incidents. In this way most of the plays have been revived,
notably the *Birds* and the *Frogs* in modern Greek by the Greek Art
Theatre under Karolos Koun.

The actors in Greek tragedy, whose costumes we know mainly
from Greek vase-paintings of theatrical scenes, wore elaborate
Ills. 5, 6 robes, often brightly coloured and heavily embroidered, and high
Ill. 2 boots (*cothurni*) in imitation of their god, Dionysus. Later their robes
Ill. 23 were padded and their height increased by a head-dress (*onkos*) and
by thick soles under the boots. This, in the vast open-air theatres of
the time, gave them an impressive dignity suitable to the characters
they portrayed and enhanced their stage presence. The most important feature of their costume was the mask, said to have been intro-

16

duced by Thespis. In light wood, cork or linen, this enabled the three *Ills. 2, 11, 23*
actors in a tragedy to play several parts each, and also, in a theatre
staffed entirely by men, to impersonate women. Each mask – more
than thirty types are known to have existed – indicated not only the
age, standing and sex of the character, but the dominant emotion –
fear, rage, hate, despair. The actor, denied the use of facial expression
and limited by his costume to broad sweeping gestures, was forced
to rely on the range and expressiveness of his voice for most of his
effects. Even after the reforms of Euripides – who was criticized by

7 Actors dressed as birds, from a vase-painting of *c.* 500 BC. Although earlier than
Aristophanes' comedy, this scene may indicate how the chorus in his *Birds* was
dressed. The costume perpetuates the traditional use of animal disguises in early
religious ceremonies

8 (*left*) Hellenistic statuette of a comic actor wearing a mask, from Tralles in Turkey

9 (*above*) Archaic Punic comic mask from Tunis

10 (*right*) Hellenistic comic mask from Athens

11 (*far right*) A marble replica of the mask of a tragic heroine. This is a late Roman example of the 'fair, long-haired, tragic heroine' but is probably modelled on earlier Greek masks

Aristophanes in one of his comedies for dressing his actors 'in rags' – the Greek tragic actor remained a static, godlike creature, speaking and singing in harmony with specially composed music, all of which is lost, and sinking his individuality in the character he portrayed. The chorus, who needed more freedom of movement, wore the dress of the people they represented, and light masks.

The costume of the comic actor was, as might be expected, less hampering, since he needed to be something of an acrobat. He usually wore soft slippers (*socci*), flesh-coloured tights, a short tunic, *Ills. 12, 13* grotesquely padded, and in the comedies of the time of Aristophanes, *Ill. 10* a large red leather phallus. Masks were exaggerated for comic effect. The attendants of Dionysus in the satyr-play wore short furry breeches to which were attached a tail and a phallus.

18

12–13 (*right*) Actors in Old Comedy, statuettes of the mid-fourth century BC. On▶ the left, a slave who is pretending to be deaf, or who has just received a box on the ear; right, two drunken slaves or revellers, wearing tights, padded jackets and the phallus

Of the theatres in which the Greek plays were first performed little survives, but it is possible to reconstruct the essential details, either from later buildings, or from the architectural evidence of the Theatre of Dionysus in Athens, which has several times been *Ill. 1* remodelled. The heart of the theatre was the original dancing-place, the flat circular space with the altar of Dionysus in the centre which was used by the chorus. This orchestra, as it was called, is admirably *Ill. 14* preserved in the theatre at Epidaurus, which is still used for an annual summer dramatic festival. The musicians probably sat or

14 A modern performance in the restored theatre at Epidaurus, showing its steep auditorium and well-preserved orchestra

stood on the altar steps. In a horseshoe shape round the orchestra, on rising ground, sat the audience, first on the bare hill-side, later on wooden benches, later still on stone or marble seats. In the centre of the front row were the elaborate stone seats reserved for the priest of Dionysus, to whom the god himself appeals for help in Aristophanes' *Frogs*, and other high officials and state visitors. Entrance was at first free. Later a small charge was made. Poor citizens were then given the necessary entrance money, since attendance at the City Dionysia was practically compulsory.

Behind the orchestra there was, probably from very early times, a stage building reminiscent of the front of the original temple. It served the practical purpose of providing the actors with a background and a sounding-board, and of concealing the dressing-rooms, the stage machinery and such properties as might be needed – the red carpet in the *Agamemnon*, the head of Pentheus in the *Bacchae*, Hector's shield in the *Trojan Women*. It was pierced by a large central double door with a smaller door on each side, by which the actors came and went. The chorus entered along two passages between the stage building and the auditorium which could also be used by the audience as it assembled. The most important part of the stage machinery was the crane (*machine*) by which the god could descend from heaven to sort out the complications of the plot (whence the expression *deus ex machina*), but there was also a wheeled platform on which a pre-arranged tableau could be shown, and a machine for imitating thunder. There was no scenery in the modern sense of the word, but the stage wall provided an increasingly elaborate architectural background, and on each side of the stage were the *periaktoi*. These are believed to have been triangular prisms which could be rotated to indicate symbolically a change of scene by means of a painted tree, a column, or waves.

It seems reasonable to suppose, in view of the size of the theatres, that there was, in front of the stage building and behind the orchestra, a raised platform for the actors, to make them easier to see, and to single them out from the chorus. Certainly in later times there was *Ill. 1* quite a high stage, with a marble frieze below and a short flight of steps up from the orchestra.

By the time the great stone buildings which we think of as typically Greek were in use, the control of the theatre had passed from the dramatists to the actors, as happened frequently in later theatre history, and the great days of Greek drama were over. Comedy was *Ill. 15* paramount, but the only writer of note was Menander, who was born about 342 BC and died in 292. Only five of his plays have survived, and these are incomplete, but he had an immense reputation in antiquity, and enough fragments of his work remain to enable us to assess the main features of his 'New Comedy', as it was called, to

15 Menander in his studio with New Comedy masks, from a relief now in Rome. The masks are those of three of Menander's chief characters: a young man, a courtesan and an angry father. The girl on the right, who is perhaps holding another mask, may be the Muse of Comedy, or Menander's mistress, Glykera

16 A scene from a Roman comedy, before AD 79, from a Pompeiian wall-painting. It appears to depict a jeering slave who has surprised a pair of lovers

17 The Roman theatre at Sabratha, the largest in North Africa. Built about AD 200, this has the typical Roman semicircular orchestra, raised stage and elaborate three-storey *frons scaenae*

distinguish it from the Old Comedy of Aristophanes. It is markedly different, being pleasantly humorous, politically inoffensive, dealing superficially with comic situations of contemporary urban life, and hardly satiric at all, though still bawdy. Its fabricated plots tell of family matters, missing children, delayed marriages, mislaid treasure, in all of which the wily and astute slave plays a leading part. It is, in fact, a romantic comedy of manners which has lost all traces of its religious origins, and in which the chorus no longer has a place.

Ills. 18, 19

It was this type of Greek comedy, played in the vast Hellenistic theatres with their high stages and elaborate scene-buildings, which the Romans came into contact with as they extended their empire southwards into Greece. Easily understood and assimilated, it was imported into Italy, where it underwent some significant changes, and gave rise to the works of the two main writers of Roman comedy

Ill. 16

18–19 (*right*) Actors in New Comedy, probably characters in plays based on, though not necessarily by, Menander. The statuette on the left represents a potter or drinker, the one on the right a money-lender or dealer, or a thieving slave

20 A scene from Terence's *Adelphi*, in a later copy of a fourth- or fifth-century original. It shows Aeschinus and his brother Ctesipho confronted by the slave-dealer Sannio (led by their slave Syrus) from whom they have stolen a girl Ctesipho loves

25

(*fabula palliata*), Plautus and Terence. From it they took their plots and many of the stock characters, the irascible old men, the young profligates, the officious slaves, who make up the *dramatis personae* of their plays.

Plautus, of whose plays twenty survive, was primarily a translator and adaptor, basing his comedies on Greek originals now lost, but transferring the action to Rome and introducing recognizable details of Roman life and manners. His characters are sharply differentiated types. Among them can be found the braggart soldier (*miles gloriosus*), the miser, the parasite, the identical twins (whose adventures provided Shakespeare with the material for his *Comedy of Errors*), and always the browbeaten but resourceful slave whose actions provide the mainspring of most of the comedies. Plautus was an excellent craftsman, and his plays act better than they read. Terence, a freed slave from Africa, had more originality and was a better writer, since, owing to the kindness of an aristocratic patron, he was better educated. In his plays, of which six survive, there are *Ill. 20* fewer topical allusions and less buffoonery than in Plautus, and the application of his plots and dialogue is more universal. Perhaps for these reasons they became unpopular with audiences whose taste ran more to rope dancing, gladiators, and players of pantomine. But like Seneca, whose tragedies were written to be read and not for the stage, both Plautus and Terence were destined to have an enormous influence on the dramatists of a much later and far different age from their own.

While the written comedies of Plautus and Terence languished for lack of audiences, the short rustic farce of southern Italy, the *fabula atellana*, gained in popularity. Its appeal was based on the purely Roman humour of the clowns Maccus and Bucco, the foolish old man Pappus, and the hunchbacked slave Dossennus. Imported into Rome, it abandoned the use of dialect, and replaced its impromptu plots by formal written texts, of which a few titles survive. In the form in which it flourished under the dictatorship of Sulla it provided the only truly indigenous type of Roman drama. It evidently had very little literary value, and its appeal was immediate and ephemeral. But it deserves to be mentioned because of the curious parallels

26

21 A Roman mime play, before AD 79, showing the elaborately built-up stage with three entrances and an upper storey. On stage, a young hero, two warriors, and two slaves at the rear, one with a torch, the other with a wine-jar, evidently making preparations for a feast

it presents to the early manifestations of the later Italian popular drama, the *commedia dell'arte* (see Chapter 3).

The theatres of the Roman world were very different from those of Greece. They were built on flat ground, not on a hillside, with a vast surrounding wall of masonry, often elaborately decorated. *Ill. 17* With the disappearance of the chorus the last link with the dithyramb had been severed, and the orchestra was no longer needed. The focal point of the Roman theatre building was therefore the high stage, with tiers of benches in front and an elaborate stage wall, the *frons* *Ill. 21* *scaenae*, behind, often two storeys high. This stage had obvious affinities with the primitive temporary platforms – the *phlyakes* stages

27

22 On a *phlyakes* stage with supporting pillars and a side entrance (*see also Ill. 20*), a miser, Charinus, is trying to protect his treasure-chest from thieves. A vase-painting of the mid-fourth century B C. It was probably from temporary stages like this that the typical Roman stage (*see Ill. 17*) developed

– on which farcical mime-plays had been performed in southern Italy up to about 300 B C. One can see from the many extant vase-paintings of *phlyakes* performances how the high platform with *Ill. 22* panels or curtains developed, and also how grotesquely costumed and exaggeratedly comic the mime-players were in the travesties of Greek tragedy or in the plays based on the amorous adventures of Zeus and the Seven Labours of Hercules which made up much of their repertory.

By the first centuries of the new era Roman theatres had been built all over Italy, in Spain and France, and in the colonies of North Africa. Some of them are still in an excellent state of preservation and

28

23 Tragic actor with mask, showing the high wig (*onkos*), a wall-painting from Herculaneum, therefore before AD 79. Judging by his untidy hair, the seated actor has just taken off his tragic mask, which can be seen on the far right. The man at the back is probably his dresser

one can see how imposing they must have been when they were *Ill. 17* newly built. They had every embellishment, including a curtain which disappeared into a trough at the front of the stage. For the spectators there were awnings, fruit-sellers and, on hot days, showers of perfumed water. But they were beautiful empty shells, housing a dying art. The performances seen in them could not compare with those in the simple wooden buildings of early Greek times. Their staple fare was bawdy and obscene mimes and farces dealing mainly with drunkenness, greed, adultery and horseplay, or lavish acrobatic spectacles featuring scantily clad dancers. Actors, who in Greece had *Ill. 24* been citizens of good repute, were no longer esteemed. Roscius,

29

whose name has become synonymous with good acting, was perhaps an honourable exception, but even Cicero, who defended him in a lawsuit, thought of drama as something to be read. Theatrical performances, once the glory of Greece, and of some importance even in Republican Rome, became under the Empire little more than a vulgar form of popular entertainment. The time came when they were forbidden altogether. Forgetful of its religious origins and its glorious past, the theatre, as so often in its history, seemed to die of its own inanity, only to revive, more strongly than ever, in an unexpected direction.

◀ 24 (*left*) 'Bikini'-clad girls dancing in a Roman aquatic spectacle, from a mosaic of the late third century A D. 'Water-ballets' were very popular with Roman audiences, and for these, and for the production of *naumachiae* (mock sea-battles), the orchestra – even that of the Theatre of Dionysus in Athens (*see Ill. 1*) – was sealed round and flooded

25 Roman masks of a slave and a flute-player

The Medieval Theatre

Throughout the history of the theatre there is nowhere to be found a complete break in continuity of development. Between the decay of one form of theatrical presentation and the rise of another, however different, there must always have been some connection, some current flowing, however far underground, to convey the fundamentals of the art from one era to another. After the disappearance of classical drama came the age of the liturgical or church drama of western Europe. It was for a long time thought that there was no connection between the two; that one died with the invasion of the barbarians and that after a gap of several centuries the other was born. This is to underestimate both the force of the mimetic instinct in man and the stubbornness of inherited traditions. The Dark Ages were perhaps not so dark after all, theatrically speaking.

It is true that the later Roman theatre had no great dramatists. Plays were read and quoted from, but not acted. Even the famous nun of Gandersheim, Hroswitha, who in the tenth century took Terence as a model for her dramatized lives of saintly women, may not have written with performance in mind. But we know, on the evidence of manuscript illustrations, that certainly the plays of Terence, and probably those of other writers, were often read aloud *Ill. 28* while actors mimed the story. Meanwhile, the humbler entertainers of the classical world wandered across Europe, alone or in small *Ills. 26, 27* groups. Among them were acrobats, dancers, mimics, animal-trainers with bears or monkeys, jugglers, wrestlers, ballad-singers, story-tellers. Carrying with them the germ of the theatre, ready to take root again when conditions proved favourable, they lived as best they could and handed on the skills and technical tricks bequeathed to them by earlier generations of mime-players. Their existence is proved by the attacks made on them by the more austere Fathers of the Church, attacks which contributed not a little to the

32

26 Medieval entertainers in fools' dress, similar to that of the Roman fools and court jesters; an illuminated manuscript of *c.* 1340 from Flanders

decay of the classical tradition, since from earliest times Christians were strictly forbidden to attend theatrical performances or to appear in them. Yet in Byzantium, it seems, efforts were made to adapt the old pagan theatre to the needs of the new religion, and there are traces of religious plays being performed for the edification of the faithful, perhaps under the influence of the Empress Theodora, *Ill. 29* who was a mime-player before she married Justinian. Slight though the traces of this Christianized theatre are, they exist, and must be remembered when we consider the widespread development of the new liturgical drama. Even if we remain faithful to the conventional view of the latter's origins, we must not overlook the possibility of

27 A medieval glove-puppet booth, *c.* 1340, from the same manuscript

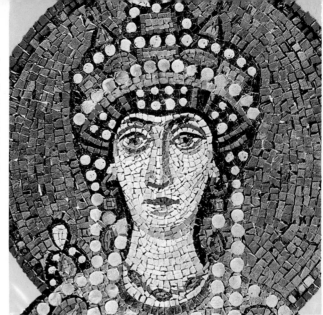

29 (*right*) A contemporary mosaic portrait of the sixth-century Byzantine Empress Theodora, formerly an actress, from San Vitale, Ravenna. Her husband Justinian published an edict permitting a nobleman to marry an actress provided she renounced her profession

the influence on it, even as late as the twelfth or thirteenth century, of the Byzantine theatre of the ninth or tenth.

It is in any case sufficiently ironic that the drama, so strictly forbidden to Christians – often by men who, like St Augustine, had enjoyed it before their conversion – should renew itself in the very heart of their cult. Just as Greek drama developed from the worship of Dionysus, so medieval liturgical drama developed from the Christian liturgy, particularly from the Easter celebrations, since the Resurrection, far more than the Nativity, was the focal point of the Christian year. The process was a slow one, and uneven. In some places the Church was more experimental, in others more conservative. But in general a clear pattern emerges, showing a definite progress from a simple act of faith in a ritual setting to a full-scale pageant on the life of Christ, acted in Latin and utilizing the whole of the church building. With the introduction of the vernacular, and the removal of the performance to an area outside the church, the way was open for the growth of a national theatre in each country. But as long as Latin remained the universal language of Christendom, the liturgical or ecclesiastical play continued to be the chief means of religious instruction for a largely illiterate population.

Ills. 30–2

35

◀ 28 (*left*) A play by Terence being read and mimed; below he is seen presenting his book to a patron; from a manuscript of *c.* 1400

Like the dithyramb, the lyrical portion of the Easter morning service provided the germ of future developments. There were, in early Christian festivals, sung portions known as *tropes*. The *trope* for

Ill. 31   Easter consisted of a short dialogue, together with some rudimentary stage directions. It is known from its opening words as the '*Quem quaeritis*' – 'Whom seek ye?'. This was sung by a priest in a white

Ill. 30   robe, representing the angel at the empty tomb, to three choirboys representing the three Marys who visited it on the first Easter morning – 'Whom seek ye in the sepulchre, O children of Christ?' To which they replied, 'Jesus of Nazareth the crucified, O child of Heaven.' 'He is not here, He has risen again as He foretold. Go,

36

◀ 30 (*far left*) The Three Marys at the Tomb, from a manuscript of *c.* 980. This illustrates the Easter *trope* shown in *Ill. 31*, and antedates the liturgical drama, being no doubt based on the scene during the Easter Mass when three choirboys approached the shrine or hollow side-altar from which the cross deposited there on Good Friday had been removed

31 (*left*) The Easter *trope* '*Quem quaeritis?*' ('Whom seek ye?'), from which European liturgical drama developed; from a Dublin Sarum Processional of the fourteenth century. The stage direction at the top of this extract instructs the Angel of the Resurrection to appear and speak to the women

32 (*right*) An alabaster plaque of the Resurrection from Nottingham, showing the Risen Christ and three soldiers asleep, a scene very probably inspired by a liturgical drama

announce that He is risen from the dead.' Then priest and choirboys, turning to the congregation, led them in a joyful Easter hymn.

It is impossible to chart the theatre's progress accurately, or to assign developments to any particular place. Liturgical plays are found all over Europe. The Mystery plays of England, the *mystères* of France, the *sacre rappresentazioni* of Italy, the *autos sacramentales* of Spain, the *Geistspiele* of the German-speaking lands, as well as the scattered examples from central and eastern Europe, all have in common their theme and the assumption of devotion and belief in their audiences. And just as the dithyramb was expanded to include stories of gods and heroes, so the simple scene of the three Marys at the

37

34 The Annunciation, the Nativity and the Resurrection, from Wakefield, York-shire. Wakefield is known to have had a long tradition of liturgical acting, and it is reasonable to suppose that these scenes approximate to what was seen on-stage

◄ 33 A French open-air performance of a religious drama, *Le Martyre de S. Apolline*, *c.* 1460, from a miniature by Jehan Fouquet. It shows a raised, fixed stage with simultaneous décor of six 'houses'. A ladder connects Heaven with the *platea*, or playing-place, and Hell has two storeys, with the devils above and Hell-Mouth below. The man with a book and a wand is the producer

tomb was enlarged by the addition of earlier and later scenes taken from the Bible, working forward to the Resurrection and eventually to the Second Coming, and backward beyond the Crucifixion and the Trial of Jesus to the Nativity, and so to the prophets of the Old Testament who foretold His coming. From the great storehouse of literature represented by the Bible were taken also such dramatic stories as that of Noah's Ark, Jonah and the Whale, Daniel in the Lion's Den, Samson and Delilah, and many others. And when they had exhausted the Bible, writers turned to the stories of saints and martyrs. Some of these told of saints whose conversion had taken place while they were acting in obscene burlesques designed to ridicule the new religion, and these provide interesting information on the last days of the Roman theatre.

Ills. 32, 34

Ill. 42

Ill. 34

Ill. 33

The first liturgical plays were written for performance by priests and choirboys in a church. As more incidents were added, laymen were allowed to appear, though not as yet any women. More space was needed as the cast list grew longer and the actors took over areas formerly occupied by the congregation. The lay-out of the acting area, whether the play was being done in a small church or in a vast cathedral, was roughly the same. The altar with its crucifix was the central point. On its right (from the priest's point of view as he faced the congregation) was Heaven, on its left Hell. The prophets spoke their lines from the pulpit. On each side of the central nave were the sites needed for the scenes in the play. They might include

Ill. 36 Bethlehem, Nazareth, Herod's palace, the Temple at Jerusalem, with
Ill. 35 the money-changers, the house of Caiaphas and the palace of
Ill. 42 Pilate, the Mount of Olives, Gethsemane, Golgotha and the tomb of the Resurrection. These sites had many names – mansions, houses and booths were some of them. The space between was the unlocalized 'playing-place' (the *platea*) which was to persist for hundreds of years and to prove so useful to future dramatists like Shakespeare, since it could represent any place the writer chose to make it. The whole church thus provided a multiple setting in which all the scenes needed for a performance were in full view of the audience all the time.

It is not known how soon the rapidly developing new drama moved out of the church. One reason for its removal may have been overcrowding; another the license and bawdry that crept in. In some places it was ejected as soon as its original simplicity had been lost; in others it lingered on until the sixteenth century. The twelfth-century Anglo-Norman play *Adam*, one of the earliest to include speeches in the vernacular, was certainly set out of doors, with the church doors forming a background through which God and the chief actors came and went, while the devils ran about in front of the raised platform. In Spain, on the other hand, the first reference to a religious play which was acted in a nobleman's hall and not in a church dates from the mid-fifteenth century. Long before that time the religious play was fully developed. It was as cosmic as anything by Aeschylus, and as much a part of its audience's life. Scepticism had no doubt crept in, as it had done in Athens with Euripides. But by that time the simple restatement of a known truth had become a conscious and complex work of art.

There were two ways of presenting the innumerable small scenes which made up the play-cycles, of which four or five are known in England and many more on the Continent. The first method was static, the second perambulating. In the first the 'houses' were arranged in a semicircle, as in the play of St Apollonia, or in a straight line, as at the Valenciennes play, with the audience in front. *Ill. 33* *Ill. 36* There was also an early form of theatre-in-the-round, with the 'houses' grouped round a central space, and the audience on raised tiers all round. This method of production was evidently used in Cornwall, where the remains of similar amphitheatres can still be seen. In each case the action progressed from one 'house' to another as the script demanded. It will be seen from the settings of the St Apollonia and Valenciennes plays that Heaven is still on the actor's right and Hell on his left.

35 Christ driving out the money-changers from the Temple, a scene from a fifteenth-century Passion Play performed in St Stephen's Church, Vienna. This scene, with its opportunities for violence and horse-play, is found in several liturgical dramas

Nazareth

le Temple

Hierusalem

vne salle

36 (*above*) The setting for the Valenciennes Passion Play, 1547. Here the 'houses' are more numerous than in the *S. Apolline* (*Ill. 33*) and are arranged in a straight line. In addition to Hell-Mouth there is a torture-chamber and a lake for St Peter

Within the image: Le limbe des peres · Lenfer · La porte doree · Maison des euesques · La mer

37 (*below*) The Triumph of Isabella, Brussels, 1615, including pageants of the Annunciation (centre middle-ground), followed by Diana and her Nymphs, and the Nativity (centre, left-hand page), with an angel perched on the roof

But sometimes – and this is particularly true of England – each scene in the production was mounted on a two-storey 'pageant' or cart, like those used in royal processions and triumphal entries, and a succession of such carts then paraded round the town. The actors repeated the play at each stopping-place in front of a group of spectators who remained where they were to await the next pageant. When plays were no longer acted in churches they were taken over by the secular authorities, and by the trade guilds. This arrangement of the different scenes on carts made possible a division of labour by which each guild assumed the responsibility for a particular scene, usually one connected with its work. Noah's Ark was staged by the shipwrights, the Tower of Babel by the carpenters, Jonah and the Whale by the fishmongers, and so on.

The religious content of the liturgical plays (or Bible-histories, as they are now called) need not be stressed. The Christian story is part of the heritage of Western civilization. One feature remains to be considered, however, and that is the comic element. It is important in the development of the theatre because it was the interpolation of

39 (*above*) Medieval devil's mask from the Tyrol, an animal head with curved horns and ass's ears

38 (*left*) Christ's Descent into Hell, showing the influence on the early sixteenth-century Flemish painter (school of Hieronymus Bosch) of the stage portrayal of Hell-Mouth (*see Ills. 33 and 36*)

comic scenes which did not appear in the original stories that led to the use of the vernacular. And this in its turn was the chief factor in the emergence of a national theatre in each separate country of Europe.

Greek tragedy, though it may have had touches of humour, more in the acting perhaps than in the text, reserved its buffoonery for the traditional satyr-play which followed. But almost from the beginning the medieval play, which was a tragedy with a happy ending, fused the two together. In the Easter play the first comic characters to be introduced were the merchants at whose shop the Marys stopped on their way to the tomb to buy the spices needed for the embalming of Christ's body. In the Christmas play it was easy to introduce comic characters among the shepherds. One of the best known is Mak the Sheepstealer, from the Chester cycle. Noah's wife became a shrew, the workmen at the Tower of Babel were given comic dialogue, Herod 'raged' amusingly when he heard of the Christ-Child's escape from the massacre of the Innocents. And always the greatest comic character was Satan himself, with his attendant devils, who after the   *Ills. 33, 36, 38*

45

scene of the Last Judgment gleefully shovelled the lost souls into Hell-Mouth. These devils were also allowed to intrude into many scenes where they had no business to be, simply in order to satisfy the popular demand for comic byplay. They wore masks as horrifying as any of the classical masks, and they probably provided interludes of acrobatic dancing and farcical miming between the scenes.

Ills. 39, 41

A link with the theatre's distant past can perhaps be found in these comic characters. The Byzantine theatre could have passed on to the actor-priests something of the traditions of classical acting, but it is surely from among the wandering entertainers that the players of comedy were drawn. Nor was that all. Someone must have had to direct the liturgical play. Amateurs with clear voices and good memories might do well enough in the serious parts, but as the plays grew more complex even they would feel the need for guidance. So would the crowds of soldiers and townsfolk. The devils too would have needed a variety of skills beyond the scope of most amateurs, and a restraining hand if their fooling was not to become tiresome. The medieval theatre has sometimes been called primitive, even simple. If there was simplicity, it must have been in the early days, when the congregation was linked in worship with the priestly actors. There was nothing simple about the play once it escaped from the church, or even before. To judge by the stage directions in the extant texts, the performances must have been extremely complicated, and they demanded a vast number of properties and working machinery. The raised wooden platform stage concealed traps, there were cranes by which God and his angels could descend from Heaven, and in the Mons play of 1501 the mechanism of Hell-Mouth, which opened to belch out clouds of smoke and closed to swallow up the damned, was so complicated that it took seventeen men to work it. The stage carpenters thought nothing of producing floods, fires, and earthquakes. Realistic executions were called for, with bloody wounds, severed heads and limbs. There was plenty of scope for livestock – rabbits, sheep, a ram for sacrifice, asses for Balaam and for the Flight into Egypt. Costumes were elaborate, and sometimes splendidly embroidered. Leather provided supple suits for the devils, breeches for the men, gloves for God. There was a profusion of

Ill. 40

40 The Three Wise Men, from a sixteenth-century Flemish Nativity Play, carrying incense, gold and myrrh. There is a slight suggestion of the Orient in their head-dresses and flowing robes

jewellery. There were gilded haloes, and for God and the archangels gilded masks. There was also the instrumental or vocal music, performed by gaily dressed groups. All of this combined to produce a moving, colourful spectacle set against painted 'houses' to which the deep red or black costumes of the devils lent sombre undertones. *Ill. 41* It is not surprising that the miniature depicting the play of Saint Apollonia shows on the stage a functionary who appears to be *Ill. 33* directing a rehearsal, or even a performance, with the help of a prompt-book and a long wand.

41 Two medieval devils, (*left*) Devil Bell and (*right*) Astaroth; pen drawings from a manuscript of 1539, Zurich. The elaborate costumes, with horns, tails and animal masks, can also be seen on the devils in *Ills. 33* and *36*

The Bible-history, and the later play of abstract vice and virtue, the Morality play, of which *Everyman* is the supreme example, made up the official theatre of the Middle Ages. Performances of a complete cycle of Biblical plays might take place under the auspices of the civic authorities every four, five or ten years, while selected scenes could be done more often. The subject-matter was Christian, but traces of the architectural background of the classical theatre can be found in the construction of the outdoor stage with its aligned 'houses', in the use of masks and machinery, and particularly in the imported comic and bawdy elements. There is also the less tangible but still perceptible feeling of theatrical traditions and experience, handed on, garbled perhaps but still valid, through generations of wandering players. The plays themselves were often extremely well written, exciting and dramatic. The audience was accustomed to pass rapidly through the whole gamut of emotions. In quick succession they experienced the wonder of Creation, the humour of Noah's wife, the curious predicament of Jonah, the tenderness of the Nativity, the savagery of the massacre of the Innocents, the tragedy of the

Ill. 34

42 Scenes from the Valenciennes Passion Play, 1547 (*see also Ill. 36*), from the Carrying of the Cross to the Deposition in the Tomb – the latter a sarcophagus which, unlike the one shown in *Ill. 30*, is large enough to contain the actor until the moment of the Resurrection

Crucifixion, the joy of the Resurrection, and the solemnity of the Ills. 32, 34, 42 Last Judgment. When a national drama finally developed, the audience in each country, conditioned by the liturgical play, was ready to receive whatever the dramatists might have to offer.

These old plays can still be successful in production. This has been proved by the revival of the York cycle in front of York Minster, of the Wakefield cycle at the Mermaid Theatre in London, of *The Play of Daniel* by an American company on tour, and by the Polish Resurrection play seen at the Aldwych in London in 1967. There is no unbroken tradition of liturgical play-production. The Bible-history died out in most European countries under the impact of the Renaissance and the Reformation. Even the famous Passion Play at Oberammergau is a late revival. Everything has to be rediscovered. But it often proves well worth discovering, and the plays reveal in production more links than one might have supposed with what went before and what is to come after.

While the vast liturgical plays were extending their range, and attracting to themselves whatever there was of theatrical talent in the

43 A scene from *Maître Pierre Pathelin*, c. 1465, the most famous of all medieval French farces. The rascally lawyer Pathelin, who has defrauded a shopkeeper, Guillaume, of a length of cloth, pretends to be dying, while his wife Guillemette parleys with Guillaume at the door

larger centres of population, there was also a continuous thread of secular drama. To this tradition belong the Mayday games and the Mumming plays in rural England, the *soties* or 'tomfooleries' which began with the French Feast of Fools, the farces of the student
Ill. 43 companies, of which the most famous is *Maître Pierre Pathelin*, the comic interludes of the German *Meistersinger*, the rough-and-tumble plays given in the open air on temporary stages in market-places in
Ill. 44 the Low Countries. In eastern Europe too, travelling bands of entertainers kept alive the tradition of the theatre, though it was not to come to fruition there for many hundreds of years. In western Europe the theatre moved more quickly from one phase to another.

44 A farce performed on a portable stage during a sixteenth-century country fair; detail from a painting by Pieter Balten. It shows a husband returning unexpectedly to find his wife hobnobbing with the village priest

CHAPTER THREE

The Theatre of the Italian Renaissance

The medieval religious play reached the peak of its development in the fourteenth century. The fifteenth witnessed its decline, which was hastened by the impact of the Renaissance. This great cultural upheaval began when Constantinople fell to the Turks in 1453, and subsequently the theatre, like all the other arts, underwent a metamorphosis due to its widespread repercussions. By the end of the fifteenth century the enthusiasm of wealthy Italian patrons of drama for plays based on classical models had seriously impaired the standing of the *sacre rappresentazioni*; in Paris the acting of religious plays was forbidden in 1548; in England the Reformation, combined with political expediency, brought them to an end by 1588; and though both the Reformation and the Counter-Reformation had their plays, they were used more for propaganda than for theatrical purposes. Jesuit drama, whose greatest period was yet to come, was scholastic rather than theatrical, and was quick to take advantage of the new classicism, mingling Hercules, tritons and nymphs with saints and martyrs. School drama was very largely educational, and still written in Latin. It was in Spain that the religious play had the longest life. After a late flowering it was forbidden there in 1765.

With the rediscovery of the works of classical drama came the realization that medieval stages, whether for indoor or outdoor performances, were not suitable for their production. Basing themselves on the architectural works of Vitruvius, written *c.* 16–13 BC and first published with illustrations in 1511, theatre architects applied principles of Roman theatre architecture to Italian buildings. With the physical aspects came also the recognition of classical form and restraint, two principles, alien to the sprawling and all-embracing Bible-history, which were to be codified and enforced with greater severity than in classical times. But this was inevitable, as was the fact that it was the late, ornate Hellenistic and Roman theatres that were used as models rather than the simple fifth-century Greek precincts, and that the tragic excesses of Euripides and Seneca, and the more easily accessible comedy of Menander, Plautus and Terence, took precedence over the works of Aeschylus and Aristophanes.

The influence of the new learning spread outwards from Italy in a series of shock-waves, reaching the further shores of western Europe after a time-lag which in some ways lessened the force of the impact and allowed a more thorough assimilation with native culture. Although to Italy must always go the glory of having initiated the Renaissance world, it is sad to have to record that the serious theatre was the least important part of it. Yet two important aspects of theatre – as apart from drama – must be credited to the Italian genius. The first is the form of the new theatre building, with its proscenium arch, and the second is the development of painted scenery. Both these aspects of the theatre are connected with the amazing contemporary development all over Italy in all the plastic and pictorial arts.

Although a careful study of the theatres built under the influence of Vitruvius shows how false in many ways was the Renaissance conception of classical theatre, we must nevertheless take as our point of departure what the new practitioners in theatre building actually designed, because it is from that that our later theatres developed. The key documents in this appraisal are the pictures of *Ills. 45–9* stages in editions of Terence published in 1493 and 1497. One shows a group of scholarly male spectators, possibly a university audience, facing a raised platform between classical pillars with an architectural *Ill. 45* background. Others show a permanent pillared set with actors on *Ill. 47* the platform stage. The four divisions of the background may correspond to the classical stage wall pierced with doors, or to the *frons scaenae* of the Romans, but they also have interesting affinities with the medieval stage, for each doorway represents a 'house' with a name above it. The use of Latin for these superscriptions again indicates an educated and not a popular audience. When we compare *Ills. 33, 36* these two stages with those of the St Apollonia or Valenciennes plays, which may in their turn have undergone some slight influence from the Humanist theatre, what is striking is not so much a radical departure from medieval practice as the imposition of order and

52

5–9 Terence on the Renaissance stage

5 (*above*) An academic audience waits for a performance, entertained by a musician in front of the stage, labelled 'proscenium'

6 (*top right*) Calliopius, who appears as the reciter of a Terence play in *Ill. 28*, speaks the prologue to the *Heauton Timorumenos*

7 (*centre right*) A scene from the *Adelphi*

8 (*bottom right*) A scene from the *Eunuchus*

9 (*below*) A scene from the *Andria*. These three woodcuts are almost certainly based on actual performances

50 (*above*) Part of the stage and auditorium of the
Teatro Olimpico, Vicenza, 1580–4, designed
by Palladio and completed by Scamozzi. The
Olimpico, with a façade obviously based on the
frons scaenae of the Roman theatre (*see Ill. 17*)
is the final flowering of Renaissance academic
theatrical architecture

51 (*above right*) Part of the auditorium, seen
from the stage, of the Teatro Farnese, 1618–19,
designed by Aleotti. This theatre, with that of
Scamozzi at Sabbionetta, is a forerunner of
the later European opera-house. Its designer, or
perhaps his pupil Giacomo Torelli (*see Ill. 103*),
provided it with side-wings and backcloth in
place of the fixed archways of earlier theatres
(*see Ill. 50*)

52 (*right*) A design for a stage-set in diagonal
perspective by one of the Bibiena family
(probably Francisco, 1659–1739). It is typical of
the Bibienas' elaborate and grandiose projects

54

53-5 Three stage settings from Serlio's *Architettura*, 1545: *left to right*, the Comic Scene, the Tragic Scene, and the Satyric Scene. The influence of these three designs, particularly the Satyric Scene, dominated the European theatre for several hundred years, and adaptations of Serlio's trees and cottages formed the setting of innumerable melodramas (*see Ill. 171*)

restraint on the former 'houses' or booths. The forty individual localities of a Mystery cycle are reduced to four, exactly similar. *Ills. 48, 49* They are usually in a straight line, but could also be grouped into a *Ills. 46, 47* three-sided arrangement jutting out into the centre of the stage, or set up like a box at one side. There is evidence here of more flexibility than we find later on.

When we come to consider Palladio's well-known Teatro *Ill. 50* Olimpico in Vicenza, with its superb *frons scaenae*, we realize that it is a typical Renaissance theatre in an academic tradition. But so far from being, as was once thought, the starting-point of the modern theatre, it is now considered the final result of a dead-end development, and the future is seen to lie with the development of the Terence *Ill. 49* stage shown in the 1497 Venice edition of his plays – an open loggia with a small semicircular amphitheatre – by Scamozzi at Sabbionetta *Ill. 51* and Aleotti in the Teatro Farnese at Parma. It is from these that the horseshoe-shaped auditorium and proscenium-arch stage with its elaborate curtain, typical of later theatre buildings all over the world, were finally evolved. They initiated a style which is only now being ousted from its supremacy by open stages and theatre-in-the-round.

56

The mention of opera-houses reminds us that one outstanding result of the Italian revival in classical style was the great art of opera. A simple play with music, on a mythological or legendary subject, in which the words were paramount was, by the genius of Monteverdi, transmuted into a new art form in which music was all-important. The subject of opera, like that of ballet, is too vast to be dealt with here, though its absence leaves a gap in theatrical history. It would perhaps be more profitable therefore to consider that other adjunct of the opera-house, scenery. This also has its roots in Italy. From there it spread across western Europe until it became a tyranny from which zealous reformers strove to liberate the stage, not always successfully.

Serlio, author of a book on architecture of which the second part, dealing with the theatre, appeared in 1545, was the first scenic artist to publish his designs. His three perspective settings, intended for a theatre in the banqueting-hall of a noble or princely dwelling-house, provided a basic concept which was adhered to by all European scene-designers for the next four hundred years. The sets intended for comedy and tragedy show houses on each side of a street, painted on *Ills. 53, 54*

56–7 Seventeenth-century masque costumes: (*left*) a 'wild man' or 'monster' by Stefano della Bella; (*right*) a costume representing Prudence, by Henri Gissey

60 (*above*) A *commedia dell'arte* troupe at the Court of Henry of Navarre, c. 1578–90, by François Bunel the Younger. A masked *zanni* indicates the horns of cuckoldry above Pantalone's head

61 Pantalone, with Arlecchino and two servants, serenading Donna Lucia, c. 1580 ▶

58–9 Two seventeenth-century masque costumes by Lodovico Burnacini, probably for Harlequin though unlike the original character (*see Ills. 61, 65, 70*)

wings and a backcloth. The set for a satyr-play, about which the
Italians knew nothing more than that it was a rustic farce, was a
Ill. 55 country scene of trees with small cottages on each side of the stage.
These three sets form the basis of the work done for the great
Italian entertainments that led to the development of the proscenium
arch, which was originally a pierced wall dividing a room into acting
area and auditorium. They influenced the scenery of the English
masque, the Spanish Court theatre, Molière's theatre in Paris and
nineteenth-century melodrama. They are essentially theatrical, and
even when Serlio's symmetrical scene in perspective, which was
adopted by all his successors, including the Bibienas, was supple-
Ill. 52 mented by the new diagonal perspective perfected by the younger
members of the Bibiena family, Serlio's groupings of buildings and
trees still formed the basis of contrasted town and country scenes.

Of the plays and splendid entertainments given on the Renaissance
Ills. 56–9 stages little remains but the designs for scenery and costume. The
erudite inheritors of the classical tradition wrote with their pens
rather than their heart's blood, and the only ones worthy of mention,
even briefly, are Ariosto, whose comedies are based on Latin
originals, Aretino, less classical and nearer to everyday life, and three
authors remembered for one play each – the cardinal Bibbiena for
Calandria, the statesman Machiavelli for *Mandragola*, and the poet
Tasso for *Aminta*, the first flowering of pastoral comedy. And
perhaps to these may be added the ill-fated Giordano Bruno, whose
Il Candelaio was banned and had what was probably its first stage
performance in Italy in 1905, but whose philosophy, which led him
to be burnt at the stake, may have influenced Shakespeare when
he was writing *Hamlet*.

Even though we may regret the lack of great dramatists, we must
concede that for the beauty of her theatre architecture and her stage
scenery, as well as for the development of opera and ballet – the
latter arising from courtly entertainments in which guests and players
mingled in a final dance – Italy deserves her reputation as the cradle
of the modern theatre. But there was another and even more
important aspect of the Italian theatre which has not yet been touched
on, whose vitality and exuberance may have drained away from

other areas the energies of the theatrically minded, and that is the
commedia dell'arte.   Ill. 60
   This form of theatre, which appears parallel with the growth of
the serious academic theatre, depended primarily upon the actor and
not the playwright. Its dialogue, from a simple exchange between
two comedians to a full-scale play involving a main and a sub-plot
and a number of actors, was entirely improvised, though a skeleton
plot or scenario was provided to keep the players within bounds.
There were also long stock speeches which, once formulated,
written down and learned by heart, could be adapted to almost any
circumstance. But these were used mainly by the more serious
characters, the young lovers, and also perhaps by the old fathers, the
pedant lawyers and the braggart soldiers. The *zanni*, or comic
servants, whose antics made up the greater and most popular part of *Ills. 62, 65,*
the entertainment, had less to say, since much of their humour was *68, 69*
visual, consisting of variations on standard jokes, the *lazzi*, or slighter
comic touches, and the *burle*, longer acts often involving a practical
joke. Both *lazzi* and *burle* afforded the actor great scope for improvisation. By tradition the *zanni* could take the basic situation of the
play in performance as far from its prescribed path as they pleased,
provided they brought it back to a point where the scenario could be
picked up again. That called for a high degree of skill and a quick
wit. But all that we know of the *commedia dell'arte* shows that its
practitioners were unequalled in their profession, combining the
attributes of dancer, singer, acrobat, low comedian, mime and
pantomimist, together with incredible agility of mind and body. A
subtle command of gesture was also essential, as the comic actors
wore masks and so were denied the use of facial expression.   Ill. 66
   The practice of improvisation was no doubt helped by another
outstanding peculiarity of the *commedia dell'arte*. The company was
made up of actors who always played the same part. This was not
type-casting as we know it today, but the lifelong assumption of a
disguise with which the actor became so identified that he often lost
his own personality in the process, or rather, so merged his own
personality in that of the type he played as to create a distinct
personage. In many cases the actor abandoned his own name for that

62 (*left*) Coviello, who came from Calabria, with a Sicilian friend, playing the guitar and singing, by Bertelli, 1642. He was one of the older men, often the companion of Pantalone, though he sometimes figured as a *zanni* with Pulcinella, whom he somewhat resembled

63 (*right*) Pantalone, by Callot, 1618. He is easily recognizable as Shakespeare's 'lean and slippered pantaloon' in *As You Like It* (II. 7), and later became the foolish old man of the English harlequinade

64 (*far right*) Il Capitano, in Venetian glass from Murano, second half of the sixteenth century

of the character, and so made it even more completely his own. Each *commedia dell'arte* mask – the word is used for the person as well as the the thing – belonged to a clearly identifiable group, and it was almost unheard-of for an actor to pass from one group to another, except perhaps in the case of the young lover. If, in later life, he lost his figure or his looks, or developed some useful comic attribute – a paunch or a nutcracker profile – he might abandon his youthful heroics for slapstick and comedy.

The young lovers, who were not particularly interesting in themselves, provided the mainspring of the comedy by their efforts to meet and marry. The heroine usually had a maidservant or confidante called Rosetta or Colombina. Her father, husband, or guardian, who *Ill. 63* tried always to prevent her escape, was a Venetian called Pantalone. He is often depicted as an amorous old man, as Zeus was on the *phlyakes* stages. He and his elderly friend, a Bolognese lawyer (Il Dottore) named Graziano, had comic menservants and sometimes shrewish housekeepers. A character somewhat apart from these domestic groups was Il Capitano, a bragging, cowardly soldier, a reincarnation of the *miles gloriosus* of Plautus. He usually assigned to himself some high-sounding title, such as Spezzaferro, Spavento da Vall'Inferno or Matamoros. This last, meaning 'Death to the Moors', was perhaps the most appropriate, since from his earliest appearance, in 1520, Il Capitano seems to have been recognizably Spanish. Perhaps his grotesque appearance, with long crooked nose and enormous moustaches, and his treatment at the hands of the *zanni*, who mock him, trip him up, and prove his valour to be nothing but cowardice, may reflect the feelings of Renaissance Italians towards their hated Spanish tyrants.

Ills. 64, 99

63

Best known of all the stock types are the comic servants. Once the plot had been set in motion, it was their job to keep it going. They were the most numerous and most protean of the *commedia dell'arte* players, and included types from several districts of Italy. It was usual for at least two comic servants to appear in each scenario, one quick-witted, to help the intrigue along, the other a simpleton, to act as a foil to his fellow's wit. Among them were Arlecchino, Pulcinella, Pedrolino, Scapino, Mezzetino, Scaramuccia, and Brighella. These are all names which in modified forms crop up again later in the history of the theatre.

Ill. 65
Ill. 69

The origins of the *commedia dell'arte* have been hotly disputed. Efforts have been made to derive it directly from the Greek *phlyakes*, the Roman *atellanae*, or the Imperial mimes. There are similarities to all these in the bawdy, farcical playing and in the emphasis on stock types. Even the name *zanni* has been considered a corruption of the Latin *sannio*, the comic fool of the atellan farce. But the time-lapse is against direct descent from classical times. So is the fact that in the Renaissance theatre written plays appear to have come before the scenario-for-improvisation. In other words, the classical influence, which produced no plays of lasting value, may nevertheless have so worked on the popular mind as to give rise to a form of theatre which had its roots both in its own time and place and in that indestructible mimetic instinct in man, that aptitude of the born comedian for buffoonery, farcical comedy, and improvisation, which resulted in the rustic plays of Greece, of Rome and of Italy, and would even now give rise to similar plays in similar circumstances. All these manifestations of theatrical life resemble each other because they come fundamentally from the same source, and reflect one particular facet of the mind of man. The *commedia dell'arte* may be indebted to earlier forms of farce for some transmitted traditions. But lacking tangible evidence, it is impossible to say that there is direct influence of one form on another.

A good deal is known about the actors and scenarios of the *commedia dell'arte*, and also about the various companies, among them the Gelosi, the Confidenti, the Uniti, and the Fedeli. But the story of the actors' migrations from one company to another, and of the

Ill. 67

64

65 Arlequin saluting the audience – a characteristic pose – by Dolivar after Le Pautre, seventeenth century. This most famous character of the *commedia dell'arte*, who came from Bergamo, is here portrayed in the transitional stage between Arlecchino and the English Harlequin. He can be seen again in the background, dancing on the far left

continual touring which made up their life, is too complicated to be dealt with in a few lines. From the mid-sixteenth century to the mid-seventeenth troupes of Italian actors travelled all over Europe, in Italy, France and Germany, westward to Spain, eastward to Russia, and even as far north as England. They appeared in London several times in the late sixteenth century, and may have visited the city as early as 1547. Of all the shifting restless population of this colourful and fantastic world a few stand out as individuals. The most famous is

Ill. 67 perhaps Isabella Andreini, leading lady of the Gelosi, who for the first time made the stereotyped young girl in love (the *innamorata*) the outstanding character. But there were also famous Arlecchinos, Pantalones and Capitanos, whose real names are hidden behind those of their masks.

66 (*above*) Three *commedia dell'arte* masks, in leather, probably for *zanni*

67 (*left*) A *commedia dell'arte* troupe, *c.* 1580, probably that of the Gelosi, with Isabella Andreini as the *innamorata* confronting an angry Pantalone

There has probably never been so intensely theatrical an institution as the *commedia dell'arte* in its heyday. It owed everything to the actor, very little to drama or literature. It trained its own players, created its own conditions, travelled with its own costumes and properties, sometimes with portable stages like the one seen in Callot's engraving of the two *zanni*, Razullo and Cucurucu. A company could consist of as few as five players, or as many as twenty-five. The less gifted groups appeared in villages and small towns, the more famous ones in noblemen's halls and kings' palaces. The influence of the *commedia dell'arte* on the theatre of Europe is incalculable. Even when its characters alter out of all recognition, they can be traced back to their originals. From Arlecchino, Colombina and Pantalone come the Harlequin, Columbine and Pantaloon of the nineteenth-century English pantomine. From Pulcinella come the French Polichinelle, the English Punchinello and finally the puppet Punch with his English wife Judy. Pedrolino underwent an even stranger metamorphosis, for he became first the elegant Pierrot of Watteau, then the lovesick, solitary, mournful Pierrot of nineteenth-century Paris, and finally the jolly, gregarious Pierrot of English seaside troupes.

Ill. 68

Ill. 70

Many other characters from the *commedia dell'arte* are enshrined in the French classical theatre, for as they declined in favour in Italy they started a new career in Paris. French comedies abound in Scapins, Scaramouches, and Mezzetins. This part of their history belongs to France, as does their influence on Molière. Shakespeare too must

Ills. 151, 162

68 Razullo (with a guitar) and Cucurucu dancing in front of an open-air stage on which a play is being performed, an engraving by Callot, 1621. The stage probably gives a good idea of what the portable *commedia dell'arte* stages were like

Diese Figur kombt wie hier oben zusehe heraus, ü: nach deme sie auf ihre Manier in einen kreiß herumb getantzt, ü: nach sonderer krummer und huckender pas gemacht, endigt sich zu aller zu schauer vergnügen der Tantz.

69 Pulcinella dancing, with a smaller Pulcinella below, by Lambranzi, 1716. The stage is interesting as showing the four pairs of wings and backcloth (perhaps made up of narrow flats) which originated in the seventeenth century and are still in use today in opera- and ballet-houses. Pulcinella is the ancestor of the French Polichinelle and the English Punch

have seen the 'lean and slippered pantaloon', to describe him so accurately.

There is no space to speak of the influence of the Italian comedians on ballet, though the Peacock Theatre in the Tivoli Gardens in Copenhagen still bears witness to a long-lived tradition. Everywhere in the theatre there are traces of the *commedia dell'arte*. Even the antics of the Keystone Cops, and of Charlie Chaplin, have been attributed to the influence of the *lazzi* and *burle* of the *zanni*. But this may be merely further evidence of the inextinguishable *vis comica* in man's make-up, which has produced all these related forms of farce, and many others which remain uncatalogued. What is certain is that the influence of the *zanni* can be found in all the fools of European farce, whose first names remind us that *zanni* may be a corruption of Giovanni, for they are called John Posset, Jean Potage, *Ill. 135* Jan Bouschet, Hanswurst, Ivanovishka-Douratchok. But it is in their later romantic guise that the descendants of Arlecchino, Pedrolino and their motley companions have captured the imagination of the world. Forgetful of their bawdy, uninhibited early days, their rags transmuted into silken patches and white satin suits, they are no longer Italians or zanies, but the courtly inhabitants of an elegant world painted by such artists as Watteau, Fragonard or *Ill. 151* Lancret.

Inevitably the *commedia dell'arte* declined. The best of it was assimilated by generations of actors all over Europe, but by the end of the seventeenth century it was only a shadow of its former self. Goldoni tried to revive it by providing definitive texts for the actors while retaining the mechanics of their performance. His rival Gozzi, on the other hand, used its masks and methods for improvised comedies which mingled farce with fairy-tale. With him the *commedia dell'arte* had a last blaze of glory before disappearing for ever. Efforts have been made to revive it, but the spirit which animated it has been drawn off into other forms of theatre. Yet the fascination of this important theatrical manifestation remains, and in dealing with it we have been led chronologically far in advance of our time. It was a long-lived product of the Renaissance, to whose repercussions elsewhere we must now return.

70

70 An open-air performance of an Italian comedy, with Arlecchino bowing before ▶ the *innamorata*, Verona, 1772

71

CHAPTER FOUR

The Elizabethan Theatre

Italy, with the *commedia dell'arte*, gave modern Europe its first fully professional actors in organized companies, and also, through the work of Renaissance architects, prepared the way for the development of the indoor theatre with painted scenery and proscenium arch. England was to have the privilege of producing in Shakespeare the first modern playwright fit to stand comparison with the masters of Greek drama. He began writing while the Elizabethan theatre was still in its infancy, but the influences which moulded him, and shaped his work, are to be found as much in his own country as on the Continent.

While the sixteenth-century holiday-crowds were still enjoying performances of Bible-histories on pageant-wagons, and of Morality plays like *Hickscorner*, with its lusty personification of Freewill and Imagination, or *Nice Wanton*, on the theme of 'spare the rod and spoil the child', the first English Renaissance comedy, *Ralph Roister Doister*, was being written by a schoolmaster, Nicholas Udall, for performance by his pupils. A decade later, in 1562, a Renaissance tragedy, *Gorboduc*, based on Seneca, was prepared by two scholars of the Inner Temple, Thomas Norton and Thomas Sackville, for performance by their fellow-students in the presence of Queen Elizabeth I. These were amateur productions for an educated audience. More acceptable to a popular audience were the Interludes, one-act comedies which show a mingling of native farce with classical allusions. For instance, in *The Play of the Weather*, by John Heywood, a number of people are shown praying to Jove for weather suitable to their own needs, which conflict with those of the other characters. Heywood's Interludes, and those of Rastell and Redford, were acted by groups of players maintained as part of their household by rich men and the nobility, and were probably *Ill. 71* given in a setting of houses on each side of a street which owed

72

something to Renaissance Italy. It was from these groups of Interlude players that the first professional English actors finally emerged. They added to their repertory such popular tragi-comedies as Preston's *Cambyses* and the long chronicle-plays which used the episodic method of the Bible-history for stories from English history, and acted them, and many others now lost, on platform stages set up in innyards, which formed excellent temporary theatres. But before the theatre could develop freely, England, like Italy, needed theatre buildings, with conditions of stability in which actor and dramatist alike could relax and feel at home.

The first permanent theatre in London was built, appropriately enough, by a carpenter, James Burbage, who was also a part-time *Ill. 74* actor, obviously a man born for the theatre. Of his two sons, the younger, Richard, was the first leading English actor, the creator of *Ill. 73* Hamlet, Lear, Othello, and Richard III, while the elder, Cuthbert, acted as his brother's manager.

The building which the elder Burbage erected in 1576 was known simply as 'The Theatre'. It was an enclosed structure of wood, which, *Ill. 74* because of opposition from the Lord Mayor of London to the very

71 A scene from the *Interlude of the Four Cardinal Virtues*, in a woodcut of *c.* 1547

73

idea of a theatre, was built outside the city boundary, in Finsbury Fields. Very little is known about it, or about the other Elizabethan theatres which sprang up as soon as Burbage's venture was seen to be successful. They were, roughly in chronological order, the Curtain, *Ills. 75, 78* the Rose, the Swan, the Globe, the Fortune, and the Hope. Of these the Rose, the Fortune, and the Hope belonged to Philip Henslowe, a shrewd business man who leased his theatres to various companies, and also paid the bills for playscripts, costumes and properties while they were in occupation. In return he received a large share of the daily takings. His stepdaughter Joan married the other outstanding *Ill. 72* actor of the period, Richard Burbage's only rival, Edward Alleyn, who inherited his father-in-law's property and papers. Among the latter was his diary, an invaluable source of information on the theatre of his time. This is now in Dulwich College, which was founded by Alleyn.

The most famous Elizabethan theatre, round which controversy constantly rages, is the Globe, built by James Burbage's sons on London's South Bank in 1599 with timber from 'The Theatre'. It was here that most of Shakespeare's plays were produced, and it was after a performance of his *Henry VIII* in 1612 that the theatre was destroyed by fire. It was rebuilt the following year and remained in *Ill. 78* use until 1644, when it was demolished.

None of the Elizabethan theatres survived, and all the information about them comes from a few builder's specifications, some scattered descriptions in letters and essays, and a very few illustrations, most of them of a later date. The only one which is known to be con-temporary is a copy of a drawing of the Swan Theatre, made by a *Ill. 75* Dutchman, Johannes de Witt, during a visit to London in about 1596. It is not very clear, but it does seem to show the main features of an Elizabethan unroofed public playhouse. These were the raised platform-stage, sometimes railed, with an open space for standing spectators on three sides, and round that two or three galleries furnished with benches or stools. This roughly represents the set-up of the innyard. Behind the platform-stage was a wall, with doors or curtained doorways which gave access backstage. This wall supported a gallery for musicians or actors, surmounted by a tower housing

72–3 The two best-known Elizabethan actors, (*left*) Edward Alleyn, 1566–1626, (*right*) Richard Burbage, *c.* 1567–1619, from portraits in the Dulwich College Picture Gallery

machinery. From this tower a trumpet-call announced the opening of the play, and a flag was flown during the performance, which usually took place in the early afternoon. Over the stage itself was a canopy, known as the 'heavens'. It was supported on columns, and the ceiling was painted blue, with golden stars. If the auditorium shows the influence of the innyard, the stage and its surroundings seem to owe more to the architectural background of the Continental theatre, with a marked classical derivation. There is also some *Ill. 76* suggestion of the triumphal arches and temporary monuments set *Ill. 77* up at fixed points in the city for royal visits and processions of all kinds. The only reminders of the Bible-history stage are the unlocalized *platea* or platform-stage (which in the absence of changeable scenery could represent any place needed for the action of the play), the trapdoors in the stage, and the machinery in the tower.

75

74 (*above left*) A reconstruction of James Burbage's theatre, known as 'The Theatre', built in 1576

75 (*above centre*) A copy of Johannes de Witt's drawing of the Swan Theatre of *c.* 1596 – the only contemporary picture of an Elizabethan theatre interior in existence

76–7 (*bottom left and centre*) The design of Continental ceremonial stages such as this Rederijkers stage, Antwerp, 1561, influenced British triumphal arches like those for James I's Coronation in 1603 (*centre*, the arch near the Royal Exchange, in Cornhill), and by inference, the London stages which so much resembled them (cf. *Ill. 74*)

78 (*above*) The exterior of the second Globe Theatre, 1616

79 (*left*) The platform stage used for William Alabaster's *Roxana*, shown in a woodcut of 1632

One of the features of the Elizabethan theatre which has caused acute controversy is the so-called 'inner stage'. This is believed to have been either a room built out behind the central opening, or part of the corridor running behind the stage wall. In either case it could be revealed by the drawing of a curtain. But some theatre historians think there never was such an inner stage. There is no sign *Ill. 75* of it in de Witt's drawing, which shows only two side doors. There is, however, no reason to suppose that all Elizabethan theatre buildings were exactly alike. And if the inner stage did not exist something like it must have been erected at the back of the main stage for such scenes as that in *The Tempest*, where Miranda and Ferdinand are 'discovered' playing chess. As we shall see later, the evidence of the *Ill. 92* Spanish stage speaks strongly in favour of the inner stage, as does perhaps the Terence-stage also.

In his description of the Swan, de Witt said the interior had a flint-and-mortar wall between wooden columns 'painted in exact imitation of marble'. The Elizabethans were excellent architects and great lovers of decorative work, and there is no reason to suppose that their theatres were less lavish than their other public buildings. The marble pillars may have been part of a scheme of gold and red and blue to which the bright costumes of the actors, the stage hangings, and the banners and pageantry of the royal or military processions in the play all added their quota of gaiety. The greater part of the actors' wardrobes was made up of discarded robes given to them by wealthy patrons. These would have seemed very splendid to the audience, which included persons from every walk of life, men and women, young and old. They would also have been contemporary in style, whatever the period of the play, but with some conventional details for certain characters, such as a breastplate and kilt for a Roman soldier, a turban for a Turk, long robes for other Orientals, and a gaberdine for a Jew. The only drawing known of Elizabethan actors *Ill. 81* in stage costume, showing a group from *Titus Andronicus* in 1595, is a good example of the mixing of contemporary and conventional dress.

The companies which appeared in the Elizabethan theatres were all under the patronage of some noble person, since masterless men,

78

even actors, were still classed officially as 'rogues and vagabonds'. Burbage and Shakespeare belonged to the Lord Chamberlain's Men, Alleyn to the Admiral's. But the rules governing each company varied, particularly as the actors gained in confidence and stability. In Shakespeare's company the actors owned their own playhouse, prompt-books, costumes and properties, and each held shares in the undertaking which entitled him to a fixed part of the profits. This was probably something like the way in which the *commedia dell'arte* companies had been organized, except that they had no permanent theatre buildings. Alleyn's company, however, paid rent to Henslowe and received salaries from him.

As in Greece, there were no women on the Elizabethan stage. Boys, specially selected for their slight, graceful build and light

81 (*above*) Characters in *Titus Andronicus*, from a manuscript by Henry Peachum, 1595, with Aaron as a blackamoor

82 (*right*) Richard Tarleton, *c.* 1590. He was described as short, thick-set, slightly hump-backed, with a squint and a comically flattened nose

83 (*far right*) William Kempe dancing, woodcut of 1600 from his own account of his morris-dance from London to Norwich, undertaken for a wager. Kempe succeeded Tarleton in the affections of the public

voices, were apprenticed to older actors and trained to play such parts as Juliet, Rosalind, Viola and Portia. The comedians of the troupe played the older women like Juliet's Nurse or Mistress Quickly. As in Italy, all the actors had to be dancers and singers, sometimes instrumentalists, for music played a large part in the plays, and in the jigs which followed them. These jigs, which were dances with sung dialogue, were immensely popular with Elizabethan audiences, and the actor William Kempe was particularly admired for his performances in them. The clowns and fools who appear in so many Elizabethan plays may, like the *zanni* of the *commedia dell'arte*, had been in the habit of extemporizing, and it is thought that Shakespeare, when he made Hamlet say to the players, 'Let those that play your fools speak no more than is set down for them', had in mind the comedian Richard Tarleton, who was famous for his improvisations. It is even possible that some of the more obscure jokes in Shakespeare's plays may be the result of impromptu remarks which became incorporated into the written script. As plays were valuable properties, they were kept in manuscript as long as possible and jealously guarded by the company which owned them. Even Shakespeare's plays were not gathered together for publication until after his death. Many by lesser authors have completely disappeared, and are known only by their titles.

Ill. 83

Ill. 82·

It was indeed fortunate that Shakespeare's plays were printed, for none of his manuscripts survived, and in spite of his world-wide *Ill. 80* reputation little is known about him. Born perhaps in Stratford-upon-Avon, in one of the midland counties of England, Warwickshire, he married there at eighteen, but soon after went to London, where he became first an actor and then a playwright and a shareholder in the Globe Theatre. Having prospered in his theatrical affairs, he bought himself a pleasant house in Stratford and retired there to die in 1616, leaving two daughters married to Stratford citizens. His only son died at the age of eleven. That is practically all we know for certain about Shakespeare's life. The rest must be looked for in his plays, which are amazingly varied in style and scope, ranging from tragedy to comedy with excursions into history, tragi-comedy, romantic tragedy, and pastoral. Very often the plays escape classification, for Shakespeare was a universal genius, and in his work comedy and tragedy are as closely interwoven as they are in the lives of all human beings. Like quicksilver, Shakespeare escapes when one tries to contain him within the definitions which serve well enough for lesser writers. Most of his plays were written for the public stage, and careful study of them has revealed much information about the structure and use of the Elizabethan stage, particularly at the Globe Theatre.

In his own day Shakespeare was not as highly esteemed as he is now. His contemporaries, with the exception of Ben Jonson, looked down on him as a hack-writer who was not, like most other dramatists of the period, a university man. We owe the first reference to Shakespeare as a dramatist – a disparaging one – to one of the so-called 'university wits', Robert Greene, who called him (in *A Groatsworth of Wit bought with a Million of Repentance*) 'an upstart crow . . . and in his opinion the only Shake-scene in the country'. Greene's malice may have been prompted by jealousy, for he was not as successful as Shakespeare, nor indeed as his other university friends. Among them was Thomas Kyd, author of a revenge play, *The Spanish Tragedy*, and perhaps of an early version of *Hamlet*, both of which may have influenced Shakespeare when he came to write his finest work.

It was Kyd's friend Christopher Marlowe, a Cambridge man, born in the same year as Shakespeare but active in the theatre before him, who opened a new era in English dramatic history with his plays, which included a dramatized version of the legend of Doctor Faustus. An illustration in a printed copy of this shows Mephistopheles, like Satan in the Bible-histories, dressed in a black suit, masked, appearing through a trapdoor in the stage. *Ill. 84*

Marlowe, who was a poet as well as a playwright, abandoned the short jigging rhymed verse in which earlier plays had been written, and by his superb manipulation of the iambic pentameter prepared the way for Shakespeare's poetic drama. He might even have equalled Shakespeare in reputation had he not been stabbed to death in a tavern brawl shortly before his thirtieth birthday.

A very different sort of man from either Marlowe or Shakespeare was Ben Jonson. After receiving a good education at Westminster, he was deprived of a university education by the action of his step-father, who took him away from school and apprenticed him to his own trade of brick-laying. Unlike Shakespeare, Jonson was always conscious of his lack of university status, and allowed it to embitter him. Frustrated, quarrelsome, he was often in trouble with the authorities, and several times in prison. But nothing stopped him from speaking and writing as he thought fit. He was perhaps more strongly influenced by the Renaissance than any other English

84 A scene from Marlowe's *Doctor Faustus* (*c.* 1589), a woodcut of 1636

dramatist. Marlowe, Kyd and Shakespeare all retained in their work something of the earlier forms of English drama. Jonson, steeped in the classical authors, brought considerable erudition to the composition of his plays, and imposed on them the five-act form advocated by Horace. In this he was imitated by the first editors of Shakespeare, the actors Heminge and Condell, who cut up into arbitrary sections what should be a continuous free-flowing whole.

Jonson's tragedies are frigid and forgotten, but his satiric comedies, in the first of which, *Everyman in His Humour*, Shakespeare played Knowell, had a lasting influence on the development of English comedy, and the best of them continue to be popular on the stage.

All the authors mentioned so far wrote mainly for open-air public
Ills. 75, 78 theatres like the Swan and the Globe. But at the turn of the century many plays were written for the indoor or private theatres set up in Blackfriars and elsewhere. These had the advantage of being usable in bad weather, or even in the winter, being roofed and lit by candles. The audience, less numerous but better educated, demanded a more subtle style in plot and dialogue and more elaborate equipment. In
Ill. 85 appearance the second Blackfriars Theatre, built, like the first, in the ruins of the old monastery, was more like the Renaissance theatres of Italy than were the earlier Elizabethan theatres. It was rectangular, with a stage across one of the shorter sides and the audience seated in front of it on benches. Although it retained from the public theatre the back wall with doors and a gallery above, it seems to have had a simultaneous setting like that shown in the
Ills. 45–9 Renaissance Terence-stages, which were still being used in France. There was also, in later years, painted scenery, which came from
Ill. 88 Italy by way of the masques performed at Court.

The Blackfriars Theatre was used mainly by adult companies, but it was leased sometimes to the boy-actors drawn from the choir-schools of St Paul's and the Chapel Royal, for whom Ben Jonson wrote some excellent comedies on classical themes. They had earlier appeared with great success in a smaller theatre near by, when their chief playwright had been John Lyly, better known as the author of the novel *Euphues*. The audience no doubt delighted in the grace and artificiality of his dialogue, and his sly references to contem-

84

85 A reconstruction of the second Blackfriars Theatre, built by James Burbage in 1597. This theatre was for many years the winter home of the King's Men, the company to which Shakespeare belonged, and was also leased to the children of the Chapel Royal and St Paul's, who appeared there in a number of plays of which the most important were those by Ben Jonson, *Cynthia's Revels* and *The Poetaster*. There is no evidence for the use of footlights

porary scandals may have had an added piquancy coming from the lips of young boys. One of Lyly's plays, at least, was first performed at Court, for although England never had a Court theatre in the sense in which it was later understood on the Continent, players formed part of the royal household from the earliest times, and entertainments were regularly given at Court on feast-days. The mummings and disguisings devised for royal occasions may not have been as splendid as those of Italy and France, but they existed. Professional actors too were pressed into service, and Shakespeare's *Twelfth Night* may have been seen at Court before it appeared on the public stage. This would have involved a certain amount of reorganization, for the play would have been given in a hall adapted for the purpose, with a few light canvas structures representing bowers, rocks, or rooms arranged in advance for the actors' use, and not on a bare platform-stage, as at the Globe.

88 (*right*) Inigo Jones' Tragic Scene. There is no proof that the design was ever ▶ used, but it was evidently meant for a private playhouse in which a Palladian arch could be combined with scenic devices

86–7 (*below*) Two costume designs by Inigo Jones: left, Penthesilea, from *The Mask of Queens*, 1609; right, Oberon, from *Oberon, the Fairy Prince*, 1611

It was, however, the Court masques of the early seventeenth century that were important in the development of the English theatre, particularly those produced by Inigo Jones from 1605 to 1613, for several of which Ben Jonson wrote the words. Jones, who was an artist and an architect, travelled widely in Italy and came into close contact with scenic artists there. From them he took the idea of a painted backcloth with side wings which he used in the productions staged at Whitehall. It is interesting to see how closely his Tragic Scene corresponds to that of Serlio. Jones' designs for scenery and costumes, many of which have been preserved, are elaborately ornate, and could not have been used in the public theatres of the time. They demanded not only the enclosed conditions of a great hall or private theatre, but also some form of proscenium arch. They also tended to distract attention from the dialogue, which caused Jonson to give up writing masques, not wishing, as he said, to

Ills. 54, 88

Ills. 86, 87

89 A platform-stage
with footlights (found
for the first time on an
English stage) and a
curtained booth at the
back, from the
frontispiece to Francis
Kirkman's *The Wits*;
or, *Sport upon Sport*,
published in 1673

compete with the carpenter and scene-painter. The use of scenery
had already spread from the Court to Blackfriars by 1637, and might,
in some modified form, have reached the public playhouses had it
not been for the Civil War, which put an end to theatre-going.

After the age of Shakespeare the English theatre, perhaps inevitably, suffered a decline. There were good actors, but none as good
as Burbage and Alleyn; good playwrights, but none as good as
Shakespeare and Jonson. There were no innovations in public-
theatre design or production to revive interest in the art of the
theatre. The buildings were getting shabby. The last one, the
Fortune, was built in 1600. The Hope, which opened in 1613, was
only the old Bear Garden, converted for use as a playhouse. The

90 Itinerant actors, and a platform-stage set up in a market-place, c. 1651–76. Although this may depict conditions in France in the mid-seventeenth century, its details are probably valid for any European troupe of itinerant actors

private theatres attracted a limited audience, the Court plays were designed for the personal entourage of the monarch. In such plays as survive we can see a definite change in style. In the hands of the playwrights Beaumont and Fletcher, who began their collaboration in 1608, high tragedy and low comedy, as understood by Shakespeare, became entangled with romance, or were discarded altogether in favour of pastorals like *The Faithful Shepherdess*. The satiric humour of Jonson lost its bite and degenerated into the mild ridicule of the citizen and his wife in *The Knight of the Burning Pestle*. Plays like these were intended for the amusement of a sophisticated audience far removed from the groundlings of the Globe who had enjoyed the robust bawdry of Shakespeare's clowns and the savagery of Jonson's *Volpone*. The only outstanding talent to emerge before civil war broke out in 1642 was that of John Webster, whose *White Devil* and *Duchess of Malfi* were strong Italian Renaissance tragedies of political intrigue written in splendidly passionate poetic dialogue and staged with extreme realism.

When war was finally declared the theatre was the first casualty. The theatres were closed and acting forbidden, and the actors dispersed to join the army or find some other means of livelihood. The Puritan so graphically portrayed by Ben Jonson in *Bartholomew Fair* had triumphed, and London was to remain officially without a theatre until 1660, though surreptitious performances of short plays were sometimes given. Some of these were published later in *The*

Ill. 89   *Wits*, whose frontispiece shows actors on a stage similar to that of the Globe, but with footlights, a startling innovation.

English theatrical tradition took a long time to recover from the shock of eighteen years without a theatre. People lost the habit of playgoing, the older generation of actors vanished almost without trace, and when the theatre resumed its activities in 1660 it had none of that strong sense of continuity which distinguishes, for example, the French theatre, though France, and through France Spain, were to have a great influence on the new English scene.

CHAPTER FIVE

The Golden Age of Spain and France

Although the development of the English and the Spanish theatres runs parallel, and their theatre buildings show many similarities, there seems to have been little or no contact between them, probably as a result of the political situation. English acrobats are mentioned as touring in Spain only a few years after the opening of The Theatre in London in 1576, and they may have taken back news of Madrid's new buildings to Burbage and Henslowe. But the plays of Spain's Golden Age seem to have been as unknown to English dramatists as theirs were to the Spaniards. It was not until the Restoration that Spanish dramatic literature, through the intermediary of France, made any impact upon England.

The early history of the Spanish theatre, with the development of religious plays in the vernacular, secular farces from popular sources, and Renaissance comedies played against a street scene reminiscent of Serlio's perspective design, resembles that of Italy and other European countries. It was at first closely bound up with the emergent theatre of Portugal, and indeed one of the first playwrights, Gil Vicente, was Portuguese. In his plays, and in those of his contemporaries, two themes which were to be important later on – the pastoral and the romantic – are already apparent. It was perhaps to satirize the chivalric and romantic tendency of the time that there appeared in 1499 *La Celestina*, a prose work in dramatic form which though not intended for the stage (it is in twenty-one acts) was probably read aloud, as the plays of Terence and Seneca were, and had a great influence on the work of later playwrights through its racy and realistic dialogue.

One of the first 'men of the theatre' in Spain, in the modern sense, was Lope de Rueda, an actor-manager and author of a number of short farces or *pasos* designed to amuse the audience between the acts of the more serious plays in which he toured with his company,

91 Lope de Vega (1562–1635), Spain's first important playwright, and virtually the founder of the Spanish theatre, in an engraving by M. S. Larmona

92 (*below*) The Corral del Príncipe, Madrid; a seventeenth-century reconstruction by Juan Comba. The resemblance to the Elizabethan 'innyard' auditorium is striking (*see Ills. 74, 75*). A point to be noticed is the indication of an inner stage (see p. 78)

93 (*below right*) A masked ball in the Teatro del Príncipe, Madrid, 1766, a painting by L. Paret. In comparison with *Ill. 92*, this shows the marked influence on Spanish theatre architecture of the typical Italian opera-house

playing in noblemen's halls and in the 'yards' or *corrales* between buildings. These, like the innyards of England, provided ready-made playing-places, and when the first professional theatres were built they incorporated several features of the *corral*. The audience stood in the courtyard (*patio*) or sat in the surrounding galleries and boxes. There was a special gallery for women, and behind the stage, which projected out into the auditorium, was a balcony reached by a flight of steps. The back wall had doors and windows, and there was definitely an inner stage, like the much-disputed inner stage of the Elizabethan theatre, which could be revealed by drawing back a curtain. There were also trapdoors in the stage floor and machinery for lowering cloud-borders, thrones or divine apparitions from above. The whole thing, in fact, was remarkably like the theatres of London. Several of these theatres were built in different parts of Spain, but the two most important were the Corral de la Cruz (1579) and the Corral del Príncipe (1582), both in Madrid. When, many years later, the Madrid theatres were rebuilt in the Italian fashion, the most important retained an echo of earlier days in its name, the Teatro del Príncipe.

Ill. 92

Ills. 74, 75

Ill. 93

The professional actor in Spain was much influenced by the visits of the *commedia dell'arte* companies, particularly that led by Ganassa. Under Italian influence structural changes were introduced into the design of the stage to facilitate the production of plays, and a high standard of acting was set. Among the authors, many of them directly influenced by classical dramatists, particularly Seneca, or by contemporary Italian writers, whose works were performed in these theatres, was Cervantes. Besides the immortal *Don Quixote* he wrote ten plays and a number of short interludes or *entremeses* given between the acts of his full-length plays, of which the best was his one tragedy, *Numancia*. At this time plays in Spain were bought outright from the dramatist by the manager of the company which wished to perform them. The actors made yearly contracts with the managers, drawing a fixed salary, in the style of Henslowe's companies in London rather than in that of Shakespeare's Globe.

The theatre in Spain was firmly established by the brilliance and
Ill. 91 fecundity of Lope de Vega, the first outstanding Spanish playwright. He is credited with having written twelve hundred plays, of which only about seven hundred and fifty survive. Such an enormous output argues not only a great facility in composition, but an insatiable demand on the part of the audience for new works, a demand which Lope de Vega, known in his own days as 'a monster of nature', was quite capable of satisfying. His plays, which are written in free-flowing verse, deal with every possible subject – religious, historical, pastoral and social – and portray an idealized Christian, indeed Catholic, society firmly divided into three estates, kings, nobles, and commons (usually peasants). The king, with the help of his nobles, rules; the commons are ruled. But rulers have duties as well as rights, the peasants have rights as well as duties. This is the background of such a play as *Fuenteovejuna* (*The Sheepfold*), which depicts not only the revolt of the villagers against a brutal overlord (thus qualifying, in some quarters, as the first Communist play of class warfare) but also the revolt of the overlord against the king. The nobleman thus fails in his duty to his underlings as well as to his superior, and must be removed from office before harmony can be restored.

94

A fruitful source of comedy in the works of Lope de Vega is the contrast between the wicked town (in which most of his middle-class audience lived) and the virtuous countryside. Indeed, as with Ben Jonson, the censuring of the faults of urban society was a rich source of satiric drama, particularly in the works of Lope de Vega's younger contemporary, Juan Ruíz de Alarcón, who was born in Mexico and taken to Spain when very young. He was a cripple, and the ridicule attracted by his physical deformity may perhaps explain and excuse the bitterness apparent in his work and his constant hostility to other writers, particularly Lope de Vega. Though his plays are ingenious and well constructed, they were less popular in Spain than in France. His sobriety and elegance made him more accessible as a model for French writers than the exuberant Lope de Vega.

When even Lope de Vega's abundant energy began to flag, he was succeeded as Spain's chief playwright by Pedro Calderón de la Barca, of whose plays more than two hundred survive. The early ones are comedies of intrigue – variations on the theme of honour – and moral and social comedies written for the public theatres. The best known of them is probably *El alcalde de Zalamea*, a study of vice and virtue in a setting which recalls Lope de Vega's vision of the orderly class-conscious society of contemporary Spain. For the Court Theatre at the palace of Buen Retiro, the Coliseo, which opened in 1640, Calderón prepared mythological spectacles of great splendour, intended to make full use of the latest Italian devices in the way of perspective scenery and concealed lighting with which it was equipped. It is interesting to see, in the designs for one of his Court productions, the obvious use of wings and backcloths, which make the illustrations more realistic than is usual in theatre designs of the time. The success of these Court spectacles contributed not a *Ill. 95* little to the decline of the commercial theatre, after Calderón's death, in favour of imported Italian opera.

Even in his youth Calderón, who became a priest in 1651, had written a number of religious plays, *autos sacramentales*, and in later life he wrote nothing else. Professor A. A. Parker, in his study of Calderón's religious works, says of him that 'he is a theological poet

95

94 Design for a Court Theatre in Spain, attributed to F. Ricci, *c.* 1680, and showing the influence of the Spanish Baroque architects, the Churrigueras, who flourished from 1680 onwards

and dramatist in a deep and legitimate sense, and as such his achievement is not only valuable, but unique'. The best known of his *autos* is *El gran teatro del mundo*, on the theme of 'all the world's a stage', with each man playing throughout his life the part allotted to him by God at birth. Although Calderón lacked Lope de Vega's facility and Alarcón's mordant satire, he was a subtle writer and a most excellent craftsman, and his plays were destined to exert an important influence on the European theatre, an influence which penetrated even to England.

One other contemporary of Lope de Vega whose work was to reappear frequently in European dramatic literature was Tirso de

95 A stage setting for one of Calderón's plays, 1690, with side-wings and backcloth in the Italian style. In the background is a ship which is about to be wrecked,
in the foreground are Cupid, Aeolus, a chorus of sea nymphs, Neptune and Mars

Molina, a writer of deep psychological intensity, at his best in the
portrayal of women, and the author of the first play on the legendary
story of Don Juan.

If the form of the early Spanish stage resembled that of England,
its plays were very different, and the most difficult for an English
audience to appreciate are those that turn on the famous *pundonor*, or
point of honour. In them action takes precedence over character, and
the moral theme is simplified to the point of abstraction. There are
no half-tones. A bad action is recognized as such even by its perpe-
trator. There are no mitigating circumstances, and the evildoer must
be punished, even if the punishment recoils on an innocent head.

It was this particular aspect of the Spanish theatre – perhaps the most characteristic, if not necessarily the most popular or prolific – that was to influence France so strongly that the modern French theatre dates its inception from *Le Cid*, a play on the early life of Spain's national hero written by Pierre Corneille, and produced in 1637. Its plot exemplifies perfectly the Spanish *pundonor*, for it shows a son avenging an insult to his aged father by killing the father of his own fiancée. Up to 1637 the French theatre had followed much the same path as the theatre elsewhere. But in 1548 the Confraternity of the Passion, which held the monopoly of acting in Paris, was forbidden to appear in the debased and secularized religious plays which formed its traditional repertory. This left the commercial theatre free to develop in its own way. The process was delayed by the ravages of civil war, and the sixteenth century, which saw the firm establishment of the' professional theatre in England and Spain, was still a period of experiment and confusion. But the influence of the Renaissance finally prevailed over the indigenous farces and *soties*, as

Ill. 101

Ill. 43

98 (*right*) French actors at the Hôtel de Bourgogne, Paris, *c.* 1630. On-stage are ▶ Turlupin, Gaultier-Garguille and Gros-Guillaume (*see also Ills. 99, 100*) interestingly reminiscent of Arlecchino, Pantalone and Pedrolino (or Pulcinella)

96 (*below*) Italian *commedia dell'arte* players in France, from the *Recueil Fossard*, *c.* 1577. In spite of the French names given to the characters, the central figure is obviously Pantalone and the woman Franceschina

LE DOCTOR CORNVTE
PANFIRLIPPE VALET   FRANCISQVINE GIGOGNE   SVEIR

97 A simultaneous setting by the designer Mahelot, with a wood, a street and a house, for Alexandre Hardy's *Cornélie*, performed at the Hôtel de Bourgogne, Paris, between 1625 and 1635

well as over the Bible-histories, and the new drama was established with plays on classical themes by scholars of the new learning. Unlike English dramatists, who mingled grave and gay in equal proportions, French writers, following what they believed to be the classical model, made a sharp distinction between the two, a distinction which was to be upheld and indeed intensified by the later dramatists of the seventeenth century. It faltered somewhat in the hands of the first professional French playwright, Alexandre Hardy, however. His numerous tragi-comedies were written for a troupe of actors and actresses – the French stage was never an all-male preserve but had young and beautiful leading ladies from the very first – who can fairly be considered the first fully-professional French players to appear in Paris, though they had been preceded there by some

Ill. 96   *commedia dell'arte* troupes. Under Valleran-Lecomte they established themselves in the old theatre of the Hôtel de Bourgogne leased to

Ill. 98   them by the Confraternity of the Passion. This was a long narrow room – Paris never had unroofed theatres like those of London and Madrid – with a platform-stage at one end. In front of it was a pit for standing spectators only, extending back to tiers of rising benches, with boxes at the side. Both stage and auditorium were lit by candles, and all the plays were presented in the old-fashioned simultaneous

Ill. 97   setting which can be seen in the designs by Mahelot, stage-designer for Valleran-Lecomte's company. These show that Italian scene design had not yet ousted the older forms. The plays themselves were to some extent exercises in rhetoric, since each actor advanced to the edge of the stage to declaim his lines, and then retired to make way for his successor.

It was not long before Paris had several theatres, all planned after the same model, where a curious mixture of plays can be noted, remnants of the old Mysteries and Moralities surviving side by side with new plays written under classical or Italian influence. Most of them were pastorals or tragi-comedies; comedy in the true sense seems not to have been popular. Farces, however, were still much in favour, and the most famous actors of the day were the farce-players

Ills. 98–100   Turlupin, Gaultier-Garguille and Gros-Guillaume. But there were a number of good serious actors ready to interpret the plays of France's

100

100 A composite painting, *c.* 1670, in which French actors of the 1630s, some of ▶ them derived from characters of the *commedia dell'arte*, mingle with players of thirty years later, among them Molière and Poisson

99 The chief comedians, right, of the Hôtel de Bourgogne, *c.* 1630. There are hints of the *commedia dell'arte* masks in these three, but they have evolved into truly French comic figures, whereas the swaggering Capitano of earlier times has now dwindled, left, into Le Capitaine Fracasse, a *figurant* (or super)

outstanding dramatists when they finally appeared. Montdory and Mlle de Villiers, with an experienced company, had no hesitation in *Ill. 101* tackling *Le Cid* when it was produced at their theatre in the Marais.

The form of Elizabethan drama flowered naturally in the hands of dramatists who were also, for the most part, actors. The form of French tragedy was imposed from without, with the codifying of the three unities of time, place and action, derived by literary critics from the works of Aristotle. They were first adhered to in the pastoral, which became popular after the appearance of a translation of Tasso's *Aminta*. The history of the battle for the unities belongs to the domain of literature rather than of the theatre. The restrictions they imposed, which would have been intolerable to English writers, suited the French love of order and seemliness, and those plays in which the writers adhered to the unities seem to have been more successful with the public than those which did not. The necessity for setting the action within a confined space – a courtyard or a room in a palace – and of resolving the conflict within a limited time, usually twenty-four hours, certainly heightened the tension and made an impact upon the spectator.

Corneille, to whom goes the honour of inaugurating France's greatest dramatic era, was a native of Rouen, where his first play, a comedy, was performed by a strolling company which had come to present some of Hardy's plays in the town. He had moved to Paris, written several more plays, and been chosen by Richelieu to fabricate dramatic literature to order – a servitude to which he was temperamentally unsuited – when his attention was drawn to *Las Mocedades del Cid*, a chronicle-play on the exploits of the great Spanish hero by Castro y Bellvís, a contemporary of Lope de Vega. On this he based *Ill. 101* his tragi-comedy *Le Cid*, which, though accused of violating the precious unities and therefore not received with universal acclaim by the critics, nevertheless established him as the leading playwright of France. He proceeded to consolidate his position with a series of excellent tragedies on classical subjects. He also dipped into Spanish *Ill. 102* drama again and produced a good comedy, *Le Menteur*, based on Alarcón's play about a man who lies so readily that when he speaks the truth he is not believed.

101-2 Engravings from a 1764 edition of Corneille's plays: (*left*) *Le Cid*, 1637; (*right*) *Le Menteur*, 1643

103 A setting by Giacomo Torelli for Corneille's spectacle-play *Andromède*, 1649

Corneille continued to write until about ten years before his death, and among his works is a charming classical spectacle *Andromède*, written to show off the Italian scenery and machinery imported into

Ill. 103 France by the great Torelli. In his later years he found himself engaged in rivalry with the young Jean Racine, a playwright destined to carry on and perfect the form of tragedy initiated by Corneille. Racine's best play, *Phèdre*, shows all his gifts to perfection. The lyric beauty of its dialogue, the subtlety of its psychology, the tension of its tightly wound plot make it a masterpiece of dramatic literature. Its leading character, which is a test-piece for all actresses

Ill. 104 aspiring to greatness, was first played by Mlle Champmeslé, who was also the interpreter of many of Racine's other heroines, among

Ill. 106 them Bérénice in the tragedy of that name, and for a time his mistress.

Ill. 105 Racine wrote only one comedy, *Les Plaideurs*, based on Aristophanes' *Wasps*. Of his nine tragedies, the finest, apart from *Phèdre*, is probably *Britannicus*, which is still in the repertory of the Comédie-Française.

Racine was fortunate in writing for a theatre that had several established companies rivalling each other in splendour and in the excellence of their acting. But his growing reputation suffered at the hands of a vicious cabal, who puffed to success a play by a second-rate dramatist, also on the subject of Phaedra, while causing Racine's to fail on its first production. The resentment he felt, coupled with the offer of a lucrative post at the Court of Louis XIV and perhaps some belated scruples resulting from a rigid upbringing, caused him to abandon the theatre at the height of his powers. His only subsequent dramatic works were the tender and poetic Biblical plays *Esther* and *Athalie*, written at the request of Mme de Maintenon for performance at Saint-Cyr, the convent school she had founded for the daughters of impecunious noblemen.

One of the first people to encourage Racine in his theatrical career

Ills. 108, 111 was Molière, the greatest comic dramatist of France, and perhaps, with the exception of Aristophanes, of the European theatre. The son of a minor Court official, he was educated at a Jesuit college where he was a fellow-pupil of the Prince de Conti, later his patron, and Cyrano de Bergerac. He may have taken part in the performances for which Jesuit schools were renowned, and this, together with a

104

104 Mlle Champmeslé (1642–98), the first
leading lady of the Comédie-Française

105–6 Engravings from a 1676 edition of
Racine's plays show (*left*) a scene from his only
comedy, *Les Plaideurs*, 1668, based on
Aristophanes' *Wasps*; (*right*) *Bérénice*, based on
a passage in Suetonius, and first performed
at the Hôtel de Bourgogne in 1670 with
Mlle Champmeslé (*Ill. 104*) in the leading role

friendship formed with a family of actors named Béjart, probably turned his thoughts to the theatre. After a half-hearted attempt to study law, he left home at the age of twenty-one and dropped his real name of Jean-Baptiste Poquelin in favour of Molière. He made his first appearances with the Béjarts and some of their friends in a converted tennis-court in Paris – the shape of the room used for the game of tennis made it easily adaptable for theatrical purposes, as can be seen from the existing one at Hampton Court, near London, and many French tennis-courts were used in this way. Unfortunately L'Illustre-Théâtre, as it was called, was not a success, and Molière went with his friends into the provinces to lead the usual life of the itinerant actor of the time. For over thirteen years the company, of which he soon became the director, toured France, acting in improvised farces in *commedia dell'arte* style (many of them adapted by Molière himself) and gaining valuable experience, until on 24 October 1658, a date memorable in French theatre history, it appeared at the Louvre before Louis XIV and his Court. A tragedy was coolly received, but when the actors appeared in one of Molière's own comedies, now lost, they proved irresistible, and soon found themselves settled in Paris, sharing a theatre with a *commedia dell'arte* troupe, and paying rent to its leader Tiberio Fiorillo, known as

Ill. 107

107 Clowns fighting, an illustration from a treatise on theatrical dancing, 1716. This scene of one clown beating another is common in *commedia dell'arte* scenarios, and as a piece of 'comic business' it passed into French comedy and probably into the early plays of Molière

108 Molière (1622–73) as ▶ Caesar in Corneille's *La Mort de Pompée*, in 1659, a portrait by Paul Mignard

109 An open-air performance of Molière's *Le Malade Imaginaire* at Versailles, 1674,
given before the King and his Court. The very large stage, splendidly decorated

and lit by five large chandeliers, was needed for the ballets given in the prologue
and between the acts

110 Armande Béjart, Molière's wife, in *Psyché*, 1670, a *tragédie-ballet*, written by Molière in collaboration with Corneille (*see Ills. 101–3*) and Philippe Quinault, with music by Jean-Baptiste Lully. The first performance was given in January 1671 in the Salle des Spectacles in the Tuileries, built by Vigarani, before Louis XIV and his Court

111 (*right*) A scene from *Les Femmes Savantes*, in which Molière ridiculed the cult of learning among would-be fashionable ladies. This engraving of 1682 shows the single set in which the play took place, replacing the older simultaneous setting of the Hôtel de Bourgogne (*see Ill. 97*). On stage Chrysale (played by Molière) is remonstrating with his wife Philaminte for dismissing the maid Martine merely because her speech is ungrammatical. The play was first produced at the Palais-Royal in March 1672

Scaramouche. The two leading actors got on very well together, and Molière was always ready to acknowledge how much he learned from the Italians. He was at first forced to adapt his productions to their set scene of houses round a square, reminiscent of Serlio's scene for comedy. Later, when both companies moved from the Petit-Bourbon to the Palais-Royal, he had ample space for his scenery and orchestra – and by then the Italians were paying him rent, so quickly had he advanced in his profession.

From the moment he settled in Paris until his death fifteen years later, at the early age of fifty-one, Molière's life was bound up with

Ill. 110

his theatre. He even married an actress in his company, Armande, the youngest member of the Béjart family, twenty years his junior. It was an unhappy marriage, but it was for Armande that Molière wrote some of his best women's parts, including Elmire in *Tartuffe*,

Célimène in *Le Misanthrope*, Armande in *Les Femmes Savantes*, Elise in *L'Avare*, and above all Lucille in *Le Bourgeois Gentilhomme*. In these plays and in many others Molière and his company appeared *Ill. 111* with almost unbroken success. He was also responsible for several sumptuous entertainments given at Versailles and for plays acted at Court. But it was on the stage of the Palais-Royal that he made his last appearance, in *Le Malade Imaginaire*, on 17 February 1673, dying a few hours later.

Molière's great achievement was that by his own efforts he raised French comedy to the level of French tragedy. Unlike those who had gone before him, and whose comedies were often translated from or based on Italian and particularly Spanish plays, he put down roots in French soil and wrote his plays from his own observations of life around him. His characters are contemporary and French to the backbone, recognizable as such even by spectators of other countries and later ages. This is one of the reasons why his plays defy translation. They can be adapted, as they have been constantly and often with success – by Miles Malleson in England, by Lady Gregory, with her Kiltartan Molière, in Ireland. But it is only the letter which remains. The spirit has evaporated.

During his lifetime Molière saw many changes in the theatre, some of which he helped to bring about. The most important was probably the change-over from the old simultaneous multiple setting used in the Bible-histories and bequeathed to the secular theatre to the single all-purpose set which helped, in tragedy, to preserve the unity of place. In comedy it was probably adopted under the influence of the *commedia dell'arte*, whose peripatetic life made them adepts at simplification. France also came under the influence of Italian scene-designers with their painted scenery and elaborate machinery, used by Molière for productions like *Andromède* and *Psyché*, and later snapped up by Lully for his operas and ballets.

Ill. 103

Molière, who is the supreme example of the dedicated 'man of the theatre', combining in himself the functions of actor, manager and dramatist, was not only a writer and player of comedy, but provides the connecting link between France's two finest writers of classical tragedy. He first appeared in Paris in *Nicomède*, by Corneille, whom he much admired, and he put on at his own theatre Racine's first play, *La Thébaïde, ou les frères ennemis*. After his death the brilliance of the French theatre was somewhat dimmed. But he left an imperishable memory, for his company, under the management of his widow and her second husband, also an actor, was amalgamated by Louis XIV with two other companies to form the Comédie-Française, the national theatre of France. Its other name is La Maison de Molière, whose traditions it continues to uphold.

The English Restoration Theatre

While Charles II was in exile he and his followers had become accustomed to watching plays staged in the style used before 1642 for English Court masques, with actresses, painted scenery and machinery imported from Italy, and a proscenium arch with a curtain. It is therefore not surprising that when he returned to England in 1660, he should have encouraged their adoption in the new public theatres. Everything favoured a fresh start, with exciting innovations. The old theatres, after eighteen years of neglect, were unusable. The companies that had played in them were disbanded, the audiences dispersed. The old plays too were out of date. Even Shakespeare was barbarous, and had to be tailored to fit the new age. Many of the perversions of his plays which later appeared in translation on the Continent were really due to rewritings by Restoration dramatists, who dressed up *Macbeth* with singing witches, added new characters to *The Tempest* and gave *Romeo and Juliet* a happy ending.

The two men to whom Charles II by Royal Patents gave the task of reviving the theatre were Thomas Killigrew and William Davenant. Both had been active as playwrights before 1642, and had seen their plays produced in the private theatres which had already begun to feel the influence of Continental staging. Davenant, moreover, who was the godson – some said the illegitimate son – of Shakespeare, had helped in the preparation of Court masques, and in *Ills. 86–8* 1654 had managed to stage in London a 'play with music' now considered the first English opera. This made for continuity, as did the fact that some of the actors in Killigrew's company had had some experience of acting, even if only in the short drolls fashioned, *Ill. 89* like *Bottom the Weaver* from *A Midsummer Night's Dream*, out of old plays, an activity which had sometimes landed them in prison.

The new theatres showed an interesting mixture of English and Continental practices. Roofed like Blackfriars, they retained a *Ill. 85* memory of the Elizabethan platform-stage in the form of an apron or forestage. But behind the apron-stage was a proscenium arch with a window opening into a music-room above it. The arch framed the painted flats, and the back shutters running in grooves which replaced the former solid back wall. These back shutters could be opened or closed to indicate a change of scene – a practice which seems to have been peculiar to the English stage, and may be a survival of the medieval use of the unlocalized *platea*. Another feature which was destined to linger on in English theatres for over two hundred years was the door opening on the forestage on each side of the proscenium arch. These – there could be as many as three each side – were known as the Doors of Entrance. They enabled actors to come and go without using the space behind the arch, which some authorities think corresponds to the inner stage of the Elizabethan theatre.

Other innovations in the Restoration theatre were the new audiences, the plays they came to see, and above all the use of actresses in female parts. These charming, talented young women, who replaced the Elizabethan boy-actors, seemed to come from

112 A scene from Settle's *The Empress of Morocco*, produced at Dorset Garden Theatre in 1673. This theatre was noted for it sumptuous scenery and mechanical devices, many of them copied from the Salle des Spectacles in Paris. It was built under the patent granted by Charles II to Sir William Davenant, its manager

113 A portrait of Nell Gwynne, from the studio of Lely, *c.* 1675. She made her first appearance on the stage at Drury Lane at fifteen, and was excellent in comedy. Her short but spectacular career included playing Florimel in Dryden's *Secret Love* (1667) in male attire. She retired from the theatre to become the mistress of Charles II

nowhere; and with no training, but with abundant self-confidence, they took London by storm. Almost from the beginning they achieved and maintained a high standard and founded a tradition of great acting which continues to this day. One of the best known of these early actresses, though known not so much for her work in the theatre as for the fact that she became the mistress of Charles II, was Nell Gwynne, of Killigrew's company. Others, like Mrs Knipp and *Ill. 113* Mrs Betterton, are immortalized in Pepys's diary, a storehouse of information on the theatre of his day.

Equally revolutionary were the plays written for the new play-houses, and the audiences which came to see them. The Patents under which Killigrew and Davenant operated are still in force. One belongs to Drury Lane Theatre, which now stands near the site of *Ill. 125* Killigrew's first Theatre Royal of 1663, built over a riding yard. The other controls Covent Garden Opera House, inheritor of the traditions of Davenant's Duke's House in Lincoln's Inn Fields, and his later Dorset Garden Theatre. Since the Patents created a monopoly *Ill. 112* of acting, London now had only two theatres instead of the ten or

Theatre, is an important figure in the development of the English stage. Under the name of Lun he appeared as Harlequin in the 'Italian Night Scenes' imported from France. These vestiges of the *commedia dell'arte* featured Harlequin metamorphosed, as in *Harlequin Doctor Faustus* or *Harlequin Jack Sheppard*, and provided one of the elements of that uniquely English entertainment, the Christmas pantomime, which within living memory always ended with a Harlequinade.

The early eighteenth century saw many changes in the style of the English theatre building. The typically Georgian playhouse, of which the first was Potter's Little Theatre in the Haymarket, was less influenced by the Italian opera-house than theatres elsewhere, perhaps because the English theatrical genius remained obstinately dramatic rather than operatic. Potter's theatre, and many which were later *Ill. 117* built in the same style, was a soberly elegant little building, with tiers of boxes rising directly from the pit, and proscenium doors opening on to an attenuated forestage. Scenery was still painted on the flat. The lighting was by overhead chandeliers with wax or tallow candles, and the curtain in the proscenium arch rose and fell only at the beginning and end of the play. In 1730 an important innovation took place when the orchestra moved to a well in front of the stage.

The audience was by now becoming more numerous but less sophisticated, and it demanded not only the ubiquitous afterpiece, introduced as a sop to those who came in late at half-price, but sentiment instead of comedy and pathos in the place of tragedy. The *Ill. 116* first play in the new style, *Love's Last Shift*, was by Colley Cibber, playwright and for a long time manager of Drury Lane, whose best play was probably *The Careless Husband*. An egregious fop and a very poor Poet Laureate, Cibber is now remembered for his memoirs and for his adaptation of *Richard III*, which contained the oft-quoted lines: 'Off with his head! So much for Buckingham!' and 'Now Richard is himself again.' It remained the standard acting text of the play for over a century and a half.

The sentimentality of *Love's Last Shift* had one good result, since it goaded the architect Vanbrugh, who not only built the Queen's

118

116 Colley Cibber as Lord Foppington in Vanbrugh's *The Relapse; or Virtue in Danger*, 1696

117 The interior of the Regency Theatre, Tottenham Street, London, as it was in 1817 during a performance of *Othello*, and probably very much earlier. It shows the typical eighteenth-century auditorium with boxes at stage level rising directly from the pit, and two elegant balconies

freedom of movement and natural delivery for the stiffness and
Ill. 128 pomposity of such older actors as Quin. Of medium height, but well
proportioned, with expressive, flashing eyes and exceptionally mobile
features, he appeared in many modern plays, some of which he
wrote himself, and also in revivals of Shakespeare. He was responsible
for many improvements in the theatre, and in 1765 introduced stage
lighting concealed from the audience, producing an effect which can
Ill. 125 be studied in the engraving of *The School for Scandal*. He also removed
the spectators who had hitherto encumbered the stage, and created
something of a sensation with the splendid cut-out and romantic
scenery designed for him by the Continental stage-designer de
Ill. 120 Loutherbourg. His career ran triumphantly from his début as Richard

120 A 'cut-out' scene by de Loutherbourg, a painter from Alsace who became
scenic director at Drury Lane under Garrick and later under Sheridan, making
important reforms in lighting effects and scenery. His fires, storms, volcanoes and
cloud-effects were much admired

III in 1741 to his retirement in 1776. Most of his time was spent at
Drury Lane, where his leading ladies included Peg Woffington, his
mistress for many years, who reversed Elizabethan theatre practice
by appearing in young men's parts, and Kitty Clive, an excellent
actress in comedy who was much admired by Horace Walpole.

Ill. 121

Ill. 122

Garrick's only rival in his own day was Macklin, best remembered
for having rescued Shylock from the clutches of the low comedian
and played him as a tragic and dignified figure. This drew from
Pope the memorable, though not perhaps strictly accurate, couplet:
'This is the Jew/That Shakespeare drew'. Macklin also discarded the
scarlet of the king's livery in which Garrick still played Macbeth, and
appeared for the first time in something approximating to the 'old

Ill. 123

121 (*left*) Peg Woffington as Mistress Ford in *The Merry Wives of Windsor*, in a
painting of 1751

122 (*right*) Kitty Clive as Isabella in Fielding's *The Old Debauchees*, in 1750

123 (*left*) Charles Macklin as Shylock at Drury Lane, 1741. He dressed soberly instead of wearing rags, and spoke naturally in contrast to the ranting of Quin as Antonio (*see Ill. 128*). His Portia was Kitty Clive (*see Ill. 122*), who convulsed the audience in the Trial Scene by mimicking well-known barristers of the time

124 (*right*) Ned Shuter and Mrs Green as Mr and Mrs Hardcastle, and John Quick as Tony Lumpkin in Goldsmith's *She Stoops to Conquer*, from an engraving after Parkinson. The play was first produced at Covent Garden in 1773. The costumes are interesting, but for a view of a contemporary stage, see Drury Lane in *Ill. 125*

Caledonian habit'. Garrick replied by dressing *King Lear* in accordance with his own ideas of 'old English costume'. Neither attempt, it is fair to say, was particularly remarkable for authenticity.

Garrick's success inevitably made him many enemies, of whom the bitterest was Samuel Foote. This excellent actor took over the Haymarket in 1747, and managed by various subterfuges to evade the Licensing Act of 1737. This had been hurriedly passed under Walpole in an effort to restrain the satiric attacks on the Government by Henry Fielding, at the same theatre. Its chief result had been to drive Fielding from the theatre to novel-writing, but it had also confirmed the monopoly of Drury Lane and Covent Garden, and hindered the expansion of the smaller unlicensed theatres. Foote, who eventually managed to get permission to open the Haymarket in the summer when the Patent theatres were closed, was also a satirist, who made himself universally feared and admired by his mordant wit and cruel mimicry. He wrote most of his own material, and excelled in brilliant but ephemeral sketches of contemporary manners which caused him to be nicknamed 'the English Aristophanes'.

Garrick was succeeded in the management of Drury Lane by Sheridan, who in spite of his preoccupation with politics gave much of his time to the theatre. With Goldsmith he represents the revolt of the reasonable man against the excesses of sensibility. The robust humour of Goldsmith's *She Stoops to Conquer* derives from Shake- *Ill. 124* speare and the Elizabethans, that of Sheridan's *The Rivals* and *The School for Scandal* from Congreve and Restoration comedy, with as much wit but less licence. Both of Sheridan's plays have remained in the repertory of the English theatre, *The Rivals* offering an excellent role for a low comedian in Bob Acres, first played at Covent Garden in 1775 by Quick, and *The School for Scandal* two equally good high-comedy roles in Sir Peter and Lady Teazle, first played at Drury Lane in 1777 by Tom King and Mrs Abington.

Ill. 125

Goldsmith wrote nothing more for the theatre, though his novel, *The Vicar of Wakefield*, dramatized a hundred years later, provided a charming vehicle for Ellen Terry. Sheridan's later plays included *A Trip to Scarborough*, a rewriting for a more squeamish age of Vanbrugh's *The Relapse*, in which the celebrated Mrs Jordan played

125 The Screen Scene from Sheridan's *School for Scandal*, with Tom King and Mrs Abington as Sir Peter and Lady Teazle. This engraving gives an excellent idea of Drury Lane in 1777. Built in 1672, it was extensively altered by the Adam brothers in 1775. The shaft of light coming from the wings on the actors' left confirms the use of side-lighting at this date

Miss Hoyden; *The Critic*, a burlesque of heroic drama which is still effective on the stage; and a pantomime, *Robinson Crusoe*. In 1794 Sheridan replaced the much-altered theatre of 1674, which was in poor condition, by a much larger building designed by Holland. There, pandering to the prevailing taste for spectacle and pantomime, he continued the profligate course that almost brought the theatre to bankruptcy, and drove his best actors to Covent Garden. He also indulged in constant litigation with the managers of the unlicensed theatres, whose success alarmed him, particularly Astley's, famous for its equestrian shows, Sadler's Wells, under the management of   *Ill. 126*

126 Anglers outside Sadler's Wells Theatre, 1796, a drawing by Cruikshank. This theatre, which later came into prominence under Phelps (*see Ill. 191*), was built by Rosoman on the site of a former concert-hall near a medicinal spring. A second Sadler's Wells on the same site was opened in 1931 by Lilian Baylis. It was demolished in 1996 and rebuilding commenced in 1997

Tom King, and the Royalty under John Palmer, both fugitive actors from Drury Lane.

Another actor, destined to play a big part in English theatrical history, who preferred to disassociate himself from Sheridan's ruinous policy was John Philip Kemble, who with his sister, Mrs Siddons, moved to Covent Garden in 1802. Here one of Kemble's first acts as *Ill. 127* manager was to engage the remarkable 'Young Roscius', Master Betty, a thirteen-year-old tragedian who surpassed even Mrs Siddons in popularity. He had a great vogue, and it is said that when he appeared as Hamlet Parliament was adjourned on a motion of the younger Pitt in order that the members might attend his performance. As an adult actor, however, he had no success, and passed the rest of his long life – he was well over eighty when he died – in complete obscurity.

In September 1808 Covent Garden was burnt to the ground. Five months later Drury Lane suffered the same fate. It was the end of an epoch. The new buildings which arose on both sites, vast white elephants which were to break the hearts of actors and managers alike, ushered in a new phase in the history of the English theatre.

127 Master Betty ('The Young Roscius') as Hamlet, 1804

CHAPTER SEVEN

The Theatre in Eighteenth-century Germany

The reforms in costume attempted by Macklin and Garrick in London in the 1770s were not the first tentatives in this direction. In Germany the first break with tradition came as early as 1741, when the reformer and theatre critic Gottsched persuaded Carolina Neuber, leader of the company which was to perform his Roman tragedy, *Der sterbende Cato*, to put her actors into classical dress, with disastrous results. Perhaps the quest for too high a degree of accuracy is anti-theatrical, and costume, in becoming historical, ceases to have a history of its own. Certainly an earlier urge towards authenticity would have deprived the theatre of the work of many designers whose fantastic inventions, intended for Court masques, operas, and other spectacular entertainments, nevertheless spilled over into the ordinary playhouses and enlivened many a dull play. They even, at times, influenced the fashion of the outside world, as did the designs of Bérain, one of the greatest artists in stage costuming, under Louis XIV, or those of François Boucher under Louis XV. The latter's wide-panniered skirt with rococo details, familiar in the theatres of the whole of Europe, reached as far as London, where it was worn by Quin as Coriolanus.

The reference to Carolina Neuber, or Die Neuberin, as she was called, indicates that Germany is now making a determined if somewhat belated appearance on the European theatrical scene. Several factors had combined to hinder the development of an indigenous German theatre, among them constant warfare, religious faction, the overpowering influence of visiting French and Italian companies, and above all the lack of a focal point like that provided for France and England by their capital cities. Actors and playwrights were thus deprived of that close contact with a tightly-knit society which produced the pungent satire of the French *sotie* and the charm of the English interlude. Nor was the acrobatic agility of the Italian comedians or the religious fervour of the Spanish *autos*, both from countries with no focal point, within the compass of the German theatre at that time. The characteristic personage of early German *Ill. 129* farce is the *Narr*, or Fool, in his cap and bells, who, though he began as a Court jester, has affinities both with the comic devil of the Bible-history and the sly *zanni* of the *commedia dell'arte* – but only such as are common to all comedians, and not necessarily attributable to outside influences. Even the tide of the new learning had little effect on the German theatre, and the best plays, of little interest today, were those written in support of the Reformation and the Counter-Reformation. These, even when designed to reinforce the Protestant argument, were still performed in the old medieval (and therefore Catholic) simultaneous setting. The secular farces – there was as yet no serious secular drama in Germany – had been taken over by the

128 (*left*) The tragic hero
in plumes and panniered
skirt. James Quin
(1693–1766) as Coriolanus
in the play of that name
by James Thomson, at
Covent Garden in 1749

129 (*right*) A German
Fool, or *Narr*, in cap and
bells, end of the fifteenth
century. This engraving
shows Claus Narr, court
jester to the Electors of
Saxony between 1461
and 1518, strangling his
goslings to save them
from drowning

130–1 Scenes from a
School Drama by Johann
Rasser, 1574. The open-air
platform stage, probably
erected in a market-place,
is very like the Terence
stage (*see Ills. 45–9*), with
a curtained booth and
the audience on three
sides. (*above*) A mother
protects her son from his
irate tutor while a second
child, his satchel over his
shoulder, makes for the
exit. (*below*) A dispute
between two peasants

Ills. *130, 131*
Ills. *132, 133*

guilds of Mastersingers, and could therefore be staged a little more lavishly than when they had been given by groups of amateurs on temporary platform-stages. But even the plays of Hans Sachs, well known to opera-goers through his appearance in Wagner's *Die Meistersinger von Nürnberg*, were presented very simply (in the 1550s) on an improvised stage in Nuremberg's abandoned Marthakirche. This constituted Germany's first theatre building, with the audience in the body of the church facing a raised stage curtained at the back and sides. Existing steps and the pulpit were pressed into service, and the actors, no longer visible throughout the play as in earlier productions, came and went through gaps in the curtains, carrying with them the props and stage furniture which the action called for. The general

Ill. *48* effect must have been something like that of the Terence-stage. Sachs, who wrote with great facility in a not unpleasing doggerel four-beat line, composed some long academic tragedies and comedies, usually on classical or Biblical themes, so it is reasonable to suppose that he was acquainted with the Terence-stage. But his fame rests mainly on his short Carnival plays, which turned the rough humour of the original *Fastnachtsspiel* into a simple folk-tale, purging it of indecency without discarding its sense of fun. Though his plays are not very original, they are marked by many deft touches, a sense of characterization, and some feeling for dramatic effect. They were produced by the author who also trained the actors in what seems to have been a fairly realistic style. Costuming was simple, consisting of traditional robes for divine and noble personages, and everyday dress

Ill. *132* for lesser mortals.

It was, curiously enough, the wandering troupes of English actors – the *Englische Komödianten* – who had the greatest influence on the nascent German-speaking theatre, both in Austria and in Germany. The first of these companies, under Robert Browne, appeared at Frankfurt in 1592, and shortly afterwards a company under Sackville was established at Wolfenbüttel in the Court Theatre of Heinrich Julius of Brunswick. The Duke was himself a playwright. His extant plays show considerable English influence, having in them much that can be traced to Shakespeare, as well as some affinities with the *commedia dell' arte*.

132

Der Teuffel leſt keyn
Lantzknecht mehr inn die
helle faren.

Hans Sachs.

132–3 (*right*) An early German dramatist, the mastersinger Hans Sachs (1494–1576), a cobbler by profession, and (*left*) a woodcut from the title-page of one of his plays

There are scattered mentions of other English companies in the early seventeenth century. They played at the big annual fairs, in noblemen's halls, or in the larger towns, either indoors or out. Some of them even penetrated into Scandinavia. As they travelled light, their scenery must have been non-existent, and the stages erected locally for them were modifications of the normal Elizabethan structure. They consisted of a large jutting-out platform with a room at the back and perhaps a gallery above. This allowed of greater mobility than the long narrow stage of the Marthakirche, and the actors took full advantage of it, playing with all the agility of contemporary London actors, reinforced by the acrobatics of the *commedia dell'arte*. The repertory consisted mainly of Elizabethan comedies and tragedies, often severely cut, played in English with the help of music, dancing and dumbshow, and enlivened between the acts by the patter in Low German of the Fool. This all-pervasive character found his way even into the burlesque version of *Hamlet*, which as *Der bestrafte Brudermord* later became one of the most popular pieces in the repertory of the German travelling companies. The Fool, though of English origin, quickly absorbed some of the characteristics of the German *Narr*, and was played by Sackville as Jan Clant (Clown) or Bouschet (Posset), by Robert Reynolds as Pickelherring, and by John Spencer as Hans Stockfisch.

The influence of the English Comedians was no doubt deplorable from a literary point of view, and led to the later popularity of the crude plays of bloody deeds in high places – the *Haupt- und Staats-*

Ill. 139 *aktionen* – but by their productions they accustomed the public to action and passion on the stage, and helped to curb the tendency of German dramatists to excessive discussion. For them the play was indeed the thing, and in ramming that point home they revolution-ized German drama. Even after German troupes had taken over the work of the English companies, their name remained useful for publicity purposes, being synonymous with all that was most admired and successful in the theatre. Their activities were hampered by the Thirty Years War, but they appeared in Germany again during the English Puritan interregnum which drove them from London. The constant passage of actors to and from the Continent must have led to a good deal of cross-fertilization in the theatre, and has posed some interesting problems in comparative literature, outside the scope of this book, of which the use made of the Faustus legend both in England and in Germany is a case in point. The last English troupe in Germany is mentioned in 1659, by which time popular staging had

Ill. 134 begun to feel the influence of Italian perspective scenery. This came in by way of the elaborate Court spectacles, mostly operatic, given in theatres built for the reigning princes by Italian architects, and also through the splendidly staged Jesuit school plays, with texts in Latin,

Ill. 136 which were dominated by Italian scenery and machinery. There was as yet no permanent public theatre in Germany where the plays of her first serious dramatist, Andreas Gryphius, could be seen, and they were performed by Protestant schoolboys. Based on French classical drama, they were written in lofty and somewhat monotonous verse, and would probably not have been well received by an audience which still delighted in the *Haupt- und Staatsaktionen*, whose extempore productions retained many of the faults of the English Comedians without their virtues. These were particularly popular in Vienna, and it was not long before the local form of the fool, Hanswurst, who seems to have evolved from John Posset (alias *Ill. 135* Johann Guttwen), ousted all the earlier imported forms. In the hands of the actor Stranitzky, Hanswurst became a completely original comic figure. Discarding the earlier loose white belted tunic and trousers, reminiscent of the costume of Pedrolino, he was dressed like a peasant from Salzburg, in a loose red jacket with a small fool's ruff, yellow pantaloons held up by red braces, a blue heart on his chest embroidered with the initials H.W., a tufted wig, a beard, heavy eyebrows, and a green pointed hat. He dominated most of the plays in the repertory of the Kärntnertor, the first permanent home of German-language comedy, and in the hands of Stranitzky's successor Prehauser underwent a mellowing process which corresponded to the alteration in the plays themselves, from improvised farces to a more sophisticated portrayal of recognizable Viennese types. Two later comic figures of the Viennese folk-play were Kasperle, the puppet-theatre equivalent of the English Punch, and Thaddädl. The latter, who belonged to a very different age and theatre from that of Hanswurst, was a falsetto-voiced, clumsy, infantile booby, perpetually infatuated. The plays in which he appeared were no longer improvisations, but texts specially written for him, or rather for the actor who immortalized him, Anton Hasenhut.

In the early eighteenth century efforts were made by serious-minded persons, both in Germany and in Austria, to banish the old comedies in favour of something more dignified, and to replace the pre-eminence of the professional actor, who had been paramount in the German theatre of the seventeenth century, by that of the literary dramatist. The reformer Gottsched, whose work was not confined *Ill. 137* to the theatre, particularly detested the improvised plays centred on a debased Harlequinade, with their rowdy foolery and easily satisfied audiences. Helped by the intrepid Carolina Neuber, he was *Ill. 138* successful for a time in banishing Harlequin from the stage and in replacing him and his antics by sober works in the French classical manner, written in prosaic alexandrines. Unfortunately Gottsched

134 (*above*) A seventeenth-century German stage, with wings, back-cloth and hanging chandeliers, but no footlights. The play is a romantic or chevalresque comedy, the winged cupid at the back presaging a happy ending

135 The English actor John Goodwin as Hanswurst, a stage in the development of the German clown showing the influence of the English Comedians in the seventeenth century

136 (*above*) The splendour of the Jesuit school productions: the arrival of Neptune, from *Pietas Victrix* by Nicolaus Avancinus, Vienna, 1659. The play had forty-six speaking parts and called for a large crowd of supers in addition

137 The German critic and dramatist Johann Christoph Gottsched (1700–66), and his wife Luise Adelgunde Victoria *née* Kulman (1713–62), who together translated and adapted a number of French classical plays for the company of Carolina Neuber (*see Ill. 138*)

138 The first outstanding German actress and theatre manageress, Carolina Neuber (1697–1760), seen here as Elizabeth I of England in a translation into German of Thomas Corneille's *Essex*. Neuber's efforts to reform the German stage failed to oust the *Haupt- und Staatsaktionen* (*Ill. 139*) from popular favour

was working in a style which was already out of date. The result was dull and did not last long. By the middle of the eighteenth century translations of Shakespeare's plays had opened up a new world of the imagination to the German playgoer, who had also become aware of the success on the contemporary French stage of the *comédie larmoyante* and the *drame bourgeois*. But Gottsched's influence had not been wholly bad. The discipline he sought to impose on the inchoate stage of his time was salutary, and his conception of the theatre as a civic institution was to bear fruit later on.

The chief opponent of Gottsched was the young Lessing, who acquired his knowledge of the theatre backstage with the company

139 A troupe of itinerant German actors getting ready to appear in a *Haupt- und Staatsaktion* in Nuremberg, *c.* 1730; an engraving by P. Decker. These were plays dealing with dramatic events in high places, with comic interludes supplied by Harlequin and Hanswurst (seen on the extreme left)

of Carolina Neuber. She produced his first comedies, which were written in the style of Molière, whom he much admired. But his first important work, *Miss Sara Sampson*, is a domestic tragedy clearly influenced by Richardson's novels, then very popular in Germany.

Lessing, whose work as a dramatic critic is no less important than his plays, was connected in 1765 with one of the first attempts to establish a permanent national theatre in Hamburg, where his *Minna von Barnhelm*, the first masterpiece of German comedy, was acted in 1767. The Hamburg venture, which was doomed to failure, was headed by two remarkable men, Ackermann and Ekhof, who had a great influence on the German theatre of their day. Ekhof in

139

particular abandoned the wooden declamation and stiff posturing of earlier actors under Carolina Neuber and Koch for the supple and natural style already in vogue elsewhere. Both Ekhof and Ackermann belonged originally to a company led by Schönemann, who had been a harlequin in a travelling troupe, and when his predilection for horse-dealing ruined him, they took over. In the reorganized company were Ackermann's two daughters, both excellent actresses, and a son of Ackermann's wife by a previous marriage, Friedrich

Ill. 140 Schröder. He was one of Germany's greatest actors, and the first to play many of Shakespeare's parts in translation, from Hamlet to King Lear. Unfortunately, Schröder's jealousy of Ekhof caused the latter to leave the company, and for some years he toured unhappily before going first to Weimar, where he met Goethe and may have supplied him with some of the material for *Wilhelm Meister*, and then to Gotha. It was at Gotha that the year before his death he engaged a young actor named Iffland, destined to play an important part in the theatre of Goethe's day. Ekhof lived long enough to see the acting profession in Germany, largely through his own efforts, achieve respectability. The change in status can be judged by the fact that Christian burial, refused to the actor-manager Velten in 1692, was freely accorded to Ekhof in 1778.

After Ackermann's death Schröder who, like Ekhof, appears in *Wilhelm Meister*, with his sister Charlotte (as Serlo and Aurelie), took over the leadership of the company and instituted many reforms, particularly in stage costuming. The period which followed was perhaps the most glorious in his career. As well as revealing the theatrical qualities of Shakespeare's plays to a young audience which knew them only on the printed page, he produced *Emilia Galotti*, by the ageing Lessing, and the first play of the young Goethe, *Götz von Berlichingen*. But in spite of his success he was not happy. Tiring of constant friction with his mother, who still held the purse-strings, he

Ill. 143 left Germany for the Vienna Burgtheater. The four years he spent there made a permanent impression on the Austrian theatre, and he may be said to have inaugurated the subtle and refined style of ensemble playing which later became the hall-mark of a Burgtheater production. It was Schröder too who first trained and guided the

great Brockmann, a leading actor at the Burgtheater from 1778 *Ill. 142*
until his death in 1812.

Schröder's time in Vienna coincided with the efforts of Joseph II to continue the reforms begun by his mother, the Empress Maria Theresa, by making the Burgtheater a national home for serious and improving drama and banishing the popular theatre to the suburbs, where it flourished more strongly than ever under Marinelli at the Theater in der Leopoldstadt.

140 Friedrich Schröder (1744–1816), the first interpreter of Shakespeare in Germany, as Falstaff in a production of 1780. Schröder adapted Shakespeare to suit the taste of the time, allowing, for example, Hamlet and Cordelia to survive. Here he wears Elizabethan doublet and hose with the plumed hat of the tragic hero

144 (*left*) Goethe as Orestes with Corona Schroeter as Iphigenia, in a Court production of Goethe's *Iphigenie auf Tauris* at the castle at Ettersburg in 1779; a painting by G. M. Kraus

145 (*right*) The Court ▶ Theatre at Weimar during the directorship of Goethe (1784–1825)

      The German stage at the end of the eighteenth century was
Ill. 141 dominated by Goethe, who devoted part of his abundant genius to the
service of the theatre. His *Götz von Berlichingen* was the first German
play to be written under the influence of Shakespeare. Though he
later reverted to his earlier admiration for French dramatic literature,
his play became the manifesto of the *Sturm und Drang* writers, setting
a pattern which was followed by most of the younger dramatists,
Ill. 146 particularly Schiller. Goethe's next dramatic works were historical
and domestic dramas, of which *Clavigo*, with its Spanish setting, still
acts well. But in later life he wrote more as a poet than a dramatist,
Ill. 144 with such plays as *Iphigenie auf Tauris* and *Faust*, a cosmic drama in
two parts. It has been staged in its entirety, but in the vastness of its
conception and the strength of its execution it transcends the limits
of the normal playhouse.

It was during Goethe's management of the Court Theatre at
Weimar – one of his many official positions there, which from 1799   *Ill. 145*
to 1805 he shared with Schiller – that most of the latter's plays were
staged, from *Wallenstein* to *Wilhelm Tell*. But his first, the epoch-
making *Die Räuber*, had had its première at Mannheim, with Ekhof's
protégé Iffland as Franz Moor. Iffland, who was later to appear at
Weimar with great success, was also a popular playwright, and a
good actor in serious comedy, but not in tragedy, having an excellent
technique but no depth. Luckily he trained his young actors in the
sobriety of Schröder rather than in his own virtuosity, and handed on
many excellent traditions to the actors of the Romantic period,
particularly Ludwig Devrient. The culminating point of his career
came in 1796, when he became director of the National Theatre in
Berlin, where he remained until his death in 1814. He produced a

146 Friedrich von Schiller (1759–1805), one of Germany's greatest playwrights, a portrait by Anton Graff. From 1799 to his death Schiller was jointly responsible with Goethe for the productions at the Court Theatre in Weimar

Ill. 146

number of old and new plays, among them those of Shakespeare and Schiller, in the grandiose romantic settings which were prepared for him by the architect and designer Schinkel. His actors were accounted better than those of Weimar, where Goethe, in reaction against the brutal realism of the *Sturm und Drang* movement and the naturalism of the *bourgeois* domestic drama, had introduced a more dignified and poetic style of acting. This unfortunately led to some stiffness and declamation, though crowd scenes were still well and realistically handled. But the literary content of Schiller's plays, combined with those of Goethe and Lessing, as well as translations of Shakespeare and Calderón, sufficed for a time to place Weimar's Court Theatre at the forefront of the German theatrical scene.

But even Weimar had to admit the melodramatic plays of Kotzebue, which are a portent of what is to come. The early nineteenth century, inheritor of the turmoil of the French Revolution, with its repercussions all over Europe, was to be once again a period of great acting and poor plays – poor in a literary, not a theatrical sense, for a prodigious amount of work in the way of scenery, costumes, music and stage effects was to go into the production of the melodramas and romantic plays which trace their ancestry back to the youthful excesses of *Götz von Berlichingen* and *Die Räuber*, ignoring entirely the later and more restrained excellencies of Goethe's *Torquato Tasso* and Schiller's *Maria Stuart*. In such an atmosphere the plays of a dramatist like Kleist, whether comic, as in *Der zerbrockene Krug*, or heroic, as in *Der Prinz von Homburg*, were bound to be *Ill. 180* unappreciated, and they had to wait to make their effect until audiences were in a more receptive frame of mind.

147 *Die Verschwörung des Fiesko zu Genua,* by Schiller, in a production at the Court Theatre, Weimar, in *c.* 1810. It was first produced in Bonn in 1783 and several times revived

CHAPTER EIGHT

France before the Revolution

While Germany was struggling to establish permanent theatres and develop a national school of play-writing, France was going through a somewhat difficult and barren period. The death of Molière had brought to an end a glorious epoch. The newly established Comédie-Française was in many ways an admirable institution. It had as its *Ills. 110, 104* leading ladies Molière's widow and Mlle Champmeslé, and as its *Ills. 148, 150* leading actors Molière's pupil Baron, famous in tragedy, and Poisson, famous for his portrayal of Crispin, in comedy. But perhaps because it was a little too conscious of its official backing and subsidy, it tended to impose on the French theatre as a whole a traditional style and repertory which brooked no opposition and left very little room for experiment. Maintaining the form without the content, tragedy declined into sensationalism and melodrama, while comedy lost its universal appeal and concerned itself rather too much with contemporary trivialities. Meanwhile, the Italian actors, under their leader *Ill. 149* Giuseppe Biancolelli, known as Dominique, had obtained from Louis XIV, in the teeth of bitter opposition from the Comédie-Française, the right to play in French. They were successful in the plays of Dufresny and Regnard, comedies which allowed them ample scope for impro- *Ill. 152* visation, but in 1697 a fancied slight to Mme de Maintenon caused them to be banished from Paris, and they did not return until after the King's death in 1716, when they again occupied the theatre in the Hôtel de Bourgogne, which had become known as the Comédie-Italienne, to distinguish it from the Comédie-Française, housed since 1689 in d'Orbay's new building. The Italians' acting and repertory alike had become outmoded, but by a process of trial and error they succeeded in recapturing the interest of the public, and in time evolved what was virtually a new form of theatrical art, combining Italian ebullience and dexterity with French wit and elegance. It was this combination of talents which enabled the Italian actors, under

148

148 The actor and playwright Michel Baron (1653–1729), a portrait by Rigaud. Baron was responsible for the early training of Adrienne Lecouvreur (*see Ill. 157*)

149 The leading actor of the Comédie-Italienne, Giuseppe Biancolelli (*c.* 1637–88), known as Dominique, in the costume of Il Dottore

Lelio and the younger Dominique, to interpret so ably the comedies of Marivaux. These, which retained from the *commedia dell'arte* the tradition of using the actor's name for the part he was playing, were all variations on a single theme – that of young people in love, whose difficulties, though momentary and often of their own making, are universally applicable. Action is replaced by psychological insight,

Ill. 151

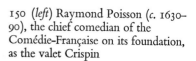

150 (*left*) Raymond Poisson (*c.* 1630–90), the chief comedian of the Comédie-Française on its foundation, as the valet Crispin

151 (*below left*) Actors of the Comédie-Italienne, Paris, where the plays of Pierre de Marivaux (1688–1763) were first given; a painting by Nicolas Lancret

152 (*right*) The Italian actors who were banished from Paris in 1697 after a play entitled *La Fausse Prude* had offended Mme de Maintenon

153 (*below*) French actors, probably those at the Comédie-Française, in a tragedy, *c.* 1720; after Watteau

permanent theatres, to become part-founders with the Italians of the Opéra-Comique, and to provide one of the outstanding theatrical attractions of Paris in the nineteenth century.

Meanwhile, audiences at the Comédie-Française, deprived of Le Sage and neglectful of Marivaux, were enjoying the tearful comedies – *comédies larmoyantes* – of Nivelle de la Chaussée, which, with the moral *drames* of Denis Diderot, mark the main contribution of the eighteenth century to the literary history of the French theatre. Both are the logical outcome of the influx into the playhouses of a middle-class audience demanding strong emotional situations in a recognizably contemporary setting. The doctrine of the equality of man brought the tragic hero from the palace into the parlour, while the sensibility of an audience which included far more women than before enjoyed being touched to tears even at a comedy. It was the misfortune of France, as of other countries at this time, to have no dramatist capable of making great theatre out of the material to hand. Luckily there was no lack of good actors, playing in well-proportioned and well-equipped theatres which had not yet been demolished to make way for the enormous playhouses of the next century.

Before tragedy finally declined into *drame bourgeois* it enjoyed one last brief blaze of glory at the hands of that universal genius, Voltaire, who like Goethe devoted part of his time and energy to the theatre. He built several private playhouses, the best being that at Ferney, his last home, and he was himself a good amateur actor and a great promoter of theatrical activities. But even his earliest tragedies, which are classical in form and continue the illusion of greatness, show traces of the influence of Shakespeare, whom Voltaire was the first Frenchman to admire, though with reservations. His later plays are unashamedly *drames bourgeois* and even *comédies larmoyantes*. In them he mingled tragedy and comedy, and employed crowd scenes and spectacular effects in a way which completed the divorce of French tragedy from its seventeenth-century roots. The crowds and spectacles, however, served one good purpose. They led to the removal from the stage of the audience, who can still be seen encroaching on the acting area in the engraving of the first production

154

156 A scene from Voltaire's *Sémiramis* at the Comédie-Française in 1748, showing spectators seated on both sides of the stage

of *Sémiramis* in 1748, but who have been banished to the audi-   *Ill. 156*
torium by the time of the revival in 1759. Three years later Garrick
was able to effect the same long overdue reform in London.

It is interesting to note, since Garrick's name has come up, that he
was the only English actor of his day to be admired on the Continent,
where he travelled extensively between 1763 and 1765. He was
particularly esteemed in France, where he had many friends, and
though he never appeared on the French – or indeed on any foreign
– stage, he gave several solo performances in private houses in Paris,
amazing the spectators by the mobility of his face, the expressiveness
of his gestures, and the enormous range of his voice. They were more
used to the traditional declamation and statuesque poses of their
own leading actors. If Garrick learned much from the French
theatre, and made use of his knowledge at Drury Lane, in return
his natural style of acting may have influenced some of the French
actors who watched his performances, particularly the great Lekain,
friend and protégé of Voltaire.

settled in Paris in 1761. His earlier efforts in Venice to revive the moribund and verbally indecent *commedia dell'arte* by providing its actors with written texts had for a time met with success. An interesting mingling of the old and new styles is apparent in his *Servant of Two Masters*, a play which has proved popular in translation in Russia, in England, and in the United States in a production by Max Reinhardt. His most successful period was from 1748 to 1753, when his plays were given at the Teatro Sant'Angelo in Venice by a company under Medebac, for which he wrote such masterpieces as *La vedova scaltra*, *Il bugiardo*, and, perhaps his best-known work, *La locandiera* (of which there are at least seven English translations). The heroine, Mirandolina, the mistress of the inn, later proved a popular part with many actresses, particularly Duse.

Unfortunately, Goldoni left Medebac to write for Vendramin's company at the Teatro San Luca (now the Teatro Goldoni), which was larger and really more suited to spectacular shows than to his intimate comedies. Although he had to contend not only with the attacks of his rival Gozzi but also with those of a mediocre playwright named Pietro Chiari, he remained with Vendramin for eight years, writing during this time some of his best plays, including *I rusteghi* and *Le donne curiose*, both used later for the libretti of operas by Wolf-Ferrari. Of his French plays the first, and most successful, was *Le Bourru bienfaisant*. He also left an excellent volume of memoirs, written in French, which is useful for the theatrical history of his time.

French drama was to have one last brilliant phase before the upheavals of the Revolution with two fine plays by Beaumarchais, *Ills. 161, 163* *Le Barbier de Séville* and *Le Mariage de Figaro*. These are too often thought of merely as the source of Rossini's and Mozart's operas. But in their original form they are highly entertaining comedies, and continue the tradition of Spanish influence on French dramatic literature which began with *Le Cid*. Between them they sum up the life and character of their extraordinary and many-sided author. He was himself the precocious page Cherubin, the handsome Almaviva (he was three times married), and above all the resourceful Figaro, jack-of-all-trades, often in trouble but always landing on his feet, clever and unscrupulous. Politically both plays were considered

160

dangerous, and it took much time and energy to get them past the censor. *Le Barbier de Séville* was acted in 1775 to amuse an audience which still felt secure from the Revolution it predicted, but by 1784, when *Le Mariage de Figaro* was first produced, the public was beginning to recognize the dangers which lay before it. The criticisms of Figaro, older and wiser, are no longer directed against an individual, but against society as a whole.

Both these plays were produced at the Comédie-Française, which had now left the theatre it had occupied since 1689 for a new building on the present site of the Odéon. Its leading actors were Préville, who *Ill. 162* had succeeded Raisin, known as 'le petit Molière', as chief comedian, playing Figaro in *Le Barbier de Séville*, and Molé, the Almaviva of *Ill. 161* that play and of its sequel, *Le Mariage de Figaro*, in which Louise *Ill. 163* Contat played Suzanne. Molé, who was outstanding in comedy, was by a curious irony destined to be the first French Hamlet, in an adaptation by Ducis. He was also the teacher and later the close friend of the leading actor Talma, who was to guide the Comédie- *Ill. 170* Française through the ravages of the French Revolution, and having weathered the storm, to see it established more firmly than ever under the aegis of Napoleon.

In Italy, apart from Goldoni and Gozzi, the only playwright worthy of note is Alfieri, the devoted lover of the Countess of Albany, wife of the Young Pretender. His two best tragedies, by common consent, are *Saul* and *Mirra*, both on Biblical subjects. The other seventeen are on classical themes. All are marked by extreme severity of style and austerity of form, and observe strictly the three unities already discarded in France. Alfieri also wrote some comedies, now forgotten, which may however be due for reappraisal, and, like Goldoni, an interesting volume of memoirs.

For the rest, Italy was given over to opera, and the dramatic genius of Apostolo Zeno and Metastasio was employed in the writing of libretti. Some of these were set by many different composers and produced with sumptuous décors by the best stage-designers of the day, inheritors of the traditions of the Bibienas, Burnacini, and Juvarra. Among them one of the most interesting was Jean-Nicolas Servandony, who studied and worked in Italy, and on one occasion *Ill. 164*

172 (*left*) Mrs Siddons (*née* Sarah Kemble, 1755–1831), one of England's most famous tragic actresses and the outstanding member of a great theatrical family; a sketch made of her in youth by George Romney

173 (*below left*) John Philip Kemble (1757–1823), the eldest son of the Kemble family and brother of Mrs Siddons. A stately, formal actor, at his best in tragic and heavily dramatic parts, he is seen here as Shakespeare's Coriolanus, in a portrait by Sir Thomas Lawrence

174 Drury Lane Theatre in 1808, after the rebuilding by Sheridan in 1794. Mrs Siddons called it 'a wilderness of a place', and the immense auditorium led the actors to enlarge their gestures and amplify their voices to the detriment of their technique

Ills. 172, 173

animals – dogs, horses, even elephants. The serious dramatists were unable to compete with such distractions, and it was on inferior new plays of good craftsmanship that the fine actors of the day wasted their powers. Both John Philip Kemble and his sister Sarah Siddons appeared in adaptations of Kotzebue, Kemble as Rolla in *Pizarro* (by no less a person than Sheridan) and Mrs Siddons as Mrs Haller, the erring wife in *The Stranger*, one of her favourite parts. Yet both could rise to the heights of Shakespearian tragedy when they wished. Kemble's Hamlet and Mrs Siddons's Lady Macbeth were highly thought of. But tragedy did not fill the playhouses, and neither of them had much gift for comedy. In this they were outshone by their youngest brother Charles. Stephen, the second brother, who was so fat that he could play Falstaff without padding, was neither a good

175 An 'all-purpose' setting for historical plays designed by William Capon (1757–1827). Capon had designed many sets both for Covent Garden and for Drury Lane, but they were lost when the theatres were destroyed by fire in 1808 and 1809. This set was for the new Covent Garden, opened by Kemble in 1809

actor nor a good manager. Charles, however, excelled in fine-gentleman parts – Romeo, Orlando, Mercutio, Mirabell, Charles Surface, and Young Absolute. All these, it will be noted, were revivals, for nothing new of permanent value was being written. In the same way Charles's daughter Fanny, one of the leading actresses of her day, made her reputation both in England and in the United States, where she married and retired from the stage for a time, in such parts as Juliet, Portia, Beatrice, Lady Teazle, and Belvidera in *Venice Preserved*.

As managers and actors John Philip and Charles Kemble were much concerned with the provision of costumes and scenery for their theatres. By the 1820s both Covent Garden and Drury Lane, in common with theatres everywhere, had replaced their candles and oil-lamps by gas lighting, an innovation which was to have far-reaching results. The main attractions of gas were the increase in illumination and the fact that the intensity of light could be controlled at will. The wavering flames – which unfortunately did little to dimi-nish the risk of fire – still imparted, though more brilliantly, the shimmering effect which was one of the chief attractions of candle-light. It was the mysterious atmosphere this gave which was most bitterly regretted when, towards the end of the nineteenth century, gas was superseded by the hard, steady glare of electricity.

One of the designers employed by the Kembles was William Capon. His work shows the influence of de Loutherbourg, but his *Ills. 175, 120* passion for 'authenticity' led him to design a number of neo-gothic settings 'suitable for Shakespeare's plays' which dominated scene-design during the next half-century. The great names in scene-painting during this time were Clarkson Stanfield and the Grieve family. The latter's ascendency lasted through three generations. John, the founder of the family, worked for Kemble. The moonlit scenes of his son William were particularly admired, and he was the first scene-designer to be called for by the audience. John's grandson Thomas, who worked for Charles Kean, was noted for the brilliance of his sets and the artistic unity of their composition.

Together with a desire for accuracy in settings went that for historically correct costumes. It was for Charles Kemble's production

176 (*left*) George Frederick Cooke (1756–1812) as Richard III, wearing the plumed hat and high boots of the Restoration tragic hero combined with Elizabethan doublet and hose, surmounted by a short ermine-trimmed cloak

178 (*right*) Edmund Kean ▶ (1787/90–1833) as Othello, after a painting by Lambert. Kean first played this part in London at Drury Lane in 1814, and thereafter many times

177 An historically accurate costume designed by James Robinson Planché (1796–1880) for a production of *King John* by Charles Kemble at Covent Garden in 1824

176

of *King John* at Covent Garden in 1824 that the playwright Planché,
who was also a noted antiquarian, designed costumes which were
Ill. 177 based on sound scholarship and a thorough knowledge of heraldry,
and so set a precedent which was followed by Charles Kean, son of
the Kembles' only rival, Edmund.

Ill. 178   Edmund Kean, a foundling child who grew up in the theatre, was
a rough, untutored genius, at his best in strong villainous parts like
Richard III, Iago, or Marlowe's Jew of Malta, Barabas. As Shakespeare's Jew, Shylock, he electrified the audience at Drury Lane by
jettisoning the red hair and beard which even Macklin had not dared
to discard, and making the character a swarthy fiend with a butcher's
knife in his grasp and blood-lust in his eyes. Kean, who was a heavy
drinker, was an unbalanced and unpredictable actor, but he was
perhaps needed in a theatre dominated by the 'noble' John Philip
Kemble and the 'gentlemanly' Charles. George Frederick Cooke,
who might have helped to redress the balance, was as alcoholic and
unreliable as Kean, and spent most of his life in the English provinces.
Ill. 176 Yet when he played Richard III at Covent Garden he gave such a
remarkable performance that Kemble swore never to play the part
again; and when he made his first appearance in the United States
at the Park Theatre, New York, he was given a tumultuous welcome.
But the audiences who had acclaimed him as the greatest tragic actor
they had ever seen fell away when his habitual intemperance and
unreliability returned. After a disastrous tour he returned to die in
New York, where Kean, who thought highly of his capabilities,
erected a monument to him.

Kean's son Charles, who also toured extensively in the United
States, was a quieter, more polished player, very unlike his tempera-
mental father. In the days of affluence which followed Kean's
triumphant début at Drury Lane in 1814 Charles had been sent to
Eton in the hope of keeping him off the stage. But when the father's
behaviour grew too scandalous to bear, Drury Lane dismissed him
and Charles took his place both as actor and as breadwinner for the
family. Father and son acted together only once, at Covent Garden,
as Othello and Iago. Edmund collapsed on stage and died shortly
afterwards. With none of his father's genius, Charles was nevertheless

178

180 A design of *c.* 1875 by George II, Duke of Saxe-Meiningen (1826–1914) for a scene in *Der Prinz von Homburg*, by Heinrich von Kleist (1777–1811), which formed part of the repertory of the Meininger company

a powerful rival in Mayer's Theater in der Josefstadt, and in 1801 Schickaneder, the librettist of Mozart's *Magic Flute*, opened the famous Theater an der Wien. This was the culminating point of his career as impresario, playwright and actor, during which he had appeared with equal success in *Hamlet*, folk-comedy and opera, and in the *Singspiele*, or ballad-operas, so popular with his royal patron Joseph II.

The day of the extempore farce was over, but a new type of popular play, the *Zauberstück*, took its place. This mixture of magic, farce and parody, which was akin to the English pantomime, had its roots far back in the baroque theatre. In the hands of three immensely productive writers, Gleich, Meisl and Bäuerle – this last the creator of the comic figure Staberl, popularized throughout Austria by the

Ill. 184   actor Karl Carl – it prepared the way for the great comedies of Raimund and Nestroy, who were to dominate the Viennese theatre for so long. Raimund, the leading comic actor of his time, served his apprenticeship in the popular theatre. He soon realized that his unique combination of wistful irony and delicately sentimental pathos needed specially written material, which he decided to provide for

Ill. 181   himself. This resulted in such plays as *Das Mädchen aus der Feenwelt* and *Der Alpenkönig und der Menschenfeind*. These are moral tales in which mortals learn from magic beings the basic truths of life, and in which spectacle, charade, transformation scenes, music and singing all receive new life from the genius of this typically Viennese playwright.

Raimund was the product of Romanticism and of the old order,

Ill. 184   which lasted longer in Austria than anywhere else. Nestroy, who succeeded, and destroyed, him, was a man of the new world whose dissatisfactions culminated in the revolutions of 1848. A facile writer, and a pilferer of plots, his bitter destructive satire often brought him into conflict with the authorities. But he bounced up again, dazzling his audiences with improvisation and superb character-acting. Though wittier than Raimund, he had less imagination and less heart. He excelled in parody, Wagner being one of his main targets. After him the phenomenon of the folk-theatre declined into Viennese operetta, which conquered the theatres of the world to the beat of waltz-time.

There was no dramatist in France to do for the serious theatre what Grillparzer did for Austria with his tragedies, of which *Der Traum ein*

Ill. 182   *Leben* echoed Calderón's *La vida es sueño*. The fervent apostles of Romanticism did their best to fill the gap with Victor Hugo's plays,

Ill. 183   particularly *Hernani* – which led to the stormiest first night the Comédie-Française had known for some time – and *Ruy Blas*. Both show the traditional influence of Spain. There were also the plays of the elder Dumas, and Alfred de Vigny's *Chatterton*, first-fruits of the English influence imported with Shakespeare, who was fully revealed to a French audience by the visit in 1827 of a company under Charles

Ill. 185   Kemble. His leading lady was Harriet Smithson, who soon after became the wife of Berlioz. The life of the Romantic theatre was

181 Ferdinand Raimund (1790–
1836) as the 'Aschenmann' in his
own play *Das Mädchen aus der
Feenwelt, oder der Bauer als
Millionär* (1826)

short. Dumas was primarily a novelist, Hugo and de Vigny were
poets. The charming comedies of Alfred de Musset were not written
for the stage, and had to be rediscovered in Russia by a young French
actress and brought back to Paris twenty years later. The true theatre
of the time was still to be found in vaudeville and melodrama, and in
the works of the prolific Scribe, who during all the excesses of
Romanticism continued imperturbably to turn out his 'well-made'
plays, which set a pattern for dramatists everywhere. Unlike the
Romantics, who made high tragedy of everyday happenings, Scribe
excelled in bringing great historical events down to the level of the
back parlour. But his technique was superb. His closely-knit plots
and orderly tying-off of loose ends appealed to the logical French
mind, and provided a welcome relief to an audience which had been
introduced somewhat hurriedly to the splendid irrelevancies of
Shakespeare and his imitators.

182 (*above left*) A scene from
the tragedy *Der Traum ein Leben*,
by the Austrian Franz
Grillparzer, at the Vienna
Burgtheater in 1834

184 (*above*) Viennese popular
theatre: Nestroy's *Lumpazivagabundus*, 1833, with the actor-
manager Karl Carl centre stage,
and Nestroy himself on his right

183 (*left*) The uproar in the
auditorium of the Comédie-
Française during the first night
of *Hernani* (25 February 1830)
by Victor Hugo

185 (*right*) Charles Kemble and
Harriet Smithson as Romeo and
Juliet in a season of
Shakespeare at the Odéon,
Paris, in 1827, a revelation to the
young Romantics

CHAPTER TEN

The Later Nineteenth-century Theatre

Between 1830 and 1880 the theatre everywhere expanded rapidly. New buildings were put up to accommodate increasingly large but undiscriminating audiences, more people found work on or behind the stage, prolific dramatists turned out hundreds of ephemeral plays which owed more to the splendour of their settings and the excellence of the actors than to plot or dialogue. In France the Comédie-Française, though still the leading theatre of Paris, found its pre-eminence challenged by the new theatres, of which the Odéon was the most important. Founded by Picard, a playwright whose musical comedy, *La petite Ville*, went to Germany as *Die lustige Witwe* and so to England as *The Merry Widow*, it was taken over in 1829 by Harel. It then deserted musical plays for a classical and contemporary repertory which gave it the position it still holds as France's second theatre. There, and in theatres like the Porte-Saint-Martin and the Renaissance, great reputations were made by such actors as Frédérick, the first Ruy Blas, famous also for his portrayal of Macaire; Deburau, the beloved Pierrot and pantomimist of the Funambules on the Boulevard du Temple, whose many theatres were swept away by Haussmann in 1862; and Marie Dorval, the heroine of many romantic dramas, who was already famous when she went to the Comédie-Française to play Kitty Bell in *Chatterton*. Even the leading members of the Comédie-Française itself were often absent on tour. Rachel, whose appearance in Racine's plays had revived the glories of French classical drama after a period of neglect, visited England in 1841 and the United States in 1855. During her absence the Comédie-Française was glad for the first time in its career to take over plays which had been successful elsewhere. Among them was Augier's best-known work, *Le Gendre de M. Poirier*. Augier, who also wrote *Les Lionnes pauvres* and *Le Fils de Giboyeur*, was one of the dramatists of the new era which began with the Revolution of 1848, and a

Ill. 186

Ill. 187

186

187 The great tragic actress Rachel (1820–58) at Covent Garden in 1841, making ▶ her farewell appearance as Camille in Corneille's *Horace*. Note the stage boxes

186 The actor Antoine-Louis-Prosper Lemaître (1800–76), known as Frédérick (*centre*), with the novelist-playwright Honoré de Balzac (*left*) and the Romantic Théophile Gautier (*right*), painted by Gautier himself in 1840

greater realist than most of his contemporaries, of whom the best known is the younger Dumas.

Dumas's plays of social criticism, *Le Demi-monde*, *Le Fils naturel*, and *Un Père prodigue* (the last two written from bitter experience as the illegitimate son of the effervescent elder Dumas), were overshadowed by the success of his first play, *La Dame aux camélias*. This was a sentimental portrayal of the courtesan with a heart of gold, Marguerite Gautier, which has provided a splendid vehicle for leading ladies ever since its first production. The hero, the young Armand Duval, was first acted by Charles Fechter, the son of an English mother and a French father of German extraction, who was equally at home everywhere. After a successful career in Paris he went to London and then to the United States, where he remained until his death. Although his English accent was never good, he had enough fluency and self-confidence to give a good account of himself as Ruy Blas in a translation of Hugo's play. It was however his revolutionary Hamlet in 1861 which first brought him into prominence, and led to his appearing at the Lyceum in London in melodrama, under his own

Ill. 189

management. The Lyceum, like the Olympic and the Princess's, had become important in the theatrical life of London after the Theatres Act of 1843 had broken the monopoly of Drury Lane and Covent Garden. This had been a less epoch-making event than might have been supposed. The unlicensed theatres had for a long time been evading the law by inserting half a dozen songs into any play, even one by Shakespeare, and calling it a burletta. The licensed theatres too had been giving their patrons much the same fare as the unlicensed. Macready, a powerful actor who after Kemble's retirement was Edmund Kean's only rival in tragedy, had endeavoured to keep up the standard at both houses with such new plays as *Virginius*, by Sheridan Knowles; *Werner*, by Lord Byron, who was for a short time on the Committee of Drury Lane; and *The Lady of Lyons*, by the novelist Bulwer Lytton. But both Patent theatres put on melo-dramas like *The Dog of Montargis*, with its canine star, and *Hyder Ali; or, the Lions of Mysore*, which called for an entire menagerie of animal performers; and both did spectacular pantomimes annually at Christmas.

Ill. 190

Ill. 188

188 Grimaldi's Game of Leapfrog. Joseph Grimaldi as the Clown in *Harlequin Padmanada, or the Golden Fish*, a pantomime produced at Covent Garden at Christmas 1811. The frog, played by an actor in a frogskin, later appeared in an opera-hat and other fashionable accessories

189

The one person who made a laudable attempt to turn the abolition
of the monopoly to good account was Samuel Phelps. He had already
made a name for himself as a tragedian on the York circuit when
Macready engaged him to play Othello at Covent Garden. In 1843
he took over Sadler's Wells Theatre, and before he finally retired in
1862 he had staged nearly all Shakespeare's plays, some of them
virtually unknown to his audiences. *Pericles*, for instance, had not
been performed since the Restoration period. With Mrs Warner as
his leading lady, Phelps appeared in most of the productions himself.
Though he was at his best in such parts as Lear and Macbeth, he also
made an excellent Bottom. In his well-run company he trained many
young actors who were proud to say in later life that they had played
with Phelps at the Wells.

Before appearing at Covent Garden Phelps had been seen briefly
at the Haymarket, which continued to profit by the summer licence

189 (*far left*) Charles
Fechter (1825–79) as
Hamlet, at the
Princess's Theatre,
London, 1861

190 (*centre*) William
Macready (1793–1873)
as Werner in the play
of that name by
Lord Byron, with
Mrs Faucit as his wife
Josephine

191 (*left*) Samuel
Phelps (1804–78) as
Cardinal Wolsey in
Shakespeare's
Henry VIII, a painting
by the actor Johnston
Forbes-Robertson

obtained for it by Foote. It had been rebuilt on its present site in 1821, and was the last London theatre to be lit by candles, gas being installed only in 1843. In the remodelling it underwent then it lost those other relics of earlier days, the forestage and the proscenium doors. Its manager at this time was Ben Webster, member of a large and far-flung theatrical family, who in his youth had danced as Harlequin and Pantaloon in pantomime before turning to low comedy. He was excellent as John Peerybingle in his own adaptation of *The Cricket on the Hearth* – both Dickens and Scott provided adaptors with unlimited material for stage plays – but his best part was Triplet in *Masks and Faces*, by Tom Taylor, a play based on the life of Peg Woffington.

Webster had for a time been a member of Mme Vestris's company at the Olympic. Fresh from a triumphant career in Paris, this excellent actress, grand-daughter of the engraver Bartolozzi and deserted wife

191

of the ballet-dancer Armand Vestris, delighted London audiences in the sparkling extravaganzas of Planché. She married as her second *Ill. 193* husband the light comedian Charles Mathews, son of the Mathews best remembered for his protean one-man entertainments *Mr Mathews at Home* and *The Actor of All Work*, in which he played all the parts himself. Together Mme Vestris and her husband went to Covent Garden, but their management was not a success. They fared better at the Lyceum, where for Planché's extravaganza *The Island of Jewels* the scene-painter Beverley designed the first transparency seen in London. Mme Vestris, who ruled her company with a stern hand, was an excellent manager and instituted many reforms, following the example of Charles Kean in historical costuming and the use of real properties. She is also believed to have been the first manager in *Ill. 192* London to employ the box-set (three walls with practicable doors and windows and a ceiling cloth over) instead of a backcloth with wings and sky borders.

One of the plays produced by Mme Vestris at Covent Garden during her tenancy was a comedy of contemporary life, *London Assurance*, in which Mathews made a great success as Dazzle. It was the first play of a young actor, Lee Morton, who under his real name of Boucicault became famous as actor and playwright in London and New York, dividing his time equally between them. He was a prolific author, being credited with one hundred and thirty plays. Many of them were adaptations from the French, among them *The Ill. 196 Corsican Brothers* (which the equally prolific H. J. Byron burlesqued as *The Corsican 'Bothers'; or, the Troublesome Twins*), but his best work was done in his Irish dramas, *The Colleen Bawn*, *Arrah-na-Pogue* and *The Shaughraun*. In all of these his wife, Agnes Robertson, though a Scotswoman, played the heroines with great success. She was also, understandably, excellent as Jeanie Deans in her husband's dramatization of Scott's *The Heart of Midlothian*.

Webster had been succeeded at the Haymarket in 1853 by John Buckstone, another good low comedian (it was tragedians who were in short supply at this time). He already had a good reputation, having appeared in many of his own plays, of which the most successful were *Luke the Labourer* and *The Green Bushes*. The latter

192 A scene from *The Conquering Game*, by William Bernard, a one-act comedy produced at the Olympic Theatre in 1832 by Mme Vestris, with herself and her husband in the chief parts

193 (*below*) Mme Vestris (*née* Lucy Eliza Bartolozzi, 1797–1856), with her second husband Charles Mathews the younger (1803–78) in *Mr and Mrs Mathews at Home*

194 Edwin Booth (1833–93), America's first outstanding native-born actor, as Richelieu in Bulwer Lytton's play of that name (first produced in London in 1839), at the Haymarket, London, in 1861

provided the mime-player Mme Céleste with one of her best parts. At the Haymarket Buckstone gathered round him an excellent company, and had an unbroken run of success. It was said that the mere sound of his voice offstage was enough to set the audience laughing. He loved the Haymarket so much that his ghost still haunts it. During his tenancy a significant event took place, nothing *Ill. 194* less than the appearance in 1861 of Edwin Booth, the first actor from the United States to win a European reputation. He appeared with great success as Shylock, Richelieu and Sir Giles Overreach.

This, with Boucicault's career in New York, serves to show the advance made by the American theatre in the preceding fifty years. Before the end of the eighteenth century the theatre had established itself even in puritanical Boston, where a Haymarket Theatre opened in 1796. But New York still held the lead in theatrical life, particularly after the rebuilding of the Park Theatre in 1820. The elder Mathews appeared there, as did Junius Brutus Booth, Edwin's father, after a successful career in London. But the Park's supremacy was soon challenged within its own city when the Chatham opened

195 The American actress Charlotte Cushman (1816–76) as Romeo with Ada Swanborough as Juliet, at the Haymarket Theatre, London, 1855. Tall and plain, with a gruff voice, she had a hard struggle before her immense talent won her public esteem

196 (below) The duel scene in Dion Boucicault's famous melodrama *The Corsican Brothers* at the Princess's Theatre, 1852, with Charles Kean as the dying Louis dei Franchi. He also played Louis's twin, Fabien, who avenges Louis's death

in 1824, followed by the Lafayette, and by the vast Bowery, which was burnt down and rebuilt four times before it finally closed in 1878. It was at the Bowery that the first outstanding American actress, Charlotte Cushman, who had something of the regal quality of Sarah Siddons, made her appearance in her most successful role, Lady Macbeth. She was also much admired as Queen Katharine in *Henry VIII*, and as Meg Merrilees in *Guy Mannering*. She was fond of appearing in men's parts, and played Wolsey and Claude Melnotte, *Ill. 195* as well as Romeo and Hamlet to the Juliet and Ophelia of her beautiful younger sister Susan.

The first outstanding American actor to be associated with the *Ill. 197* Bowery was Edwin Forrest. This fine tragedian was unfortunately bitterly jealous of Macready, whom he blamed for the failure of his second visit to London in 1845. When Macready again visited New York, Forrest's recriminations led to the Astor Place riots in which twenty-two people were killed. Macready himself had to be smuggled out of the town and put aboard a ship for England.

During the 1830s and 1840s the number of theatres in New York increased rapidly. They were mainly managed by actors, the National by Wallack, the Olympic by Mitchell, and Burton's, one of the best, by the British-born William Burton. The only serious rival of Burton's was Wallack's (formerly Brougham's Lyceum), opened in 1852 by another London actor, James Wallack, who left a son, Lester, and a nephew, James, to carry on his work. This they did with great success, James being at his best in tragedy and strong drama, Lester in comedy and romance. It was with this theatre that Dion Boucicault was mainly associated. Boucicault's American plays included the first, and for a long time the only attempt to treat the *Ill. 198* American Negro seriously on the stage, in *The Octoroon; or, Life in Lousiana*. In this the famous Joseph Jefferson, third of the name and a second-generation American, played Salem Scudder. Jefferson, whose charming, humorous personality, typical of all that was best in the American of his time, comes over admirably in his autobiography, was also excellent as Caleb Plummer in *The Cricket on the Hearth*, *Ill. 200* and as Bob Acres in *The Rivals*. But it is for his Rip Van Winkle that he is chiefly remembered. After appearing in an unsatisfactory

196

197 The American actor Edwin Forrest (1806–72) in his most famous role, Spartacus in *The Gladiator* by Robert M. Bird

198 (*below*) The Slave Market Scene in *The Octoroon; or, Life in Louisiana*, in which the wealthy young Southern girl tries to buy Zoë, the octoroon. This play, by Dion Boucicault (1822–90), was first produced in the United States in 1859, with Boucicault's wife Agnes Robertson as Zoë and Jefferson as Salem Scudder

version of Washington Irving's story, by several hands, he went to London in 1865 and there made a success in a dramatization by Boucicault which he so altered and adapted over the years that he made it virtually his own.

One of the parts which Jefferson created was Asa Trenchard in *Our American Cousin*. It was in this play that E.A. Sothern played Lord Dundreary and gave the English language a new name for drooping side-whiskers. Written by an Englishman, Tom Taylor, it was first produced in the United States by Laura Keene, a fine actress and theatre manager who in 1856 opened her own theatre in New York. This was a beautiful house with a white and gold interior, upholstered in gold damask. She prospered for a while, but was ruined by the outbreak of the War between the States, and went on tour. Her company was playing in *Our American Cousin* at Ford's Theatre in Washington, D.C. on 15 April 1865, when Lincoln was assassinated in his box by the younger brother of Edwin Booth, who was also an actor. There was a strong strain of insanity in the Booth family which in Edwin manifested itself in melancholia, and he never fully recovered from the shock of his brother's action. But as a tragic actor he had no equal. Both he and Jefferson, who was supreme in comedy, were the forerunners of a generation of American actors which included such figures as Mantell, Gillette, Mansfield, Mrs Fiske, Julia Marlowe and Maude Adams. One actress whose career spanned the greater part of the century and almost epitomized in itself the history of the early American stage was Mrs John Drew, for many years manager of the Arch Street Theatre, Philadelphia. As Louisa Lane, she appeared on the stage as a small child, playing in England with Macready, and in the United States with the first Joseph Jefferson. In her old age she matched the third Joseph Jefferson's Bob Acres with her own Mrs Malaprop, one of her best parts. Her son John and her grandchildren the Barrymores carried on the traditions of the family into the next century, John Barrymore in particular being renowned for his fine portrayal of Hamlet.

As economic pressure forced the immigrants to the United States farther and farther west, actors accompanied or soon followed them, and it was not long before theatres were being built all over

Ill. 199

198

199 (*above*) Mrs John Drew (1820–97) as Mrs Malaprop in Sheridan's *The Rivals*

200 Joseph Jefferson (1829–1905), third of the name, as Rip Van Winkle in the version prepared for him by Dion Boucicault, which he first played in London at the Adelphi in 1865, and in New York a year later

the continent, with companies moving from one to another. Among the pioneers were the Drakes, led by 'Old Sam' Drake; Caldwell, who built the first theatre in New Orleans; Ludlow and Sol Smith, who ran several theatres from their base in St Louis; the second Joseph Jefferson, who took his family to act in Chicago; and the lovely Julia Dean, grand-daughter of 'Old Sam' Drake, who made her début in Omaha. In Nauvoo, Illinois, where the Mormons first settled after they left New York, their leader Brigham Young played in *Pizarro*, and so encouraged the Mormon passion for play-acting that later in Salt Lake City they built a fine theatre, copied from Drury Lane, with a bust of Shakespeare over the door. In Colorado and far west on the Pacific coast the gold-miners demanded entertainment, paying for it in gold-dust. All the great names of the theatre flocked to California, where the first theatres were built in about 1850. The brightest star of them all was Charlotte Crabtree, known as Lotta, who toured the mining camps from the age of ten before going to New York to play in *Little Nell and the Marchioness*, *Ill. 201* and to make a fortune out of burlesques and extravaganzas. And down the Mississippi floated the showboats, pioneered by William Chapman, a London actor, and made famous by Edna Ferber's novel *Showboat* and the musical based on it. The staple fare of these floating theatres was melodrama and pantomime or such nautical dramas as *Black-Eyed Susan*. American playwrights were still few and far between, though Anna Cora Mowatt, who was also an actress, produced in *Fashion; or, Life in New York* the first American social comedy. But it was a long time before anyone rivalled the prolific Boucicault. Meanwhile, the craze for Negro minstrels swept

201 Charlotte Crabtree (1847–1924), known as Lotta, as the Marchioness, in a dramatization by John Brougham of Dickens' *Old Curiosity Shop* (1867)

202 (*far right*) John Drew (1853–1927), son of Mrs John Drew (*see Ill. 199*), and Ada Rehan (1860–1916) in *The Railroad of Love*, Daly's Theatre, New York, 1888

across the country and reached as far as England, rivalled in popularity only by spectacular song-and-dance shows like *The Black Crook* at Niblo's Garden, or by the variety show and its successor the vaudeville show, which reached its apotheosis at the Palace Theatre in New York.

Perhaps the nearest rival to Boucicault in the United States was Augustin Daly, whose ninety plays were mainly adaptations. He is however chiefly remembered for the theatres he opened in New York and London. The latter opened in 1893 with a production of *The Taming of the Shrew*, headed by Daly's leading players, John Drew and Ada Rehan. This theatre later became a fashionable home *Ill. 202* of musical comedy. Daly is also remembered for having encouraged Bronson Howard, the first American dramatist to make a living by writing plays, by staging his initial effort, *Saratoga*. Howard's *Young Mrs Winthrop*, which marked a distinct advance in the development of native American drama, was later put on by Belasco, who like Daly was a prolific playwright and a manager who opened his own theatre in New York. His productions were spectacular, and in later life he was noted for his artistic use of stage lighting. His own plays had no literary value, but were excellent vehicles tailored to fit the players who made their names under his management. Among them were Mrs Leslie Carter in *Zaza*, Blanche Bates in *Madame Butterfly*, and David Warfield in Klein's *The Auctioneer*. The American theatre now had everything it needed except a great playwright. Clyde Fitch, though excellent in many ways, hardly qualified. His most popular plays were *Beau Brummell*, written for Richard Mansfield, and *Captain Jinks of the Horse Marines*, in which Ethel Barrymore scored her first success.

Curiously enough, it was an American manager, Hezekiah Bateman, who was to further the career of one of England's greatest actors. Seeking a theatre in which to display the talents of his daughters Kate, Virginia (who married an English actor and became the mother of Fay Compton), and Isabel, who had all been on the stage since early childhood, Bateman took over the London Lyceum in 1871 and engaged as his leading man the thirty-three-year-old Henry Irving. Irving's career up to that time had given no indication of his future greatness. He was not a naturally good actor. His voice was harsh and his gait ungainly. Throughout his career there were always critics ready and anxious to point out his faults. But with the determination of genius he overcame all his handicaps and in so doing gained great personal prestige, being the first English actor to be knighted. He scored his first success at the Lyceum as Matthias in *The Bells*, a melodrama which he persuaded Bateman to put on when the season had opened disappointingly. This study in terror made him famous overnight, and his reputation was further enhanced by the pathos of his Charles I and by his controversial Hamlet. In 1879 he took over the management of the Lyceum himself, and made it the first theatre in London. As his leading lady he engaged Ellen Terry, the second daughter of a large theatrical family, and a

203 Fred Terry (1863–1933), as Henry in one of his most popular productions, *Henry of Navarre*, by William Devereux, first seen in 1908. Fred had his stage training under the Bancrofts (*Ill. 210*) and Irving (*Ills. 205, 207*)

much-loved actress who was considered the embodiment of all that was charming and womanly. She had been on the stage since early childhood, making her first appearance in Charles Kean's company at the age of ten. In the same company was her elder sister Kate, accounted by some a finer actress than Ellen, who retired early on marriage, and whose eldest daughter, also Kate, was the mother of John Gielgud. Ellen's youngest brother, Fred, was a fine romantic *Ill. 203* actor, who with his beautiful wife, Julia Neilson, appeared in such popular successes as *The Scarlet Pimpernel* and *Henry of Navarre*.

To act with Irving was an education in itself, and among the young men he engaged and trained were William Terriss, later well-loved in nautical melodrama at the Adelphi, who was murdered outside the stage door by a madman, and whose daughter Ellaline, a delightful heroine in musical comedy, married the light comedian

204 Kate Bateman and her sister Ellen, aged eight and seven, in *The Young Couple*, specially adapted for them from *Le Mariage Enfantin*, by Eugène Scribe, in which they appeared during their season at the St James's Theatre, London, in 1851. They also played Portia and Shylock, Macbeth and Lady Macbeth, and Richard III and Richmond

205 (*above*) Henry Irving (1838–1905) as Mathias
in *The Bells*, a melodrama by Leopold Lewis
based on Erckmann-Chatrian's *Le Juif polonais*,
first produced at the Lyceum, London, in 1851.
Here Irving as the Burgomaster sees in a
vision the Polish Jew he has murdered and robbed

207 Irving and Ellen Terry (1847–1928) as
Iachimo and Imogen in *Cymbeline* at the Lyceum
in 1896. Irving took a great risk in putting on
such a little-known play, but it was a success.
Ellen Terry charmed the audience as Imogen, and
even Bernard Shaw, Irving's severest critic,
said of his Iachimo that it was 'a true impersona-
tion, without a single lapse in the sustained
beauty of its execution'

204

206 John Martin-
Harvey (1863–1944)
as Sidney Carton in
The Only Way, an
adaptation by several
hands of Dickens'
novel, *A Tale of Two
Cities*. First produced
at the Lyceum in
1899, it was an
immediate success

Seymour Hicks; Johnston Forbes-Robertson, one of the finest

Ill. 208 Hamlets of all time, an actor of great delicacy and charm, with a superb voice, who was knighted during his farewell appearance at Drury Lane (he was also a painter – for one of his portraits see *Ill. 191*); and John Martin-Harvey, also a great romantic actor. He is

Ill. 206 best remembered for one part, Sydney Carton in *The Only Way* (a dramatization of *A Tale of Two Cities*), as is Wilson Barrett for his Marcus Superbus in *The Sign of the Cross*, and Lewis Waller for his Monsieur Beaucaire and d'Artagnan. These were the popular idols of the day, particularly in the provinces, where the old stock companies had been dispersed, leaving the larger towns dependent on visiting companies. The leading actors of the day toured extensively, especially in the summer, as did the actor-managers Frank Benson and Ben Greet with their Shakespeare companies. The first eventually established the Shakespeare Festival at

208 Johnston Forbes-Robertson (1853–1937) as Hamlet in a production at the Lyceum Theatre in September 1897. This shows the entry of Fortinbras in the final scene

Stratford-upon-Avon which was later to play so important a part in English theatrical life. The second took himself and his actors to the Old Vic, in the Waterloo Road, for many years Shakespeare's London home. (The theatre reopened in 1983.)

The tradition of the actor-manager established in his own theatre, inaugurated by Irving, was carried on in London by George Alexander at the St James's Theatre, which he took over in 1891; by Beerbohm Tree at Her Majesty's, which he built in 1897 with the profits from his tenure of the Haymarket; and by Charles Wyndham, in the theatre which he built in 1899 and named after himself. In all these fine playhouses there was equally fine acting, but the plays were mostly fustian. Even Tom Taylor, whose *Ticket-of-Leave Man* *Ill. 209* was the best of many dramas of contemporary low life, cannot be accounted more than a good craftsman in the old style. It was a style which Tom Robertson, brother of the actress Madge Kendal,

209 A scene from *The Ticket-of-Leave Man* by Tom Taylor (1817–80), which had in it the first stage detective, Hawkshaw (*centre*), and also the first stage setting of a London restaurant

210 Squire Bancroft (1841–1926) with his wife Marie Wilton (1839–1921) as Sidney Daryl and Maud Hetherington in *Society*, the first play of Tom Robertson, which they produced under their own management at the Prince of Wales's Theatre in 1865

was to destroy with his early efforts at realism in his so-called 'cup-and-saucer' dramas. These were given at the Prince of Wales's

Ill. 210 Theatre by Marie Wilton and her husband, Squire Bancroft. They demanded a complete revolution both in acting and in staging. The heavy delivery and broad gestures of earlier days were superseded by a quieter and more natural style of acting. The colourful but often irrelevant décors inherited from melodrama were replaced by some-what more realistic furniture and settings. Some of the effects of the change-over can be seen in *Trelawny of the 'Wells'*, a light comedy by A. W. Pinero, a playwright who startled Victorian playgoers as much with *The Second Mrs Tanqueray* and *The Notorious Mrs Ebbsmith* (which made the reputation of that fine but uneven actress, Mrs Patrick Campbell, later the first Eliza Doolittle) as his contemporary H. A. Jones did with *Saints and Sinners* and *Michael and his Lost Angel*. Jones, who considered himself a leader in the Theatre of Ideas, was also a good craftsman – the third act of his *Mrs Dane's Defence* is a classic example of dramatic tension – but his plays are now for-

208

gotten. Of Pinero's works only his early farces are still acted and admired. Both men thought themselves realists and social critics, but both suffered from a tendency to run away from the issues they had raised, and their characters behaved more in accordance with the conventions of the theatre than with those of real life. They had none of the wit of the unclassifiable Oscar Wilde, whose brilliant and artificial comedies, of which the best is *The Importance of Being Earnest*, are still current on the stage, or of W. S. Gilbert, whose *Ill. 211* plays, popular in their own day, have been overshadowed by the success of his libretti for light opera (derived from the forgotten extravaganzas and burlesques of Planché) which are indissolubly linked with the music of Arthur Sullivan.

Jones and Pinero and countless other dramatists were influenced in their work by the French dramatist Victorien Sardou, who succeeded Scribe as the purveyor of high-class melodrama, described derisively by Bernard Shaw as 'Sardoodledum'. He wrote many of his plays for the French actress Sarah Bernhardt, the 'golden-voiced', who through her high-spirited unconventionality became a legend in her lifetime. But even those who smiled at her absurdities admitted the excellence of her acting, and she had a long and brilliant career which took her all over the world. Although at her best in emotional, melodramatic parts like Tosca and Fedora, she was willing to tackle

211 George Alexander as John Worthing and Allan Aynesworth as Algernon Moncrieff in the first production of Oscar Wilde's *The Importance of Being Earnest* at the St James's Theatre, London, on 14 February 1895

anything – Madame Sans-Gêne, Phèdre, Marguerite Gautier,
Ill. 212 L'Aiglon, even Hamlet and Pelléas. Her only rival on the Continent
was the Italian actress Eleonora Duse, for whom the plays of
d'Annunzio were written. At her best in tragedy, she was in many
ways the opposite of the flamboyant Sarah Bernhardt, quiet,

212 Sarah Bernhardt (1845–1923) and Mrs Patrick Campbell (*née* Beatrice Stella
Tanner, 1865–1940) as Pelléas and Mélisande in the 1904 production of the play
of that name by Maurice Maeterlinck

213 Eleonora Duse (1858–1924) as Magda in an Italian version of *Die Heimat* (1893) by Hermann Sudermann, at Drury Lane, London, in 1895

withdrawn, an actress of great strength and subtlety. An enigmatic person, who in seeming to shun publicity attracted it, she too travelled extensively. In 1895 she appeared in London as Magda in Sudermann's *Heimat*, playing in Italian at the same time as Bernhardt *Ill. 213* was playing the part in French. This gave playgoers the unusual opportunity of comparing the two interpretations on the spot, an unusual event celebrated by Bernard Shaw in a masterly article written as dramatic critic of *The Saturday Review*. He preferred Duse in the part.

Die Heimat seemed new and daring when first produced, and a year later it was translated into English (as *Magda*) by Louis N. Parker. Shorn of the glamour of a foreign tongue and bereft of its equally glamorous leading ladies, it proved rather shoddy stuff, typical of much that passed for strong drama in the theatre of its day. But perhaps the actor-managers were less to blame than one might think in remaining faithful to the melodrama and romance their audiences demanded, since they had to face strong competition from the mushrooming music-hall. This form of entertainment, which

215 George Robey (1869–1954), known as 'The Prime Minister of Mirth', as Dame Hubbard in the pantomime *Goody-Two-Shoes*

◀ 214 (*left*) The famous music-hall star Marie Lloyd (1870–1922) in a characteristic costume and pose. Among her best-known songs were 'My Old Man said Follow the Van' and 'I'm One of the Ruins that Cromwell Knocked About a Bit'. She first appeared at the Royal Eagle Music Hall in 1885, and worked until a few days before her death

began modestly enough in the 1850s, soon created its own stars, who travelled incessantly from one town to another, and achieved enviable reputations. Some of them are still remembered – Vesta Tilley, Little Tich, Marie Lloyd, Grock, Harry Lauder, George Robey. They were individualists, and had little in common with straight actors, but their work touched the theatre at one point, when music-hall comedians of the calibre of Dan Leno and Herbert Campbell appeared annually in the Christmas pantomime, and music-hall routines were incorporated into the story. It was this that finally led to the lengthening of the fairy-tale opening and the ousting of the last remnants of the Harlequinade once made glorious by the genius of Grimaldi, whose Clown owed nothing to Italian models, and was, like the pantomime itself, a purely English creation.

Ills. 214, 215

Ill. 188

213

CHAPTER ELEVEN

Ibsen, Chekhov and the Theatre of Ideas

Although it is not necessary for the theatre as a medium of entertainment to concern itself seriously with social problems, or to look for plays of permanent literary value, there are times when, perhaps in memory of its religious origins, the tide turns against triviality and too great a divorce between reality and illusion. Audiences then demand – or perhaps it would be truer to say, are willing to accept – plays of social protest and criticism, even of propaganda. This may result in poor playwriting and in the production of a number of plays which, being nothing but propaganda, disappear without trace once their usefulness is over. But given the perfect balance between good theatre and a social problem of universal application, it may result in substantial additions to the world's stock of imperishable dramatic literature.

Such a period began in the European theatre of the late nineteenth century with the plays of Ibsen, reinforced by those of Chekhov. Both playwrights came from countries that had not previously made much impact on the European theatre. Denmark, whose history until 1814 was bound up with that of Norway, had produced a good writer of tragedy in the German style in Adam Oehlenschlaeger, and an excellent writer of comedy, mainly influenced by Molière and the *commedia dell'arte*, in Ludvig Holberg. But though both dramatists were known and acted throughout Europe, they had no following, and remained *sui generis*. It was not until Ibsen established a European reputation with *Brand*, one of his early verse-plays, of which the best known is *Peer Gynt*, that other countries thought of looking towards Scandinavia for inspiration. It came in full measure, first with the four searing pictures of small-town life, *The Pillars of Society*, *A Doll's House*, *Ghosts* and *An Enemy of the People*, and then with the symbolism of *The Wild Duck* and *The Master Builder* and the studies of individual exploration of experience in *Rosmersholm*, *Hedda*

214

Gabler, *Little Eyolf* and *John Gabriel Borkman*. Ibsen's last play,   *Ill.* 217
When We Dead Awaken, is a powerful work, written at the age of
seventy. It is comparable in its wisdom and maturity to *The Tempest*,
the last play of Shakespeare, whom Ibsen approaches closely in the
profoundly poetic thought and form underlying even his most
realistic works.

Ibsen, who learned his stagecraft as assistant manager of the Bergen
and Oslo theatres, and through careful study of the German and
Italian theatres which he visited on his travels, had an immense
influence not only on the drama of his day but also on the art of
acting and scenic presentation. It was under his influence, combined
with that of the Meiningers, that Antoine, who did more than anyone to deliver Europe from the domination of the 'well-made' play,
founded the Théâtre Libre in Paris. Here he produced the first
French translation of *Ghosts*, playing Oswald himself. Later his
Théâtre Antoine became a rallying-point for young dramatists.
There, and at the Odéon, he produced such realistic masterpieces as
Becque's *La Parisienne* and Brieux's *Les Avariés*; as *Damaged Goods*   *Ill.* 216
the latter created a sensation in England and the United States.
Antoine's influence, which continued into the next generation with
Jacques Copeau, led to the establishment in Germany of the Freie
Bühne under Otto Brahm, who encouraged the German dramatist
Gerhart Hauptmann, and of Grein's Independent Theatre in London,
where the battle for Ibsen was not won without a determined
struggle. The influential theatre critic Clement Scott denounced
Ghosts (in a translation by the equally eminent critic William
Archer) as a 'deplorably dull play. . . handled by a bungler' and 'an
open drain . . . a loathsome sore unbandaged', 'a dirty act done
publicly . . .'. But with the co-operation of such actresses as Janet   *Ill.* 217
Achurch, the first Nora in *A Doll's House*, and Elizabeth Robins, the
first Hedda Gabler, Hilda (in *The Master Builder*) and Rebecca West
(in *Rosmersholm*), Ibsen eventually took his rightful place on the
English stage. In the United States his plays met with less opposition,
partly owing to the number of well-disposed Scandinavian
immigrants who flocked to see them, and partly to the absence of an
effective censorship. The first production to arouse widespread

interest was *A Doll's House*, with Beatrice Cameron as Nora. This was followed by *Ghosts*, with Mrs Fiske as Mrs Alving, *Hedda Gabler*, with Blanche Bates in the title-role, and *Little Eyolf*, with Alla Nazimova as Rita. Incidentally, it is interesting to note how many of Ibsen's finest parts were written for women.

The only other Scandinavian dramatists to compare with Ibsen were his fellow-countryman, Bjørn Bjørnson, and the Swedish August Strindberg, both somewhat younger. Bjørnson, like Ibsen, worked in the Bergen and Oslo theatres, and his plays often deal with the same moral diseases of contemporary society. But he differs from Ibsen in his optimism and his firmly expressed belief in a redemptive force. Some of his plays have been seen in English, but his influence was mainly confined to Europe, particularly Germany.

Strindberg provoked at first almost as much hostility as Ibsen, but *The Father*, *Miss Julie* and *The Dance of Death* are now recognized as masterpieces which explore abnormal states of mind, and denounce by implication not so much the accidental corruption of society as certain basic evils in the human heart. At the Intima Teatern in Stockholm, where he directed his own plays, with his third wife Harriet Bosse as his leading lady, Strindberg made a number of technical innovations which greatly influenced the theatre of his own day, and anticipated some of the virtuosity later apparent in many European and American productions.

In London, the Independent Theatre, which had helped to establish Ibsen in England, also staged *Widowers' Houses*, the first play of the Irish dramatist George Bernard Shaw, one of Ibsen's most ardent disciples. Shaw's plays were at first considered almost as subversive as Ibsen's, since they were concerned with such social problems as slum landlordism and prostitution, which were then judged unfit for public discussion. But even his most blatant propaganda was presented with wit and elegance, and he aimed his arguments at the intelligence of his audiences rather than at their emotions. Though some of his plays have failed to maintain their place in the repertory, particularly when the abuses that occasioned them were corrected, many continue to be successful in revival. He will also be remembered for his connection with *My Fair Lady*

216 (*above*) A reading to an invited audience at the Théâtre Antoine of *Les Avariés* by its author, Eugène Brieux, in 1901 – a protest against censorship

217 The visit of the Rat-Wife, a scene from *Little Eyolf*, by Henrik Ibsen, in the first English production at the Avenue Theatre, London, in 1896. Mrs Patrick Campbell played the Rat-Wife, Janet Achurch was Rita and Elizabeth Robins Asta

Ill. 269 (a musical based on his play *Pygmalion*), which has had a world-wide success both on stage and screen.

Shaw's long career stretched from *Widowers' Houses* in 1892 to *Buoyant Billions* in 1949, the year before his death at the age of ninety-four. His work in general is based on a sound knowledge of theatre technique, and during his lifetime he dominated the stage not only in England, but on the Continent, where many of his plays were first produced in translation. In the United States the best *Ill. 218* known was *The Devil's Disciple*, which had its first production in New York with Richard Mansfield as Dick Dudgeon. *Saint Joan*, which many critics consider Shaw's finest play, also had its première

218 Richard Mansfield (1857–1907) as Dick Dudgeon in *The Devil's Disciple* by George Bernard Shaw (1856–1950), which had its world première in a performance at the Guild Theatre, New York, in 1897

219 *(right)* Sybil Thorndike as Saint Joan in the first London production (1924) of Shaw's play of that name, at the New Theatre. Here Joan waits with Dunois and his page for a west wind to carry their army across the Loire

in New York, with Winifred Lenihan in the title-role. This was played a year later in the London production by Sybil Thorndike, whose performance proved to be one of the highlights of a long and distinguished career. *Ill. 219*

Shaw's dislike of the elaborate spectacles, particularly of Shakespeare, provided by such actor-managers as Irving and Tree, was shared by William Poel, who, in reaction against the sacrifice of the poet's text for the benefit of costume and scenery, began a series of experimental productions, mostly in adapted halls, in which, with a bare stage and unobtrusive costuming, he tried to reproduce the conditions of the Elizabethan theatre as he understood them. His *Ill. 220*

main objective was to allow the verse to flow freely, giving prominence once more to the playwright. One of his most faithful followers, Harley Granville-Barker, had already made a name for himself as a director and dramatist when, in a season at the Court Theatre in 1906–7, he introduced eleven of Shaw's plays to the general public. But the first of Shaw's plays to appear in the commercial theatre was that excellent comedy, *Arms and the Man*, which was included in a season at the Avenue Theatre in 1904 by the actress Florence Farr, who played Louka. The financial backing for this venture was provided by a remarkable woman, Miss Horniman, founder of the Abbey Theatre in Dublin, where most of the plays of J. M. Synge and Sean O'Casey were first produced. She introduced into England from the Continent, where she had seen and admired it in action, the idea of 'playing in repertory', a return to much earlier conditions in the English theatres which had been abandoned in favour of a continuous run of one play. From 1908 to 1917 Miss Horniman maintained at the Gaiety Theatre in Manchester a true repertory company, which provided the inspiration for the very different but equally important Birmingham Repertory Theatre. This was the creation of Barry Jackson, a wealthy amateur of the theatre, who also founded the Malvern Festival for the production of Shaw's later plays, and first introduced Shakespeare in

220 A production of *Hamlet* by the pioneer of simplified staging, William Poel (1852-1934), at the Carpenters' Hall, London, in February 1900. Poel played Hamlet

221

221 A scene from the Moscow Art Theatre's 1902 production of *The Lower Depths* by Maxim Gorky, directed by Stanislavsky, who can be seen far back stage right

222 *(right)* Shaw's *Androcles and the Lion*, from the first production at the St James's ▶ Theatre, London, by Harley Granville-Barker in 1913

modern dress to London audiences with *Hamlet* in 1925 and *Macbeth* in 1926, both transferred from Birmingham.

One of Shaw's plays, *Heartbreak House*, was subtitled 'a Fantasia in the Russian manner' as a tribute to Chekhov, whose *Cherry Orchard* Shaw had persuaded the Stage Society to put on in London in 1912. This was the English playgoer's first introduction to the work of Russia's greatest dramatist of pre-Revolutionary days. Like all dramatists with something new to offer, Chekhov demanded actors trained in a new style to interpret him. He found them, after some initial failures elsewhere, in the company founded by his compatriots Stanislavsky and Nemirovich-Danchenko at the Moscow Art Theatre.

Ills. 221, 223

Before the advent of Stanislavsky, whose carefully formulated 'method' of training actors later became paramount in America, the Russian theatre had developed unnoticed outside its own borders. It had some excellent actors, many of them serfs trained in the private theatres maintained by wealthy noblemen. Due to the founding of a specifically Russian literature by the poet Pushkin, it also had some fine plays, among them Lermontov's *Masquerade* and Ostrovsky's *The Storm* – both tragedies – and a superb comedy by Griboyedov with a title which defies translation, *Gore ot Uma*; *Too Clever By Half* probably comes nearest to it. Among the rest, the best known in English are Gogol's *The Government Inspector* and Turgenev's *A Month in the Country*. But all these, together with the plays of Tolstoy and Gorky – the 'stormy petrel' of the Revolution whose best work had to wait for production until after 1917 – were unknown in Europe. It was not until Stanislavsky had trained actors able to convey the subtlety of Chekhov's dialogue, which when presented in the old style had appeared incomprehensible even to Russian audiences, that first Russia and then the world became aware of his genius. Constant revivals and many new translations have made him part of world theatre, and his influence on actors and acting everywhere has been incalculable.

Ill. 221

223 The company of the Moscow Art Theatre,
founded in 1898 by Nemirovich-Danchenko
and Stanislavsky (*see also Ill. 221*), listening to a
reading by Chekhov of his play *The Seagull*,
in which they appeared in 1899. Stanislavsky,
who played Trigorin, is sitting on Chekhov's
right, Nemirovich-Danchenko is standing far left

Meanwhile, in Spain, which always seems to have stood a little apart from the main current of European drama, Adría Gual, founder of the Teatro Intím in Barcelona, in line with Grein's Independent Theatre and Antoine's Théâtre-Libre, was trying in vain to introduce Ibsen to his compatriots. Ibsen's influence shows itself mainly in two plays by Echegaray – *The Son of Don Juan*, which owes something to *Ghosts*, and *El gran Galeoto*, which deals in an Ibsenite manner with the tragic results of malicious gossip. The work of Spain's greatest dramatist of this period, Benavente, seems, particularly in his best-known play, *The Bonds of Interest*, to derive more from the traditions of the *commedia dell'arte*, while the works of the Quintero brothers, and a widespread revival of the old art of puppetry, provided further examples of the flight from reality. Yet Martínez Sierra, whose own religious and romantic plays were often more popular abroad than in his own country, made a determined effort to modernize the Spanish theatre through his work at the Teatro Eslava in Madrid, where among other plays he produced *Blood Wedding*, *The House of Bernarda Alba* and *Yerma*, strong, passionate dramas by the young García Lorca, a potentially great playwright who was killed in the Spanish Civil War. After his death the theatre in Spain withdrew once more into escapism, and remains conservative in form and content, the commercial playhouses tending to rely mainly on foreign imports.

It was Italy, under the joint influence of Ibsen and Shakespeare, who had belatedly been introduced to Italian audiences by the tragic actor Ernesto Rossi, which was to produce the outstanding playwright of the new era, Luigi Pirandello. Neither the poverty of his early years, nor the later tragedy of his wife's insanity, was able to

Ill. 224

224 The Italian actor Ernesto Rossi
(1827–96) as Hamlet at Drury Lane
in 1876, in an Italian version which
he first performed in Italy in *c.* 1857

225 *(right)* Probably the most
popular of Pirandello's plays:
Six Characters in Search of an Author,
first seen in Italy in 1921, and in
England in 1922; here seen in a
production at the Arts Theatre
Club in 1928 ▶

quench his passion for the theatre, and in 1925 he established in
Rome a company for the production of his own plays, which deal
with the illusion of life and the hopelessness of man's attempts to
recognize reality. The influence of Pirandello's philosophy on the
disillusioned generation of the 1920s and 1930s was profound.
Though *Enrico IV* is probably his finest play, the best known in
Ill. 225 English are *Six Characters in Search of an Author, As You Desire Me,
Right You Are, If You Think You Are,* and *To-Night We Improvise.*
  The new drama, which had its roots in the late nineteenth
century, naturally demanded a new approach to scenic design as
well as to acting, and a pioneer in this field was the Swiss artist
Adolphe Appia. Shocked by the disparity between the old two-
dimensional scenery and the three-dimensional actor, he endea-

226

voured to design settings eloquent in their simplicity which created *Ill. 227* not a background but an environment. His admirable sets were enhanced by dramatic lighting effects made possible by the introduction of electricity, which, in the hands of successive lighting experts, was to become of increasing importance in the interpretation of play-texts.

Another and even more powerful advocate of scenic simplicity, and one whose writings and teaching were to have an influence on the theatre everywhere out of all proportion to the amount of work by him which was actually seen on stage, was Ellen Terry's son, Gordon Craig. Finding the contemporary London theatre *Ills.* 226, 228 uncongenial, he settled on the Continent in 1908, and spent the rest of his long life battling against what he considered the egotism and stupidity of actors, the inadequacies of directors, and the crass follies of contemporary scene designers. His system, in essentials, resolved itself into a series of large screens which served as a background for the imaginative use of changing lights. These, with a few rostrums and flights of steps, were used to build up a stage picture which made no concessions whatever to the prevailing demand for realism. And when this demand began to wane, the exponents of the new freedom, who wanted to escape from the tyranny of the proscenium arch and the box-set, found themselves still condemned to work in buildings which gave no opportunity for the

226 (*left*) A set for
Macbeth ('So foul and fair
a day I have not seen')
from a series designed by
Edward Gordon Craig
(1872–1966) for a
production at the
Knickerbocker Theater,
New York, in 1928

228 Gordon Craig's set
for Act II (The
Banqueting Hall) of
Ibsen's *Kongsemnerne* (*The
Crown Pretenders*)

227 (*below left*) A set for
Act II of Ibsen's *Little
Eyolf* (1924) by the Swiss
designer Adolphe Appia
(1862–1928). Appia and
Craig between them
revolutionized the art of
scenic design in Europe
and America, partly under
the influence of the
◄ theatre of the Far East

deployment of dramatic space which they envisaged. To achieve
Craig's vision of the future, it would be necessary to build new
theatres and alter fundamentally the training of the actor.

A form of theatre which seemed to offer a solution to the anti-
realist dilemma was that of the Far East, which, though dating back
beyond the earliest manifestations of theatre in modern Europe, was
until the end of the nineteenth century quite unknown there.
Relying on travellers' tales, and the translations of a few play-texts
by such scholars as Arthur Waley, directors and designers saw in the
elaborate symbolism and apparent simplicity of the Far Eastern stage
a way out of the dead end in which they found themselves.
Interesting additions to the European theatre were made by their
efforts – the revolving stage (introduced in 1896), the 'flowery way'
through the audience, the use of masks, and the relevance of

incidental music; and new concepts found their way also into the works of a number of dramatists, notably W. B. Yeats. But in the end Europe had to solve its own problems, though pockets of Far Eastern influence remained.

It is almost impossible for the European mind to adjust itself to the traditional and ritual elements in the Far Eastern theatre, though there is much in it that anyone must admire. Particularly interesting are the evocative symbolism of the costumes, where each colour and every fold of material conveys a message, and the incredible artistry of the actors, trained from childhood in a severe discipline which teaches control of every movement of the body. It was perhaps this aspect of the Far Eastern theatre which was to have the most influence on the Western world when the time came to reconsider the basic training of young actors.

Japanese plays, which were occasionally seen in London and Paris in the 1950s–1960s, when Japanese troupes visited the World Theatre season, take two forms (apart from the puppet-play, which cannot be dealt with here) – the *Nōh* and the *kabuki*. The aristocratic

Ill. 229   *Nōh* play, with its roots deep in religious ritual, takes its subjects from myth and legend, and is essentially a drama of soliloquy and reminiscence, and not, as in the West, of conflict. The chief actor (there are only two, with a chorus of singers) is masked, as in Greek tragedy, and sumptuously costumed. Both singer and actor, he chants his lines as he glides to and fro, the stamping of his stockinged feet on the resonant pinewood floor of the stage combining with the piercing notes of the transverse flute and the beat of three drums to provide a rhythmic accompaniment to his highly stylized movements. And as each Greek tragedy had its satyr-play, so each

Ill. 230   *Nōh* has its *kyōgen*, or comic interlude, which in performance is somewhat reminiscent of the miming and clowning of the old *commedia dell'arte*.

Ills. 231, 232   The *kabuki*, unlike the *Nōh*, is a hybrid form, as its name implies (*ka* – singing, *bu* – dancing, *ki* – acting), which takes its subjects from Japanese history or from daily life in ancient times. Its actors, who are more numerous than in the *Nōh* and not masked, though their costumes and movements are equally brilliant and stylized, have also

230

229 A scene from a Japanese *Nōh* play, *The Lady Aoi*, seen at the Aldwych Theatre, London, during the World Theatre Season of 1967. A priest (*stage left*) wrestles symbolically with an evil spirit for the life of the Lady Aoi

230 (*below*) A *khōgen*, or comic interlude, *The Tied Servants*, also seen at the Aldwych. Two men, though tied up as show in the picture, manage to steal wine from a large cask

231 An eighteenth-century print of a Japanese *kabuki* theatre, showing the

hanamichi, or 'flower way', along which the actors make their entrances and exits a chorus of singers to accompany them, and in addition an orchestra of *samisen* players. A detail in both *Nōh* and *kabuki* which intrigued Western audiences was the presence of stage-hands, in dark kimonos, who came and went during the performances, adjusting costumes, and handing over or removing properties as required.

Although both the *Nōh* and a modernized form of *kabuki* still flourish in Japan, there was, from the end of the nineteenth century, some infiltration from the West, beginning, not surprisingly, with Shakespeare, first in free adaptations, and later in the scholarly translations of Dr Tsubouchi, completed in 1928. A new style of acting, inaugurated by Oto Kawakami in the early 1900s, later facilitated the production in Japanese of plays by Ibsen, Hauptmann, Strindberg and Pirandello; but it was some time before Japan

232 A modern *kabuki* play, *Kanjinchō*, at the Kabuki-za Theatre in Tokyo in 1960; a revival in modern style of one of the most representative classical Japanese plays, first performed in 1840. The actors are Koshiro VIII as Benkei and Danjūrō XI as Togashi

233 Mei Lan-Fang (1894–1961) in one of his female parts. He was the first Chinese actor to combine the dramatic techniques of the five female roles in Peking opera, and his virtuosity, while only in his early twenties, caused the part of the heroine to oust the elderly bearded male from its pre-eminent place for the first time

produced any 'modern' playwrights. One of the most interesting today is Kobo Abe, who from 1973 to 1980 ran a theatre group in Tokyo for the production of his own plays, which, like his novels, show plainly the influence of such Western writers as Beckett, Kafka and Brecht. But perhaps the solution to Japan's theatrical problems will come through the adaptation and extension of the comic *kyōgen*, which certainly deals realistically with daily life, though not as yet with the life of today.

The Chinese theatre, which since the beginning of the nineteenth century has consisted chiefly of the Peking opera, is, like the Japanese, designed mainly to afford great scope to the actor. Its productions are a flexible and harmonious blend of dialogue, song, dance and acrobatics on subjects taken from national history, legends

235

and fiction. Costumes are magnificent, but with no attempt at historical accuracy. Colours indicate rank. Yellow is for an emperor, red for an official. Temperament too is indicated by colour – blue for ferocity, red for courage – and certain properties have with the lapse of time acquired symbolic meanings. A table is a bridge, an oar a ship, a whip a horse. As in Japan, all the parts in a Chinese play were played by men, who started training as children. The only Chinese actor known by name outside his own country was the female impersonator Mei Lan-Fang, who in the 1920s and 1930s toured Europe and the United States in some of his finest

Ill. 235

Ill. 233

236

234 (*left*) A scene from a Chinese play illustrating the symbolism by which the waving of blue flags indicates the sea

235 The heroine in a Chinese play (played by a man). The tasselled whip which she is carrying indicates that she is supposed to be on horseback

parts, astonishing audiences everywhere by the delicacy and virtuosity of his performances. Later, actresses were introduced into Chinese companies, and efforts were made to encourage the survival of many types of local theatre, each with its own repertory and characteristic style of acting. In the early part of the twentieth century the influence of Western drama was felt through translations of Ibsen and other European dramatists, but with the establishment of the People's Republic in 1949 new plays were concerned mainly with revolutionary propaganda. Since the death of Mao and the fall of the Gang of Four in 1976, some earlier

Chinese playwrights have emerged from hiding; and traditional Peking and *Kungu* as well as local-style operas have been performed again, as well as plays of the *hua ju* type – new, Western-style 'spoken dramas' of social comment, often with a satirical or political content. Since 1978 the dance-drama based on traditional stories has also become increasingly popular.

Unlike traditional Japanese plays, some examples from China have passed in adaptation into the dramatic literature of the West. Voltaire drew on *The Chinese Orphan* for his *L'Orphelin de la Chine*; Klabund translated *The Chalk Circle*, which has been seen in English, as has Brecht's version, *The Caucasian Chalk Circle*; and in the 1930s both England and America enjoyed *Lady Precious Stream*, adapted by the Chinese writer S. I. Hsiung.

The theatre of India, which is as ancient as that of China and Japan, and equally traditional, is little known in the West, though her dance-forms and music have been the subject of intensive study.

236 *Sizwe Bansi is Dead*, an indictment of the policy of Apartheid; directed by Athol Fugard at the Royal Court Theatre in London in 1973, with John Kani (left) and Winston Ntshona (right)

The only Indian plays known in translation are the fourth-century *Little Clay Cart*, attributed to Śūdraka, and the fifth-century Śakūntalā, by Kālidāsa. A version of the latter by Sir William Jones, published in 1789, evoked the admiration of Goethe, and first drew the attention of European readers to the beauties of Sanskrit dramatic literature. It was produced in London in 1899 and in New York in 1924. In modern times the plays in English of the Indian poet Rabindranath Tagore have been published and read, but seldom acted. There seemed at one time a possibility that India, which had acting versions of Shakespeare in several of its vernacular languages, might produce a dramatic literature in the modern style, but it seems at present as if the creative element in Indian drama is engaged in the cinema more than the theatre.

The theatre of Black Africa is, in the main, like that of India, highly traditional across the continent. There are performances in the vernacular, occasionally in pidgin English, and in East Africa, in Swahili, which feature folk operas based on tribal songs and dances. In the large cities plays in English and French can be seen, dealing with the struggle for independence or based on incidents from earlier local history. The best known English-language playwrights outside their own countries are probably the Nigerian political satirist Wole Soyinka, author of *Kongi's Harvest* (New York, 1966), and the Kenyan Ngugi wa Thiong'o, whose *The Trial of Dedan Kimathi* featured a Mau-Mau hero (London, 1984). French-language plays, which sometimes find their way to Paris where Black actors are often found training in drama schools, can be seen on the Ivory Coast, in Guinea, Mali, and especially in Senegal and Algeria.

Collective Creation, as practised in Britain and America, is also typical of the vigorous English-language drama of the Black townships. South Africa's best-known playwright, the Afrikaaner Athol Fugard, has also worked collectively, notably in *Sizwe Bansi is Dead*. This, like others of his own plays, among them *Boesman and Lena* (1971) and *Master Harold . . . and the Boys* (1983), has been successfully produced in New York and London.   *Ill. 236*

CHAPTER TWELVE

The Modern Theatre

Up to the end of the nineteenth century the actor dominated the theatre, playwrights being generally required to provide situations in which he could be seen at his best. With the advent of Ibsen and his followers, however, the text became all-important, and actors had to adapt themselves to the new conditions. Realistic dialogue, in a conversational style, took the place of rhetoric and declamation; gestures became more restrained, and the scenery presented an accurate representation of the place and period of the play. The illusion of reality was greatly helped by the almost universal adoption of the box-set, which took the place of the romantic backcloth and wings used in melodrama. Plays too had to conform to modern conditions to survive, and those which, like Shakespeare's, were written for an open stage and an unlocalized setting, suffered cruelly from being confined behind a proscenium arch.

One of the paradoxes of the theatre soon became apparent; the more realistic the play, the more it needed in the way of accessories. The classics could be acted with little more than 'bare boards and a passion'; but the realistic playwright demanded all the paraphernalia of modern living, and in addition the complete segregation of the audience from the actors. This led to the darkening of the auditorium, and to the convention by which the proscenium arch became an opening in a 'fourth wall', through which the spectators watched what Zola, speaking of his own intensely realistic plays, called 'a slice of life'. It also had the effect of narrowing the dramatist's range to intimate, interior scenes, and to subjects which lent themselves to the one-set play with only a handful of actors.

Too much insistence on realism was bound to produce a reaction. This took the form of expressionism, a hallucinatory vision of life inherent in the later dramas of Strindberg. It originated in Germany

237 A constructivist set from the United States: the setting for O'Neill's Dynamo (1929), designed by Lee Simonson (1888–1967)

238 A revolutionary stage in Soviet Russia in the 1920s: a production of Ostrovsky's *The Forest* (first produced in 1851), directed and designed by V. E. Meyerhold (1874–1940)

in Sorge's *Der Bettler*, and was later responsible for the plays of Wedekind and Kaiser; in France, it was apparent in Lenormand's *Simoun* and *The Eater of Dreams*, both seen in London in the 1920s. These paved the way for *The Silver Tassie* and *Within the Gates*, by the Irish playwright Sean O'Casey, and for *The Emperor Jones* and *The Hairy Ape*, by America's foremost dramatist, Eugene O'Neill.

In the end, however, the expressionist play, veering as it does between conscious and subconscious states of mind, posed too many problems for actor and director alike, and remained mainly a literary manifestation. New ideas, which, like those of Craig and Appia, struck at the very roots of realism, resulted in constructivism, offspring of the Russian Revolution of 1917, which, subordinating both actor and play-text to the stage setting, abolished detailed scenery in favour of platforms, steps and significant forms meant to convey the thrusting and dynamic qualities of the new Soviet *Ill. 238* Russia. The Russian director Meyerhold, with his theory of 'bio-mechanics', went even further, clearing the stage as far as the back wall so as to leave a bare space on which he could manoeuvre his players, whom, like Craig, he regarded as puppets to be manipulated by one man – himself.

Ill. 237 Expressionism and constructivism, one literary, the other theatrical, served their turn, and then gave way to experiments seeking to bring back into the playhouse the sense of wonder and participation temporarily lost in the search for realism. Under the new dispensation even Ibsen and Chekhov were found to be poets and symbolists, as was shown in the new translations which revealed the full beauty of their plays to receptive audiences.

As in all periods of change these so-called 'new dramas' represented only a fraction of the plays produced during the period of their ascendancy. Audiences still enjoyed farce, drawing-room comedy, the whimsical offerings of J. M. Barrie, the brittle comedies of Noël Coward, and the 'well-made' cynicisms of Somerset Maugham. Austria had her own brand of cynicism with Arthur Schnitzler, whose *La Ronde* was to prove attractive to audiences everywhere; but one of her finest dramatists at this time was Hugo von Hofmannsthal, author of some excellent plays, but now in

LIMELIGHTS
WORKED FROM
5 GALLERIES
SUSPENDED
FROM THE ROOF

ENTRANCE
& EXIT

ORCHESTRA

ENTRANCE
FOR PERFORMERS

SEAT
CLOTH
WHEN
DOORS
THROWN
OPEN

EXIT

SECTION TAKEN
OUT OF FLOORING TO
SHOW THE UNDERGROUND
ARRANGEMENTS TO RAISE AND
LOWER STAGE

POSITION OF
HILL AND TREES
WHEN IN THE
ARENA

LESSER
SLIDING DOOR
WHICH FITS
INTO THE
GREAT
DOOR

GREAT SLIDING
DOOR

RAILS ON WHICH
THE HILL AND
TREES MOVES INTO
THE ARENA

PLAYER
MAKING
READY
IN THE
CORRIDORS

239 A view from the flies of the Great Hall at Olympia, London, as it appeared during
the production of *The Miracle* by Max Reinhardt (1873–1943) in 1911. This wordless
spectacle-play by Karl Volmöller, with music by Engelbert Humperdinck, was based
on an old legend about a nun who escapes from her convent and returns after many
years to find that the Madonna has taken her place

danger of being regarded only as the librettist of Richard Strauss and
the adapter of the old Morality play *Everyman* for Max Reinhardt's
Salzburg Festival.

Mention of Reinhardt entails consideration of one of the
outstanding phenomena of the twentieth-century theatre – the rise
of the producer, now, under the influence of the United States,
known as the director, and in Europe as the *régisseur*. Because of the
importance of ensemble acting in so many new plays, someone not

Ill. 239

240 (*above left*) Madeleine Renaud
and her husband Jean-Louis Barrault
in *Le Chien du Jardinier*, by
Georges Neveux, London 1956

242 (*above right*) The opening scene
of *King Lear* at Stratford-upon-
Avon, 1937, designed and
produced by Theodore
Komisarjevsky (1882–1954)

241 Louis Jouvet (1887–1951), one
of the outstanding figures of the
French theatre between the two
world wars, as Molière's Tartuffe

involved in the action was needed to supervise and co-ordinate the
work of the actors. Unlike the Duke of Saxe-Meiningen, the *Ill. 180*
prototype of the modern director, most directors began as actors,
and only later devoted themselves entirely to direction. This was the
case with Reinhardt. He dominated the theatre of Central Europe
for over twenty-five years, refusing to be confined by any one form
of theatrical presentation, setting his productions in a ballroom, a
circus, a cathedral square, or in the vast spaces of London's Olympia,
which housed his conception of *The Miracle*, a brilliant spectacle *Ill. 239*
whose crowds he manipulated with consummate ease.

243 Orestes and the Furies, a scene from the 1981 production at the National Theatre, London, of the *Oresteia*, performed in masks by an all-male cast, directed by Peter Hall, and with scenery and costumes by Jocelyn Herbert and music by Harrison Birtwhistle. This spectacular and successful production became (in 1982) the first English-language version of a Greek tragedy to be performed at the open-air theatre at Epidaurus (*Ill. 14*)

Yet Reinhardt could produce with equal artistry delicate intimate plays whose natural home was the jewel-like Residenztheater in Munich. He was eclectic in his choice of scenery, using whatever best suited his concept of the play – permanent, semi-permanent, simultaneous – together with runways, rostrums, steps and a revolving stage. His extensive travels brought him into prominence everywhere, but in 1933 he settled in the United States, where he died ten years later.

Although the director was a comparative newcomer in the history of the theatre, the first half of the twentieth century saw many reputations made in this field, each director bringing to his work some quality which stamped it as peculiarly his own. In Russia Meyerhold gave way to Vakhtangov, whose short but stimulating career in his own theatre in Moscow had a widespread influence; Taïrov, who with his actress-wife Alice Koonen introduced to the Soviet stage the works of many contemporary foreign dramatists; and Okhlopkov, who was profoundly influenced by the theatrical concepts of the Far East. In France the work of Antoine was carried on by Pitoëff and his wife Ludmilla at the Théâtre des Mathurins, and between the two world wars Paris saw the work of a famous quartet of directors – Dullin at the Atelier, Copeau at the Vieux-Colombier, Baty at the theatre to which he gave his own name, and *Ill. 241* Jouvet at the Athénée. Besides being an inspired interpreter of Molière's plays, Jouvet was responsible for bringing before the public the plays of Giraudoux, a witty and subtle dramatist who proved popular in translation both in England and America.

A Frenchman who won international renown as a director was Copeau's nephew and disciple Michel Saint-Denis, founder of the Compagnie des Quinze. Through his later drama centres in London and Strasbourg he was responsible for the training of many young actors, and he directed in the commercial theatre a number of productions which offered a highly personal interpretation of the text while remaining faithful to the author's intentions. His peripatetic career, with its consequent cross-fertilization of the theatre on both sides of the Atlantic, was paralleled by that of Komisarjevsky, a Russian-born stage-designer and director who

248

aroused fierce controversy with some of his productions of
Shakespeare at Stratford-upon-Avon, particularly a *Macbeth* with
aluminium scenery, but who triumphed with an outstanding
production of *King Lear*.

Among the many admirable directors in England at this time was
Tyrone Guthrie, remarkable for his masterly handling of crowd
scenes. He was the inspiration behind much excellent work,
particularly at the Stratford (Ontario) Festival Theatre, and at a
theatre in Minneapolis, Minnesota, both of which he founded, the
latter being later named in his honour. An infant prodigy, who was
to enjoy, perhaps more than any Englishman since Craig, a
European reputation, was Peter Brook, who, by-passing both
training and experience, directed his first play at eighteen, and after a
series of brilliant productions, took control of an explosively
experimental and creative group in Paris.

In Germany Jessner, one of the first directors there to abolish
scenery in favour of linked flights of steps (*Spieltreppe*) providing
different acting levels, and Piscator, a disciple of Reinhardt and the
precursor of 'epic theatre', were responsible for productions whose
influence spread far beyond their own country. Piscator, like
Reinhardt, finally settled in the United States, which, being now
fully-fledged theatrically, was able to produce her own directors.
Among the most successful were Guthrie McClintic, who did some
of his best work with plays which starred his wife, Katherine
Cornell, and Elia Kazan, responsible for the staging of plays by two
of America's most important playwrights, Arthur Miller (*Death of a
Salesman*) and Tennessee Williams (*A Streetcar Named Desire*). But it
was in the field of scenic design that the American theatre first made
a reputation outside its own borders, with a succession of artists
which included Lee Simonson, Norman Bel Geddes, Aline
Bernstein, Jo Mielziner and Boris Aronson. An important figure of
these early days was the designer Robert Edmond Jones, who
through his connection with the Provincetown Players helped to
further the career of the United States' first outstanding playwright,
Eugene O'Neill. O'Neill, equally at home with Greek drama,
realism, symbolism and expressionism, shocked the complacency of

Ill. 242

Ill. 257

Ill. 237

Ill. 248

244 (*above*) John Gielgud, considered
the finest Hamlet of his generation, in
the production at the New Theatre,
London, in 1934

245–6 Costume design by Motley for
(*above right*) Michael Redgrave as
Antony in *Antony and Cleopatra*, and
(*right*) Marius Goring as Richard III, in
the 1953 season at the Royal
Shakespeare Theatre, Stratford-
upon-Avon

247 (*far right*) Laurence Olivier as
Tattle in Congreve's *Love for Love*,
revived by the National Theatre at the
Old Vic, London, in its 1965 season

250

his audiences into an awareness of a world not previously explored by American dramatists, and he still stands as the main contributor from the United States to the history of world drama.

There was no lack of good actors to interpret O'Neill, both in New York and in London, where many of his plays were seen and

248　Eben (played by Charles Ellis) with Abbie, his young stepmother (Mary Morris) in a scene from *Desire Under the Elms*, by Eugene O'Neill (1888–1953), first produced at the Greenwich Village Theatre in 1924 by the Provincetown Players, in a multiple set designed by Robert Edmond Jones

admired; but on the whole the great reputations of the English-speaking theatre at this time, when so many American actors were being lured away to Hollywood, were made in London in revivals of the classics, particularly at the Old Vic under the management of

Ill. 244　Lilian Baylis – John Gielgud, the finest Hamlet of his generation;
Ill. 247　Laurence Olivier, who later led England's first National Theatre Company; Ralph Richardson, a subtle actor of great integrity; Donald Wolfit who toured indefatigably in Shakespeare; Michael

Redgrave, a fine actor in nervous, intellectual parts; Alec Guinness, a *Ill. 245* truly protean actor who, in the opinion of his admirers, spent far too much time on the cinema to the detriment of the living theatre, and Anthony Quayle, who from 1948 to 1956 was an unusually youthful director of the Stratford-upon-Avon company, where he was succeeded by the even more youthful Peter Hall, destined to *Ill. 243* control the fortunes of the National Theatre building when it finally opened on London's South Bank in 1976–7.

A partnership much admired in America, which gave equal pleasure in London, was that between Lynn Fontanne and her *Ill. 249* husband Alfred Lunt, who began playing together in 1924. Equally

249 Alfred Lunt as Jupiter and his wife Lynn Fontanne as Alkmena in an adaptation by S. N. Behrman of *Amphitryon 38*, by Jean Giraudoux (1882–1944), produced in New York in 1937, and in London a year later

Ill. 240   fruitful was the partnership between the French actor Jean-Louis Barrault and his wife Madeleine Renaud, the one trained originally as a mime, the other in the strict discipline of the Comédie-Française. With their own company they did sterling work at home and abroad, particularly with their productions of Claudel, hitherto considered a difficult and unrewarding playwright. In what many regard as Claudel's finest play, *Partage de midi*, Edwige Feuillère, one of France's outstanding actresses, provided as Ysé a brilliant and sensuous counterpart to the tormented and despairing Mesa of Barrault.

250 The Berliner Ensemble with Helene Weigel in *Mother Courage and her Children* by Bertolt Brecht (1898–1956), one of the seminal influences in the theatre today

The Second World War had a profound effect upon the theatre everywhere, though some of the subterranean influences which led to the final upheaval had been apparent before 1939. The dispersal of talents under Hitler, the growing dissatisfaction of theatre workers with the limitations imposed by the proscenium arch, the desire to enlarge the bounds of experience, the inadequacy of most of the new plays, created an unstable situation which needed only a sudden jolt to set the theatre off in a new direction. This was provided by the work of Bertolt Brecht, the dominating influence in the European theatre of the 1950s. He had for a time been Reinhardt's assistant at the Deutsches Theater in Berlin, and his early plays showed him attempting to make use both of Piscator's 'epic theatre' and his own theory of 'alienation'. This new approach to the problem of actor–audience relationship consisted in destroying by various technical methods the once-prized 'theatrical illusion', and so preventing the spectators from becoming emotionally involved in the action. Only then, he argued, can they judge the performance and the subject-matter objectively and with intelligence. It was admirable in theory, and sometimes worked well, but revivals of some of his plays under other directors have shown that his characters cannot always avoid engaging the sympathy of the audience.

Brecht, a confirmed Communist, first came to prominence in Berlin in 1928 with a new version of Gay's *The Beggar's Opera* – his *The Threepenny Opera* with music by Kurt Weill; but it was during his exile from Germany after 1933 that he wrote what are generally considered to be his best plays – *Mother Courage and Her Children,* *Ill. 250* *Galileo, The Good Woman of Setzuan, The Days of the Commune* and *The Caucasian Chalk Circle.* These and all his later plays were professionally presented after 1945 by his own company, the Berliner Ensemble, led by his actress-wife Helene Weigel. In 1956, after he husband's death, and again in 1965, she took the company to London, giving playgoers a chance to see in the original a number of plays already known in translation.

Soon after the first of these visits, a leading actress in London, Peggy Ashcroft, was seen in *The Good Woman of Setzuan,* diplaying incredible virtuosity in the dual roles of the prostitute and her male

cousin. Two years previously she had given a superb performance of
Ill. 251 Hedda Gabler which won her a gold medal from the King of
Norway. Both plays were directed by George Devine, founder of
the English Stage Company, which had a seminal influence on the
development of the modern English theatre, determining its future
Ill. 254 course with a production in 1956 of John Osborne's *Look Back in
Anger*. There had been, immediately after the war, strong signs of a
revival of poetic drama on the London stage, with Christopher Fry's
The Lady's Not For Burning and his *The Dark is Light Enough*, the
Ill. 252 latter long remembered for the excellent acting of Edith Evans, who
had made her reputation in Restoration comedy, Shaw and Wilde.
But particularly among younger playgoers, the tide turned against
Fry, as in the 1900s it had turned against the equally poetic Stephen
Phillips; it turned also against light drawing-room comedy and the

251 (*left*) Peggy Ashcroft with George Devine in the 1954 production of Ibsen's
Hedda Gabler (1890) at the Lyric Theatre, Hammersmith

252 (*right*) Edith Evans as the Countess Rosmarin Ostenburg in *The Dark is Light
Enough*, by Christopher Fry, at the Aldwych Theatre, London, 1954

253 *Ring Round the Moon*, a translation by Christopher Fry of *L'Invitation au Château*, by Jean Anouilh, produced by Peter Brook at the Globe Theatre, London, in 1950, with Paul Scofield and Claire Bloom (*centre*), Margaret Rutherford and Daphne Newton (*stage right*). Décor by Oliver Messel

use of Southern English, in favour of local accents and the speech of the semi-literate. Among playwrights who took advantage of the freedom thus conferred upon them were Arnold Wesker with *The Kitchen*, Harold Pinter with *The Caretaker*, set in an attic, and Ann Jellicoe with *The Knack*, which took place in a bedsitter.

The innovations introduced into his plays by Brecht, and his insistence that the actor must not attempt to 'become' the character he is portraying – in direct contradiction to the 'method' of Stanislavsky – led to a new style of acting and direction which has been particularly influential in the post-war experimental theatres of eastern Europe. In the English theatre Brecht's influence was apparent not only in new methods of Shakespearean production, but in such new works as Bolt's *A Man for all Seasons*, Shaffer's *The Royal Hunt of the Sun*, John Arden's Armstrong's Last Goodnight, and in all the plays produced by Joan Littlewood for Theatre Workshop. At this experimental East End theatre the author's script was used as a basis for brilliant improvisation by the director, who imposed on the actors her own concept of the play. This worked well with such modern playscripts as *A Taste of Honey* and *Oh, what a Lovely War!*, but less well for the classics.

Experimental work of much the same kind was seen in New York in the productions of The Living Theatre, founded in 1947 by Julian Beck and his wife Judith Malina. It had a chequered career, but exerted a tremendous influence on the theatre everywhere, and its outstanding productions – Jack Gelber's *The Connection* (1959), about drug addiction, and Kenneth Brown's anti-military *The Brig* – are still remembered. Driven into exile by financial and other difficulties, the troupe toured Europe during the 1960s, returning to America eventually to continue its experimental work, mainly in 'peripatetic political manifestations'.

Both Theatre Workshop and The Living Theatre were typical of the small groups which emerged – and continue to emerge – all over Europe, in the USA and in parts of South America, living from

254 *Look Back in Anger* by John Osborne, at the Royal Court Theatre, London, in 1956, with Kenneth Haigh, Alan Bates and Mary Ure. The play that launched Alan Bates (as Cliff Lewis, seated left) on his successful career

255 The final scene – the crucifixion – from *The Royal Hunt of the Sun*, by Peter Shaffer, at the Old Vic, London, with the National Theatre Company, in 1964, with Robert Stephens (*above*) as Atahualpa and Colin Blakely (*below*) as Pizarro

hand to mouth, exploring new techniques, providing their own scripts, working wherever they can find a roof over their heads, or even in the streets and parks. They can be found in cellars, disused chapels, warehouses, and, like the famous La Mama group, in cafés; in pubs, wine bars, and even, as at New End, London, in a converted mortuary. Through their combined efforts they are breaking the mould of the formal theatre, and, with improvisation and Collective Creation, lessening their dependence on the playwrights, to whom, and to their audiences, they offer an entirely new concept of theatre.

Nevertheless, substantially built playhouses continue to make a contribution to be reckoned with, though their splendour does not always guarantee the provision of plays to match.

Germany, weakened by the war and the subsequent partitioning of the country, replaced many of her bombed theatres with splendid new buildings equipped with all the latest devices; but the best German-language plays of the 1950s came from two playwrights resident in Switzerland – Max Frisch and Friedrich Dürrenmatt. Italy sent to other European countries the plays of Ugo Betti, while Eduardo de Filippo, with his brother Peppino, strove to keep alive the Neapolitan tradition of farce-playing; both were seen in London during World Theatre seasons there. Several plays by the Russian dramatist Arbusov, particularly *Old World*, were well received in the West, though Soviet Russia produced no major playwright. And in France an effort was being made to decentralize and democratize the theatre by the establishment, under Jean Vilar, of the Théâtre National Populaire. This broke the age-old domination of Paris, and led to the foundation in the provinces of centres for acting and actor-training, of which the most important was that at Villeurbanne, under the iconoclastic Roger Planchon, which eventually became the first provincial theatre to receive a Government grant, and so, after the death of Vilar in 1971, the first to take over the title of Théâtre National Populaire.

The post-war French theatre was dominated by the works of the existentialist philosopher Sartre and his contemporary Anouilh, whose numerous plays found appreciative audiences all over Europe and in America. But the most important play of the 1950s was *Ill. 256* undoubtedly Samuel Beckett's *Waiting for Godot* (first written in French), which portrayed vividly the contemporary obsession with human isolation. Two further manifestations of the spirit of the age, both originating in France, were the Theatre of the Absurd and the Theatre of Cruelty. The first, whose roots go back to 1896, with the *Ill. 258* production of Jarry's *Ubu Roi*, was based on the assumption that human life is so illogical, and language so inadequate as a means of communication, that man's only refuge is in laughter, as is evinced in the plays of Ionesco, such as *The Bald Prima Donna* and *The Chairs*. The second, which derived from the writings of Artaud, who died

256 Samuel Beckett's *Waiting for Godot*, first performed in Paris in 1953 and produced in London by Peter Hall at the Arts Theatre in 1955

insane, sought to free man from the restraints of morality and reason, permitting him to return to a primitive state of ferocity and brute power. It had an immense vogue in Europe, and came officially into England in 1964 with Peter Brook's production at the Aldwych, the London home of his Stratford company, of the German dramatist Weiss's *The Persecution and Assassination of Marat as Performed by the Inmates of the Asylum of Charenton under the direction of the Marquis de Sade*, known briefly as *The Marat/Sade*. The influence of that epoch-making event was seen in a number of plays which – like Edward Bond's *Saved* with its stoning of a baby in its pram – aroused as much protest as Ibsen's, and with as little effect.

261

257 Peter Brook's Royal Shakespeare Company production of *A Midsummer Night's Dream*, 1970, 'combining the rough magic of the circus, the puppet-theatre, and the music hall', in which the cast performs on stilts and trapezes

258 The Theatre of the Absurd: a sketch by David Hockney for Alfred Jarry's *Ubu Roi*, first produced in Paris in 1896 and revived at the Royal Court Theatre in London in 1966. Hockney's décor and costumes set the monstrous figure of Père Ubu in a landscape of Pop Art

259 Performance 'in promenade': a scene with Adam and Eve at the Creation, from *The Mysteries*, a trilogy compiled from English medieval Mystery plays by Bill Bryden and his company, produced at the National Theatre (Cottesloe), London, in 1985. The action takes place in and among the audience

260 A popular adaptation of a novel for the stage: *Nicholas Nickleby*. Nicholas (Roger Rees) meets the 'infant phenomenon' and Mr Folair of Mr Crummles' Company, a scene from the Royal Shakespeare Company production at the Aldwych Theatre, London, in 1981, directed by Trevor Nunn and John Caird

261 A set by the Czech scene-designer Josef Svoboda for a production of Sophocles' *Oedipus the King* at the Prague National Theatre, 1963. The thirty-foot-wide staircase rises from the bottom of the Orchestra pit, through the proscenium up to the grid in one broad flight. The steps are semi-transparent, with the musicians underneath, and the music was heard through perforations in the staircase

263 (*opposite*) The Royal Exchange Theatre, Manchester, a theatre-in-the-round ▶ which opened in 1976 and holds 700 spectators. The auditorium can be converted for thrust-stage performances

It was not long before the new ferment of ideas resulted in the building of open-stage playhouses, similar to those of the Elizabethan theatre, among them the The Mermaid in London; the Barbican, the City of London home of the Royal Shakespeare *Ill. 262* Company; the Chichester Festival Theatre, and the Stratford (Ontario) Festival Theatre – and a return to an even more primitive form of auditorium, the theatre-in-the-round. Among the latter were the Victoria Theatre, Stoke-on-Trent, which saw the first productions of many plays by a prolific dramatist, Alan Ayckbourn, and, in its most sophisticated modern form, the Royal Exchange *Ill. 263* Theatre, Manchester, which has been described as 'a module enclosed in clear glass and suspended from four pillars'.

America too had its theatre-in-the-round, with the Arena Stage in Washington, D.C., and many unconventional styles of staging

264

262 Interior of the Chichester Festival Theatre which opened in 1962 under the direction of Laurence Olivier. A hexagonal building, it seats 1,394 people round a thrust stage, no seat being more than 65 feet distant from it. Many of the theatre's summer season productions have subsequently been staged in London

were seen in the off- and off-off-Broadway theatres which arose in revolt against the increasing commercialism of mainstream shows.

Ill. 264

Ill. 265

Among American writers who soon became well known were Edward Albee, author of *Who's Afraid of Virginia Woolf?*, Sam Shepard, a prolific playwright first produced off-Broadway, and David Mamet, whose early plays were seen, not in New York, but in Chicago, and transferred.

Among older theatres outside London which continue to do good work, and so sustain the decentralization of the theatre that first appeared in France, is the Citizens' Theatre, Glasgow, which under Giles Havergal stages avant-garde productions of both revivals and new plays. In America, regional theatres built in most large cities have removed much of the pressure from New York.

An event which had a profound effect upon theatrical life in England was the abolition in 1968 of the centuries-old censorship after a long and bitter struggle. The freedom this gave to playwrights to deal with controversial subjects was widely welcomed, and was expressed in the immediate exploitation in public of obscenity, blasphemy, nudity, and even sodomy, as in Howard Brenton's *The Romans in Britain*.

265 (*right*) *American Buffalo* by
David Mamet, first produced
in Chicago, 1975, here in a
Long Wharf Theatre touring
production, with Al Pacino
as Teach, 1984

264 (*opposite*) Uta Hagen,
George Grizzard and Arthur
Hill in *Who's Afraid of Virginia
Woolf?* by Edward Albee, first
produced in New York in 1962
and in London, also with Uta
Hagen, in 1964

266 (*below*) Members of the
Negro Ensemble Company in
a scene from *A Soldier's Play*
by Charles Fuller, first
performed in New York in
1981, and seen in Edinburgh
in 1984

A new generation of playwrights came to prominence in the 1960s and 1970s, some, such as Edward Bond and David Hare, addressing the issues of contemporary politics and society directly, others, such as Alan Bennett and Michael Frayn, pursuing the comedy of modern social relations, and others again, such as Peter Schaffer and Tom Stoppard, dramatizing intellectual and cultural themes with wit and virtuosity. There were plenty of excellent actors and actresses to interpret them – Helen Mirren, Glenda Jackson, Judi Dench, Diana Rigg, Tom Courtenay, Ian Holm, Ian McKellen, and others too numerous to mention.

Ills. 267, 268

It was perhaps the loosening of constraints which prompted in reaction the sudden flowering of revivals and new light comedies, particularly 'musicals'. The old 'musical comedy', which evolved in the USA under the influence of the Continental light opera, was popularized in London by George Edwardes and followed by the light musical entertainments of Ivor Novello and Noël Coward. In New York it took a more serious turn, resulting in the integrated song-and-dance show, often based on an existing work, which

267 (*left*) Glenda Jackson as Nina Leeds in a 1984 revival of Eugene O'Neill's *Strange Interlude*, a part admirably suited to her strong dramatic personality

268 (*right*) Diana Rigg as Dorothy in a scene from Tom Stoppard's *Jumpers*, set on a university campus; first produced, using a revolving stage, by the National Theatre Company at the Old Vic, London, in 1972, directed by Peter Wood

269 The Ascot Scene from *My Fair Lady*, based on Shaw's *Pygmalion*, and one of the most successful musicals ever written. Lyrics by Alan Jay Lerner, music by Frederick Loewe, produced at the Mark Hellinger Theatre, New York, in 1956 and at Drury Lane in 1958. Costumes by Cecil Beaton and scenery by Oliver Smith

mingled good music, a strong plot, fine choreography, and lavish scenery and costumes to produce such works as *Oklahoma!* and *West Side Story*. In London an outstanding success was Lionel Bart's *Oliver!* Later outstanding musicals were Sondheim's *Company* and *A Little Night Music*, and Marvin Hamlisch's *A Chorus Line*. The *Ill. 270* English composer Andrew Lloyd-Webber was responsible for *Jesus Christ Superstar* and *Evita* with lyrics by Tim Rice, for *Cats* (based on poems by T. S. Eliot), and for *Starlight Express*.

The second half of the twentieth century has seen a number of interesting and far-reaching innovations in the theatre everywhere. Among them are the establishment in America of several all-Black groups, including the Negro Ensemble Company, founded for the production of plays by Black writers; the foundation, prompted by the Women's Liberation Movement, of all-women companies which aim, in the United States and to a lesser extent in England, not

269

only to produce plays by women, but to give them greater opportunities in all branches of the professional theatre; the increasing number of Community or Collective theatres, marked by a return to primitive staging, group production of scripts, or improvisation; the readiness of some countries to subsidize the theatre; and finally the establishment of new 'playhouses' in unexpected locations, and with new audiences. Against all these efforts must be set the tendency of the cinema and above all television to attract many of the best acting and writing talents, to the impoverishment of the live theatre; and the denial in some countries of the freedom needed by actors and playwrights alike if they are to function properly. Yet, in spite of everything, it seems certain that the theatre, 'that fabulous invalid' as it has been called, so often dying but never dead, will continue to flourish, reflecting and sustaining the social community which called it into being.

270 *A Chorus Line*, a 1975 musical by Marvin Hamlisch, directed and choreographed by Michael Bennett, which became the longest running show in the history of Broadway. The scene shows the line up of players who have been successful in auditions, after they, and those who failed, have revealed something of their past history in conversation with the director

CHAPTER THIRTEEN

The Contemporary Theatre
by Enoch Brater

One of the great strengths of theatre at the end of the twentieth century was its rich capacity to renew itself through dynamic international and intercultural encounters. Peter Brook's landmark production of *The Mahabharata*, a three-part, nine-hour play that Jean-Claude Carrière based on the classic Indian epic, enthralled audiences throughout Europe and became the major theatrical event of the 1987–88 season in North America. In works such as *The Conference of the Birds* and *The Ik*, Brook experimented at Le Centre International de Créations Théâtrales in Paris with the problems of representing on stage the myth, ritual and splendour of worlds imagined in specifically non-Western terms. At its best the result has been a cross-fertilization rather than an appropriation of theatrical forms and acting techniques, especially as Brook's directing style depends on the cultural expression and previous training of a company that is multi-national, multi-ethnic and multi-racial.

Ill. 272

Such a widening spectrum of globalization has led to a remarkable hybridization of the possibilities for theatre itself. In Japan the NOHO Theatre Group of Kyoto staged the plays of Samuel Beckett in a fusion of *kyogen* and experimental elements; and in 1996 the Habima Theatre in Tel Aviv, a company founded in 1917 by actors trained at the Moscow Art Theatre in the naturalistic style by Stanislavsky himself, presented for the first time in its distinguished history a new work written and performed as a modern Hebrew interpretation of Nōh and *kabuki*. In Paris Ariane Mnouchkine directed the Théâtre du Soleil in a compelling production of *Les Atrides*, a four-play, ten-hour cycle of Greek tragedies in which the actors wore opulent ceremonial costumes of Asian provenance, the stagehands were *kabuki*-like, while the choreography of the chorus emulated the

Ill. 271

Ill. 273

271 The NOHO Theatre Group of Kyoto, Japan, presents Samuel Beckett's work in a fusion of *kyogen* and experimental elements. Here the actors Akira Shigeyama *(right)* and Yasushi Maruishi star in Jonah Salz's 1987 production of *Theatre I*.

272 Peter Brook's *The Mahabharata* employed an international cast of actors when the production was mounted at the Festival d'Avignon in 1985. A combination of theatre styles from both the East and the West, this adaptation of Indian mythology toured successfully around the world.

Kathakali dance dramas of Southern India. The musical accompaniment, composed by Jean-Jacques Lemêtre, was played on a rustic handstand containing more than 140 exotic instruments and combined elements of Eastern folk improvisation, *kabuki* percussion and Western modernist techniques. The acting, fiery and grand and never inward, was classical French, even though Mnouchkine's international company was not.

Reacting against what he recently called 'the English theatre of received pronunciation', Simon McBurney, Artistic Director of Théâtre de Complicité, based in London, has similarly drawn upon the various training experiences of his own multi-national troupe to create such original stage pieces as *The Three Lives of Lucie Chabrol* and *The Street of Crocodiles*. Employing techniques based on the theory and practice of Jacques LeCoq, Complicité's work in rehearsal, with its strong emphasis on collaboration and improvisation, most closely resembles the visionary style of American playwright and director Joseph Chaikin, whose work in movement and voice for the Open Theater in the New York of the 1960s and 1970s culminated in such famous productions as *The Serpent, Terminal* and *The Mutation Show*.

The spontaneity and investigative potential of laboratory theatre, whose *raison d'être* can be traced in Jerzy Grotowski's influential

273 'The theatre is not supposed to represent psychology but passions', according to director Ariane Mnouchkine. Her 1990 production of *Les Atrides* for the Théâtre du Soleil opened to wide acclaim in France, Britain, Canada and the United States.

manifesto, *Towards a Poor Theatre*, validates once again the role of the modern theatre director as the central organizing consciousness for any performance event. Contemporary theatre is indeed a director's theatre, so much so that we now speak of Ingmar Bergman's *Hedda Gabler*, Peter Stein's *Prince of Homburg*, Giorgio Strehler's *Mother Courage*, Deborah Warner's *Titus Andronicus*, Yuri Lyubimov's *Hamlet*, Georg Tabori's *Waiting for Godot*, Stephen Daldry's *Machinal*, or Peter Brook's *King Lear*. Interrogating already established dramatic texts, or shaping new material that evolves through group exploration and participation, this new director's theatre can be both liberating and autocratic, depending on the dynamics of a given ensemble.

Ill. 274
Ill. 276
Ill. 275

Although we traditionally associate a director's theatre with the great European companies, stage life in the United States has been constructed along several parallel lines. Richard Foreman's Ontological-Hysterical Theater, Elizabeth LeCompte's work with the Wooster Group, JoAnne Akalaitis's or Lee Breuer's production history for Mabou Mines and Robert Wilson's theatre similarly place the director at centre stage. American directors have been

Ill. 278

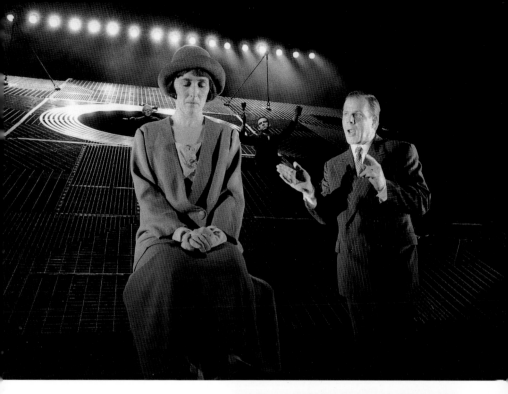

274 Deborah Warner directed *Titus Andronicus* for the Royal Shakespeare Company in 1987. From left to right: Donald Sumpter as Marcus, Jeremy Gilley as Young Lucius, Brian Cox as Titus and Sonia Ritter as Lavinia, as seen here at the Swan Theatre in Stratford-upon-Avon.

275 Fiona Shaw played the central role in *Machinal* for the National Theatre in London in 1993. Ian MacNeil designed a heavy-metal set to complement Stephen Daldry's hard-hitting interpretation of Sophie Treadwell's 1928 play.

276 Yuri Lyubimov's Russian-language production of *Hamlet* for the Taganka Theatre in Moscow. In 1989 the director mounted a production of the same play for the Leicester Haymarket Theatre in Britain.

particularly adventurous about incorporating new theatre technology into the making of unique and ambitious dramatic images. In
Route 1 & 9 the Wooster Group employed its signature television
screens to broadcast a conventional production of *Our Town*, which
then played in dramatic counterpoint to live, albeit dissonant, stage
action. In this unpredictable environment, Thornton Wilder's old
chestnut appeared oddly moving, as did selected speeches from
Chekhov read by an ailing Ron Vawter, similarly broadcast within
the fluid boundaries of the performance space for the Wooster
Group's 1993 *Fish Story*. Even when directing more canonical
material for this company, LeCompte makes use of high-tech
theatre vocabulary. Her 1997 New York production of *The Hairy
Ape*, which starred her then husband Willem Dafoe, featured a
heavy-metal set, a twelve-tone soundscape, and a non-traditional
lighting concept, resulting in the evocation of a thoroughly expres-
sionistic *mise-en-scène* to capture the tone and mood of Eugene
O'Neill's 1922 play.

277 Mikhail Bulgakov's *The Master and Margarita*, as interpreted for the Moscow stage by the Taganka Theatre under Yuri Lyubimov's direction.

278 The Wooster Group's *House/Lights* featured Kate Valk and Roy Faudree in their 1997 production. Based in New York, the collective is well known for its free-wheeling adaptations, its cross-cultural encounters and its signature television screens.

279 Philip Glass wrote the music for Robert Wilson's 1976 *Einstein on the Beach*, whose venues included the Festival d'Avignon, the Deutsches Schauspielhaus in Hamburg, the Metropolitan Opera House in New York and the Venice Biennale.

Yet no American director has been more totalizing in his embrace of theatre technology than Robert Wilson. His theatre of moving images is a caravan of vast machinery, large-scale props and flamboyant properties, gigantic scenic landscapes, atonal music, baroque costumes and high-concept lighting, all subject to rigid formalist patterns of stasis, mobility and silence. Often compared to Richard Wagner, Wilson has found a more receptive audience for his 'maximum' stagecraft in Northern Europe, particularly in *Ill. 279* Germany, than he has in the United States, though his *Einstein on the Beach*, with music by John Cage, was a theatrical sensation when it had its première at the Metropolitan Opera House in New York in 1976. Under his carefully guarded direction, elaborate and spectacular productions of *Time Rocker, A Letter for Queen Victoria, Deafman Glance, The Life and Times of Joseph Stalin* and sections from *the CIVIL warS* have travelled to theatre centres all over the world, earning a wide international reputation. More traditional playwrights like Marguerite Duras and Beckett have used new theatre technology and mechanical media in less aggressive but no less persuasive ways. Equating stage space with the space of human consciousness, both dramatists explored the possibility of voice-over previously recorded on electronic magnetic tape as a means of evoking inner worlds above and beyond the staged world on public display. Particularly in his last, great works of the 1970s and 1980s Beckett adapted to the live theatre the images of sharp black-and-white resolution he had previously refined in plays for television, just as the amplification and modulation of the human voice in *Rockaby* and *Footfalls* draw upon his knowledge and experience of radio drama.

Competing with popular forms of entertainment such as film, video and television, theatre at the end of the twentieth century has been forced to turn inwards in an attempt to rediscover its uniqueness in a commercial age of mechanical representation. But even as it has done so, theatre has not been immune to the demands of a changing audience and the society it reflects. The Women's Movement, in particular, has had a profound effect on who makes theatre, when and where. Caryl Churchill, one of Britain's leading

278

280 Caryl Churchill's *Top Girls*, directed by Max Stafford Clark, opened at the Royal Court Theatre in London on 28 August 1982. Shown here are Lindsay Duncan, Carole Hayman and Gwen Taylor from the cast that also featured Deborah Findlay, Selina Cadell and Leslie Manville. The play was revived at the Royal Court Theatre in 1991.

playwrights, was among the first of many new voices to make itself heard. Her first big success, *Cloud Nine*, began as a workshop production for the Joint Stock Company. Exploring the shifting nature of power politics based on questions of gender, race, sexuality and the paternalism of British colonialism, the script spans more than one hundred years, from Victorian England to 1970s London; but playing with time, only twenty-five years passes for Churchill's representative characters. *Top Girls* is similarly transgressive: here *Ill. 280* Churchill brings to the dinner table 'great' women from the real and fictive past, including Pope Joan, Patient Griselda, Dull Gret (subject of a well-known Breughel painting) and the thirteenth-century Japanese courtesan Lady Nijo. The rest, we might say, is history – but a history that gets itself substantially rewritten in the course of this play's stage life. Churchill's perspective in these works, quickly championed by leading feminist critics on both sides of the Atlantic, allowed her audience to study in miniature the drama of female figures as they struggle to move from the object to the subject position, a theme also brought to the London stage in new plays by Maureen Duffy, Sarah Daniels, Louise Page, Nell Dunn and Sharman MacDonald. In works including *Piaf, Queen Christina, Camille* and *Marlene*, Pam Gems has explored the sexual stereotyping underlying celebrated romantic prototypes, digging up old myths and rerooting them in the new soil of our own time. 'The theatre culture in England is superb,' observed playwright Gloria Parkinson, 'but it's the boys' culture.' Yet in the hands of prominent

279

and inventive directors such as Katie Mitchell, Sarah Pia Anderson and Deborah Warner, that culture is slowly changing.

In a pluralistic society such as the United States' it is not only the Women's Movement that has transformed the face of theatre, though indeed the field of play ranges widely, from the politically sophisticated drama of Maria Irene Fornes to the Broadway fare of Wendy Wasserstein. As the advent of the Black Arts Movement and the legacy of the Harlem Renaissance make clear, the drama of minority discourse was well under way. It was not until the volatile work of Ed Bullins and LeRoi Jones (Amiri Baraka), however, that African American drama became firmly lodged in the larger American theatre consciousness. In works ranging from Lorraine Hansberry's assimilative *A Raisin in the Sun* (later adapted into the Broadway musical called *Raisin*), to Adrienne Kennedy's probing *Funnyhouse of a Negro* and *A Movie Star Has to Star in Black and White*, to Ntozake Shange's triumphant 'choreopoem' *For colored girls who have considered suicide/when the rainbow is enuf*, to the epic range and density of Suzan-Lori Parks in *Imperceptible Mutabilities in the Third Kingdom* and *The America Play*, plays written by women can hardly be said to have played the secondary part. But it is the essentially realistic theatre of August Wilson in old-fashioned works such as *Ma Rainey's Black Bottom, Joe Turner's Come and Gone* and *The Piano Lesson*, rather than the more innovative work of other African American playwrights, that has proved to have the most staying power on American stages.

Ill. 281 In 1988 John Dexter directed an elegant production of *M. Butterfly* on Broadway, with scenery and costumes by Eiko Ishioka. David Henry Hwang's play was a suggestive compilation of cross-cultural encounters. Based on the true story of a French diplomat's love affair with a star of the Beijing Opera, a man disguised as a woman, the play offered a timely variation on the *Madame Butterfly* myth, whose stage history begins in New York with the 1900 one-act play David Belasco based on a short story by John Luther Long; four years later it was transformed into Puccini's famous opera. Although Hwang's play titillated audiences with a vivid scenario of deception and desire, illusion and reality

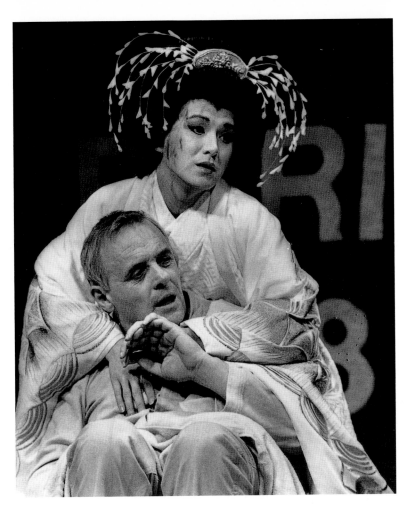

281 Anthony Hopkins played René Gallimard in *M. Butterfly* in London in 1989.
John Dexter directed John Lithgow and B. D. Wong in the original New York
production in 1988, a Tony Award-winning show with designs by Eiko Ishioka.

as experienced on an intensely personal level, from another point
of view *M. Butterfly* exposed the folly of a masculine West domin -
ating and mythologizing an absurdly fetishized and feminized East.
Although by no means as revelatory of the Asian American experience as a play such as Philip Kan Gotanda's *Yankee Dawg You Die*,

Hwang's highly theatrical display nevertheless placed Asian American drama firmly on the map. Luis Valdez's work for El Teatro Campesino has been similarly praised for the attention it has drawn to Chicano drama, just as Dee Brown's hugely successful *Bury My Heart at Wounded Knee* has found new audiences for the drama of Native Americans.

In any serious overview of contemporary theatre it would of course be impossible to ignore the important contribution of gay and lesbian drama. Sometimes associated with collectives such as the Gay Sweatshop in London or centres including The WOW Café on Manhattan's Lower East Side, where the radical group Split Britches has its home base, gay and lesbian theatre has also spawned a remarkable series of new plays. Giving dramatic expression to social and psychological issues that modern theatre has often ignored or at best merely implied, *The Boys in the Band*, which explored the relationships of a group of gay men who gather to celebrate a friend's birthday, became the rallying point for a movement that would no longer accept its marginalization. Mart Crowley's 1968 play has been followed by many variations on the same theme, including Terrence McNally's sentimental *Love! Valour! Compassion!* (1994). The increased politicization of gay theatre can be noticed as early as 1979, when Martin Sherman's *Bent* made an uneasy equation of homosexual persecution with the Holocaust and Nazi death-camps. But it was not until Tony Kushner's *Angels in America* that gay theatre assumed its full political maturity and dramatic authority. Subtitled *A Gay Fantasia on National Themes* and originally presented in two parts, *Millennium Approaches* (1991) and *Perestroika* (1992), the play certified its epic sweep by framing a homosexual love story within the wide historical context of political corruption and religious ecstasy in a rapidly changing American landscape. Kushner reminded his audience that there were no angels in America, just frail human beings. *Angels in America* has had international appeal, with major productions in Los Angeles, London, Avignon, Frankfurt, Tel Aviv, New York and Madrid.

Performance art, a highly stylized late twentieth-century event, constantly demands that its audience redefine what it understands

Ill. 282

282

282 Directed by Declan Donnellan and designed by Nick Ormerod, the National Theatre production of *Angels in America* was both intimate and epic. *Perestroika* (Part 2) starred Nancy Crane as the Angel and Stephen Dillane as Prior Walter, shown here at the small Cottesloe Theatre in 1993.

as an act of theatre itself. Great practitioners of this form such as   *Ill. 283*
Karen Finley and Rachel Rosenthal negotiate new acting spaces
for themselves, turning the landscape of a stage into the landscape
of their own bodies. Here 'performativity' becomes more central
to the kinetic presence and exploration of the body than any conventional definition of dramatic art might be able to contain.
Observing such trends, critical theorists have begun to talk about
'theatricality' rather than 'theatre', much to the dismay of more
classically disciplined (and more sceptical) theatre practitioners.
Laurie Anderson, by contrast, will take full advantage of electronic

283

283 Karen Finley performed her original work *The American Chestnut* in 1997. The performance artist is also well known in the United States for challenging right-wing control over funds administered by the National Endowment for the Arts.

284 Anna Deavere Smith as seen in *Let Me Down Easy*, originally staged in 2009. Her performance was later broadcast in the U.S. on PBS on 13 January 2012.

technology to orchestrate a performance event that is a synthesis of amplified sound, white noise and her own very human voice; on a wide proscenium all props and properties are managed and manipulated by Anderson herself, now seen in a tableau subject to the seemingly arbitrary whims of an advanced lighting board.

Another prominent performance artist, Spalding Gray, who committed suicide in New York in 2004, began his theatre work as a principal member of the experimental Wooster Group. His highly influential monologues, obsessive and doggedly autobiographical, were performed on a starkly dressed set where the microphone was his only antagonist. Self-indulgence was at full stretch, yet yearning all the while for something much larger than itself as a 'one man' talking cure. In *Swimming to Cambodia* (1987),

285 Mike Daisey performing his controversial monologue *The Agony and Ecstasy of Steve Jobs*, first produced at the New York Public Theatre in 2011. When Jobs died in the middle of the run, on 5 October, Daisey made a few minor changes.

for example, Gray detailed his participation in the film *The Killing Fields* by setting his personal experience against the wider perspective of political turmoil in Southeast Asia. Gray's innovative style sparked the imagination and energy behind three decades' worth of other solo shows, including *The Agony and Ecstasy of Steve Jobs* (2011), in which Mike Daisey speaks about what defines him as a 'tech geek' and how his exposure to Chinese factories made him think quite differently about the price others pay for the endless electronic consumption the developed world takes for granted. Yet no one has developed the one-person performance with greater political resonance than Anna Deavere Smith. In works such as *Fires in the Mirror* (1991), based on the highly charged race riots in Crown Heights, Brooklyn, and in the equally informed *Twilight: Los Angeles* (1992), Smith plays a series of different characters who tell the story in and on their own terms. In her stagings ethnicity and gender

Ill. 285

Ill. 284

286 Alex Jennings (centre, as George W. Bush) in *Stuff Happens* at the National Theatre in London. Nicholas Farrell (as Tony Blair) is to his right.

provide opportunities, not barriers. Her persona is similarly at bay in *Let Me Down Easy* (2009), an absorbing series of testimonials about death, the ailing body, and access to healthcare in an increasingly polarized United States.

Playwrights in the early part of the twenty-first century have struggled to transform the tensions of contemporary history into

Ill. 286   the substance of theatre and drama, but not for want of trying. *Stuff Happens*, the British playwright David Hare's attempt at docudrama, originally seen at the National Theatre in London in 2004 and a year later at the New York Public Theater, registers the cynical power play at the centre of the second President Bush's decision to go to war against Saddam Hussein. On offer was an attractively staged display of political deception and manipulation, but one that shed little light on the view of a situation most of the audience likely agreed with before they bought their tickets. This also held true for J. T. Rogers' *Blood and Gifts* in 2011 at Lincoln Center, where the production highlighted the shifting priorities

286

dictated by intelligence offices in the U.S., Britain, Pakistan and the former Soviet Union as daily life in Afghanistan continued to unravel. More stylized was *Bengal Tiger at the Baghdad Zoo*, the play by Rajiv Joseph in which Robin Williams took the lead as a recently escaped animal-cum-spokesman with a rich narrative afterlife, even as a city explodes around him. More successful, perhaps because the playwright keeps a greater distance between herself and the politics at work in her own back yard, was Lynn Nottage's *Ruined*, *Ill. 287* the 2009 Pulitzer Prize-winning play set in the civil war-torn Democratic Republic of Congo. The drama communicates but also personalizes the plight of women caught in a vortex of rape and violence. *Black Watch*, based on interviews conducted by Gregory *Ill. 288* Burke and therefore viewed through the eyes of those on the ground rather than a playwright's consciousness, moved swiftly from a pool room in Fife to an 'armoured wagon' in Iraq in order to capture the disintegration of a famous regiment. Neither parochial nor self-serving, this tightly choreographed production

287 *Ruined* (as seen below) opened at the Berkeley Repertory Theatre in 2011 as a co-production with the Huntington Theatre Company and La Jolla Playhouse. The 2009 New York premiere was staged by the Manhattan Theatre Club at City Center.

288 The National Theatre of Scotland production of Gregory Burke's *Black Watch* toured internationally, and was seen in London at the Barbican Theatre and in New York at St Ann's Warehouse in Dumbo, Brooklyn.

289 Pina Bausch's *Palermo Palermo* was seen at the Brooklyn Academy of Music in New York in 1991 as part of the Next Wave Festival, where her much-celebrated *tanztheater* became almost an annual event.

from the National Theatre of Scotland gave the drama inherent in this small piece of recent history the opportunity to emerge slowly and deliberately. Nothing was predetermined as an item in advance of the developing stage action. The same could not be said of *My Name Is Rachel Corrie*, stemming from the same general period. Based on the diaries and emails of a young American peace activist planted in the midst of an Israeli–Palestinian tragedy for which her experience and idealism leave her completely unprepared, the play records how she pays with her life when she attempts to stop a bulldozer from destroying an Arab house. The real story is in itself far more compelling than anything that has been arranged for the stage, even when done so by the accomplished actor Alan Rickman, who worked on this uneasy script with the journalist Katharine Viner.

The rites and rituals of contemporary theatre can be just as contentious when they turn their attention to questions of genre and emerging dramatic forms. Pina Bausch's innovative *tanztheater* is a case in point. Exhilarating, painstakingly detailed and continually inventive, her work as choreographer transforms the urgent and intimate movement of dance into the realm of emotionally lucid theatricality. Here the retreat from realism is all but complete. Signature works such as the 1978 *Rites of Spring*, in which the stage is covered with soil, and the same year's *Café Müller*, in which dancers stumble around the stage crashing into tables and chairs, established a vocabulary and grammar for a new kind of theatrical reality that became ever more poignant and precise until her death in 2009. The Spanish director Pedro Almodóvar uses scenes from Bausch's repertory as a locus of connection between two men in his film *Talk to Her* (2002), yet another moment in which different genres meet and merge to form a previously unimagined synthesis. Much of this is effectively transmitted in Wim Wenders' 3D documentary *Pina* (2011).

Such cross-fertilization between the various realms of the performing arts has contributed significantly to their dynamism and appeal. A new generation of directors has played a major role here, moving as freely as Franco Zeffirelli from live stage to opera to

Ill. 289

film and even, in some cases, to television drama. Luc Bondy, Michael Grandage, Des McAnuff, Sam Mendes and Rupert Goold bring to the stage a multidimensionality of fresh perspectives based less upon the breakdown of genre considerations than on their interchangeability and flexibility. Robert Lepage, known for his visual wizardry as the artistic director of Le Cirque du Soleil, mounted Wagner's four-part Ring Cycle for the New York Metropolitan Opera by incorporating a number of resources with his production team, including a spectacular transformative set designed with great mechanical daring, if not efficiency.

The international borders of theatre have also proved to be porous, especially so as well-established companies such as the Gate Theatre of Dublin, the Royal Shakespeare Company, the Teatro Piccolo of Milan and the Moscow Art Theatre, as well as their counterparts from China, Israel, Australia and Japan, travel around *Ill. 290* the world. Live, high-definition broadcasts from the National *Ill. 291* Theatre in London and also from the Donmar Warehouse, featuring such luminaries as Helen Mirren in *Phèdre*, Derek Jacobi in *King Lear*, and Zoë Wanamaker in *The Cherry Orchard*, were seen

290 The smash hit *One Man, Two Guvnors*, based on Goldoni's *The Servant of Two Masters* and featuring James Corden (centre) in the lead role, was one of 2011's most popular transmissions in the high-definition 'Live' series organized by the National Theatre in London.

291 Helen Mirren starred in Racine's *Phèdre* in a version by Ted Hughes in the first production to be broadcast live from the National Theatre, London on 25 June 2009.

simultaneously in more than three dozen countries, giving an entirely new dimension to accessible live theatre. The spirit of globalism could also be seen at the Comédie-Française in Paris when *Ill. 292* for the first time in its history a non-European play, *A Streetcar Named Desire*, was placed in the hands of a creative team from Mabou Mines, the celebrated American company well known for its work on Beckett and reinterpretation of classical texts. Directed by Lee Breuer in close collaboration with the puppeteer Basil Twist, and incorporating Japanese screens and wide swatches of bright colour, the production became the high point of the Tennessee Williams centenary year.

In such a provocative climate of global awareness it is not surprising to see that political theatre continues to range widely, building as it does on such diverse foundations as the pioneering work of Joan Holden with the San Francisco Mime Troupe; the equation of theatre and state terrorism in the plays of Argentine

Notes on the Illustrations

1 The Theatre of Dionysus in Athens.

2 Greek actor in costume holding a tragic mask, late fourth century BC. Fragment of a crater from Tarentum. Martin von Wagner Museum der Universität, Würzburg.

3 The Cart of Thespis, a reconstruction from a black-figured Attic vase-painting now in the British Museum. Dionysus, represented by his priest, on his way to the City Dionysia in a boat-shaped vehicle – the *carrus navalis* – accompanied by two flute-playing satyrs.

4 The theatre at Delphi stands in close proximity to the Temple of Apollo. This association between the two buildings is typical of the early Greek theatres, whose dramatic festivals were still part of a religious ceremony.

5 Clytemnestra killing Cassandra, from a red-figured bowl from Spina by the Marlay painter, c. 430 BC. Museo Archeologico Nazionale, Ferrara.

6 Apollo protecting Orestes from the Furies, an early Apulian volute crater from Ruvo, c. 370. In the final section of the *Oresteia* Orestes takes refuge in the sanctuary of Apollo at Delphi (*see Ill. 4*). Museo Nazionale Archeologico, Naples.

7 Actors dressed as birds, c. 500 BC, from a black-figured œnochoe. British Museum.

8 Hellenistic statuette of a comic actor wearing a mask, from Tralles in Turkey. This is interesting as showing the actor's face inside his mask, and also the crossed feet and clasped

hands, a characteristic attitude shown in many portrayals of comic actors. Istanbul Museum.

9 Archaic Punic comic mask from Tunis, unpainted. Musée du Bardo, Tunisia.

10 Hellenistic comic mask. Museum, Athens.

11 Roman marble mask of a tragic heroine. Museo Nazionale Archeologico, Naples.

12 Actor in Old Comedy, mid-fourth century BC, terracotta statuette from the Piraeus. British Museum.

13 Actors in Old Comedy, mid-fourth century BC, terracotta statuettes. Staatliche Museen, Berlin.

14 The restored theatre at Epidaurus. This theatre, which is acoustically perfect, is used every year for a summer festival of classical Greek plays. (The buildings at the rear have been constructed for the performances and are not permanent.)

15 Menander in his studio with New Comedy masks, marble relief. Lateran Museum, Rome.

16 A scene from a Roman comedy, wall-painting from the House of Casca in Pompeii, before AD 79.

17 The Roman theatre at Sabratha in North Africa.

18–19 Actors in New Comedy, terracotta statuettes. The one on the left wears a short tunic and cloak (*sagulum*), the other a short tunic, with the longer woollen cloak used for travelling. British Museum.

20 A scene from Terence's *Adelphi*, from the *Codex Vaticanus*, a ninth-century copy by Adelricus of the fourth- or fifth-century original, now in the

Vatican Museum. Compare the door on the extreme left with that in *Ill. 22*. The originals were done while the plays were still being performed and may therefore be taken as evidence for Roman stagecraft and costumes.

21 A Roman mime play, a reconstruction by Cube of a wall-painting in Pompeii, before AD 79.

22 A miser protecting his treasure from thieves, a vase-painting by Assteas, 360–330 BC, found at Nola in Italy. Staatliche Museen, Berlin.

23 Tragic actor, wall-painting from Herculaneum, before AD 79.

24 'Bikini'-clad girls, late third century AD, mosaic in the Piazza Armerina, Sicily.

25 Roman masks of a slave and a flute-player, mosaic. They much resemble those shown on a marble relief now in Naples, where an irate father confronts his drunken son, who is accompanied by just such a slave and flute-girl as in Menander's *Epitrepontes*. Capitoline Museum, Rome.

26 Medieval entertainers in fools' dress, from the manuscript of *Li Romans d'Alixandre*, written and illuminated in Flanders c. 1340. Bodleian Library, Oxford (264, f.84v), courtesy the Curators of the Bodleian Library.

27 A medieval glove-puppet booth, also from *Li Romans d'Alixandre* (f.54v). It bears a striking resemblance to the modern Punch-and-Judy booth. Courtesy the Curators of the Bodleian Library, Oxford.

294

28 A play by Terence being read and mimed, the frontispiece to the illuminated *Terence des Ducs*, *c.* 1400, Bibliothèque de l'Arsenal, Paris (MS. Cod. Lat. Ars. 664). Calliopius, in a small central booth, is reading, or reciting, one of Terence's plays while four masked actors mime it to music. There is a very similar illustration in a Terence Codex in the Bibliothèque National (Cod. Lat. 7907a).

29 The Empress Theodora, mosaic from San Vitale, Ravenna, *c.* 545. She became Empress in AD 527, and may have encouraged the performance in Byzantium of religious plays which preserved something of the classical traditions of acting and stagecraft for later ages.

30 The Three Marys at the Tomb, from the Benedictional of Robert of Jumièges, *c.* 980. The leading Mary is carrying a censer and perhaps an incense boat. It is interesting to compare the token sepulchre on which the Angel of the Resurrection is seated in church with the practicable oblong sarcophagus in *Ill. 34*, and the one in which the body of the actor playing Christ is being deposited on the extreme right-hand side of *Ill. 42*. Bibliothèque Publique, Rouen.

31 The Easter *trope* '*Quem quaeritis?*', from a fourteenth-century Sarum Processional, formerly in the possession of the Church of St John the Evangelist, Dublin, now in the Bodleian Library, Oxford (Rawlinson Liturg. MS. D.4). Courtesy the Curators of the Bodleian Library.

32 An alabaster plaque of the Resurrection, from Nottingham. The Resurrection, a favourite subject with medieval artists, was never portrayed in Byzantine art, and it is likely that this scene was directly inspired by the liturgical drama. Victoria and Albert Museum, London.

33 *Le Martyre de S. Apolline, c.* 1460, by Jehan Fouquet (1415–83). The brutal realism of the scene contrasts with the reticence of Greek tragedy, where acts of violence were never shown on stage. Musée Condé, Chantilly.

34 Three scenes from the life of Christ, a relief on the West front of the Chantry Chapel, St Mary's, Wakefield, Yorkshire.

35 Christ driving out the money-changers from the Temple, carving by Master Wilhelm Rollinger on a choir stall (destroyed in the Second World War) in St Stephen's Church, Vienna.

36 The Valenciennes Passion Play, 1547, manuscript by Hubert Cailleau. Bibliothèque Nationale (MS. 12536 f. 2v).

37 The Triumph of Isabella, Brussels, 1615, by Denis van Alsloot. In the procession Biblical and mythological scenes follow each other closely. These give some idea of the way in which Biblical scenes may have been acted on perambulating carts, a method particularly favoured in medieval England. Victoria and Albert Museum, London.

38 Christ's Descent into Hell. School of Hieronymus Bosch, first quarter of the sixteenth century. Metropolitan Museum of Art, New York (Harris Brisbane Dick Fund, 1926).

39 Devil's mask from the Tyrol. The devils, who were always comic, were probably played by the ambulant entertainers shown in *Ill. 26*. Their animal masks are found later in the Italian popular comedy. Tiroler Volkskunstmuseum, Innsbruck.

40 The Three Wise Men, from a sixteenth-century Flemish Nativity play. Collection Mr Ifan Kyrle Fletcher, London.

41 Two medieval devils by Jakob Ruoff (copyist Wolfgang Haller), from the manuscript of the *Weingartenspiel*, Zurich,

1539. Vadiana Stadtbibliothek, St Gallen.

42 Scenes from the Valenciennes Passion Play, 1547. From the same manuscript as *Ill. 36* Bibliothèque Nationale, Paris.

43 A scene from *Maître Pierre Pathelin, c.* 1465, a woodcut from an edition published *c.* 1500.

44 A farce performed during a sixteenth-century country fair, detail from a painting by Pieter Balten (died 1598). Rijksmuseum, Amsterdam.

45–9 Terence on the Renaissance stage. Four woodcuts from the Trechsel edition of Terence's plays (Lyons, 1493), one (*Ill. 49*) from the Venice edition of 1497. 45 An academic audience waits for the performance. What can be seen of the pillared and curtained stage, evidently erected in an upper room for the occasion, is very like that for the *Andria* (*Ill. 49*) and the *Eunuchus* (*Ill. 48*).

46 Calliopius speaks the prologue to the *Heauton Timorumenos*.

47 A scene from the *Adelphi*.

48 A scene from the *Eunuchus*.

49 A scene from the *Andria*. The numerous 'houses' of the medieval stage have been reduced to four, in imitation of the classical setting of doors set in a back wall, an interesting mingling of classical and medieval practices. The whole stage stands on a platform mounted on trestles, rather like the *phlyakes* stage in *Ill. 22*, or the *commedia dell'arte* stage in *Ill. 68*.

50 The stage and auditorium of the Teatro Olimpico, Vicenza, 1580–4. From *The Baroque Theatre*, Margarete Baur-Heinhold.

51 The auditorium of the Teatro Farnese, Parma, 1618–19, which was badly damaged during the Second World War. Its side wings and backcloth inaugurated a style which persisted until the end of the nineteenth century, and is still

295

used for opera and ballet in many of the great theatres of the world.

52 Design for stage-set by one of the Bibiena family. The exploitation by the younger Bibienas of the *scena d'angolo* opened up new vistas in European scene design. Drawing from the Yordini Collection, Milan.

53–5 Three stage settings from the section of *Architettura* (by Sebastiano Serlio, 1475–1554) dealing with perspective, published in Venice in 1545. It was translated into English in 1611. The sets, in symmetrical perspective, are intended for a temporary stage erected in a large hall.

56 Costume design by Stefano della Bella (1610–64). Victoria and Albert Museum, London.

57 Costume design by Henri Gissey (1621–73). The marginal notes give the original colours.

58–9 Costume designs by Lodovico Burnacini (1636–1707), probably intended for a Court performance in Vienna, from the Nationalbibliothek there. They show strongly the influence of the *commedia dell'arte*, and were probably intended for a *zanni*, possibly Harlequin.

60 A *commedia dell'arte* troupe at the Court of Henry of Navarre, *c.* 1578–90, by François Bunel the Younger. This painting is very similar to a sixteenth-century one in Stockholm, attributed to Franz Porbus, probably because such a scene appeared frequently in *commedia dell'arte* scenarios (*see also Ill. 96*). Musée de Béziers.

61 Pantalone serenading Donna Lucia, a painting *c.* 1580 by an unknown artist. Perhaps the servant with the book on the far right is doing the actual serenading. (For other illustrations of Pantalone see *Ills. 60, 63, 67, 96*.) Drottningholm Theatre Museum.

62 Coviello, a drawing from Francesco Bertelli's *Il carnevale*

italiano mascherato, Venice, 1642.

63 Pantalone, an engraving by Jacques Callot, 1618. A Venetian, he wears a red woollen cap and red velvet suit, with a loose black cloak, and Turkish slippers.

64 Il Capitano, in Venetian glass from Murano, second half of the sixteenth century. This braggart soldier is the prototype of Shakespeare's Ancient Pistol. For a later French version, see the figure far left in *Ill. 99*. Kunsthistorisches Museum, Vienna.

65 Arlequin, by Dolivar after Le Pautre, seventeenth century. He is wearing his original cat mask and carrying a *bat*, but his loose patched costume has become a well-fitting suit of brilliantly coloured silk diamonds. Cabinet des Estampes, Bibliothèque Nationale, Paris.

66 *Commedia dell'arte* masks. They resemble the half-mask worn by Harlequin (*see Ill. 65*), which left the mouth free, and are also reminiscent of some known to have been worn by Neapolitan Pulcinellas. Bibliothèque de l'Arsenal, Paris.

67 A *commedia dell'arte* troupe, *c.* 1580, with Isabella Andreini (1562–1604), the best-known actress of the *commedia dell'arte*, who gave her name to the heroines of innumerable scenarios. Musée Carnavalet, Paris.

68 Razullo and Cucurucu, from Callot's *I Balli di Sfessania* (a series of engravings of stock characters in the *commedia dell'-arte*), published in 1621.

69 Pulcinella, engraving by Johann Georg Puschner from G. Lambranzi's *Deliciae Theatrales* (The New and Curious School of Theatrical Dancing), 1716.

70 An open-air performance of an Italian comedy, Verona, 1772. An oil-painting by Marco Marcola. It would be tempting to attribute the play to Goldoni, but it represents what must have been a stock situation in

many of the *commedia dell'arte* scenarios. Art Institute of Chicago (the gift of Emily Crane Chadbourne). Courtesy of the Art Institue of Chicago.

71 A scene from the *Interlude of the Four Cardinal Virtues* (Temperance, Justice, Prudence and Fortitude, who, with Wilful, make up the cast); a woodcut of *c.* 1547. British Museum.

72 Edward Alleyn, a portrait by an unknown artist at Dulwich College, which Alleyn founded after his retirement from the stage as the College of God's Gift. He was the chief actor of the Admiral's Men, and the first to play many of Marlowe's heroes, including Tamburlaine, Doctor Faustus (*see Ill. 84*) and Barabas in *The Jew of Malta*. Reproduced by permission of the Governors of Dulwich College.

73 Richard Burbage – traditionally a self-portrait. Burbage, whose father built the first theatre in London in 1576, was the leading actor of the Lord Chamberlain's Men (later the King's Men), and the first to play many of Shakespeare's heroes, including Hamlet, Lear, Othello and Richard III. Reproduced by permission of the Governors of Dulwich College.

74 Reconstruction of an Elizabethan theatre of *c.* 1580–90, perhaps that built by James Burbage in 1576, by C. Walter Hodges (*The Globe Restored*, Ernest Benn Ltd, 1953, p. 73). The auditorium shows the influence of the innyard and the bear-pit, but the stage owes its Baroque façade more to the influence of Flemish theatres and triumphal arches (*see Ills. 76, 77*), combined with the curtained booth of the stages shown in *Ills. 44, 68*.

75 The Swan Theatre, *c.* 1596, copy by Arend van Buchel of Utrecht of a drawing sent to him by his friend Johannes de Witt during a visit to London. It helps to confirm evidence

drawn from other sources, particularly as regards the large open stage, the stage building with its pillars and flag, and the three galleries for spectators. Library of the University of Utrecht.

76 A Rederijkers stage at Antwerp, 1561, with a *platea* in front of a two-storey building and a curtained window above a central curtained opening. Such stages were built for the members of Flemish Chambers of Rhetoric for civic entertainments; they may have been known to James Burbage when he built his Theatre in London in 1576. Bibliothèque Royale, Brussels.

77 A triumphal arch for the Coronation of James I, 1603 – The Flemish Arch – from Stephen Harrison's *Arches of Triumph*, 1604. This shows clearly the influence of the Antwerp stage (*Ill. 76*). In some of the arches there were niches for the accommodation of living actors (the London arch had an actor representing the Thames, and Alleyn as the Genius of the City).

78 The exterior of the Globe Theatre, from Visscher's *View of London*, Amsterdam, 1616. This octagonal building probably represents the second Globe, built in 1614. The first Globe, shown on Norden's map of 1600, appears to be circular, and is so shown on an engraving by Hollar of 1644. The flag and the presence of people at the door seem to indicate that a play is in progress.

79 A Cambridge students' performance of *Roxana*, by William Alabaster (1567–1640), detail from the frontispiece of an edition of 1632. The temporary stage has a background of curtains, which resemble those of the Terence and *commedia dell'-arte* stages rather than the solid architecture of the public theatres in London.

80 William Shakespeare (1546–1616), the so-called 'Chandos' portrait. It appears to be a slightly later romanticized version of the engraving by Martin Droeshout which forms the frontispiece to the First Folio of 1623. National Portrait Gallery, London.

81 Characters in *Titus Andronicus*, believed to have been drawn by Henry Peacham, in 1595, from a manuscript at Longleat. Reproduced by courtesy of the Marquess of Bath.

82 Richard Tarleton, from an initial letter in a manuscript by John Scottowe. Tarleton was an excellent extempore actor – which may have called forth Shakespeare's rebuke to the clown in *Hamlet* (*see p. 81*). Several of Shakespeare's comic characters, among them the Gravedigger in *Hamlet*, appear to be based on his memories of Tarleton's fooling. British Museum (Harleian MS. 3885 f. 19).

83 William Kempe, a woodcut from the title-page of his *Nine Days' Wonder*, 1600. Kempe was the chief comedian of Shakespeare's company, and is known to have been the first to play Dogberry in *Much Ado about Nothing* and Peter in *Romeo and Juliet*.

84 A scene from *The Tragical History of Doctor Faustus* by Christopher Marlowe (1564–93); a woodcut from an edition of 1636. This play was first performed by the Admiral's Men for Henslowe, with Alleyn (*see Ill. 72*) in the title role, probably between 1588 and 1592. Mephistopheles, whose costume is reminiscent of that of the devils in the liturgical play (*see Ill. 41*) is appearing through the trapdoor with which Elizabethan theatres are known to have been equipped, in response to the conjurations of Faustus, safely enclosed within his magic circle.

85 The second Blackfriars Theatre, built by James Burbage on the site later occupied by the offices of *The Times*. (The first theatre, used from 1576 to 1584 by the Children of the Chapel Royal and St Paul's and Oxford's Boys – the 'little eyases' mentioned in *Hamlet* II. 2 – was in a different part of the building.) Reconstruction by the late J. H. Farrar. Reproduced by permission of the Architect of the Greater London Council.

86–7 Costume designs by Inigo Jones (1573–1652) for two masks given at Whitehall in 1609 and 1611, both with texts by Ben Jonson (1571–1638). They are in the Roman style, and show Continental, particularly Flemish, influence. Although these costumes were not designed for the public theatre, it is reasonable to suppose that they approximate roughly to what Shakespeare's audiences would have expected to see. Devonshire Collection, Chatsworth. Reproduced by permission of the Trustees of the Chatsworth Settlement.

88 Inigo Jones' Tragic Scene, which closely resembles that of Serlio (*Ill. 54*). Devonshire Collection, Chatsworth. Reproduced by permission of the Trustees of the Chatsworth Settlement.

89 The frontispiece to Francis Kirkman's *The Wits; or, Sport upon Sport*, 1673. The gallery at the back of the platform stage with spectators in it seems to confirm the presence of such a feature in the Swan Theatre (*see Ill. 75*). The great importance of this illustration lies in the evidence it provides for the lighting of the stage by overhead chandeliers and footlights. For similar lighting in France see *Ill. 100*.

90 Itinerant actors, and a platform stage, frontispiece by William Faithorne for the English translation of Paul Scarron's *Roman Comique* (1651), published in 1676.

91 Lope Felix de Vega Carpio. Many of his early plays were written for the actor-manager Jeronimo Velazquez, and may have been given at the newly opened Corral del Príncipe (see *Ill. 92*). Engraving by M.S. Larmona.

92 Reconstruction of the Corral del Príncipe, Madrid, which dates from *c.* 1582, by Juan Comba, a seventeenth-century artist. Like *Ills. 21* and *74*, it helps us to visualize the main features of the theatre it represents. Museo Municipal, Madrid.

93 A masked ball in the Teatro del Príncipe, 1766, by L. Paret. Prado, Madrid.

94 Design for a Court Theatre, *c.* 1680, attributed to Francisco Ricci. Ricci was appointed director of the Royal Theatre in the Alcázar in 1649 in the reign of Philip IV, and died in 1685 in his seventies, in the reign of Charles II. Biblioteca Nacionale, Madrid.

95 Set designed for a revival in 1690 of *La fiera, el rayo y la piedra*, by Pedro Calderón de la Barca (1608–81). This engraving is one of twenty-four now in the Biblioteca Nacionale, Madrid. The name of the designer is not known.

96 Italian actors in France, *c.* 1577, from the *Recueil Fossard*. It may represent the Gelosi Company, who acted before Henry III at Blois in 1577 (for a somewhat similar scene see *Ill. 60*). National museum, Stockholm.

97 The simultaneous setting for *Cornélie*, by Alexandre Hardy (*c.* 1575–*c.* 1631), a design from the *Mémoire de Mahelot, Laurent et d'autres décorateurs* (MS. Bibl. Nat. Paris No. 24330, f. 30).

98 Actors in a comedy probably based on a *commedia dell'arte* scenario at the Hôtel de Bourgogne, *c.* 1630. The symmetrical architectural background and the small balustrades figure in several extant designs for this

theatre (*see also Ill. 97*). Engraving by Abraham Bosse, Bibliothèque Nationale (Cabinet des Estampes), Paris.

99 The comedians of the Hôtel de Bourgogne, Turlupin, Gros-Guillaume and Gaultier-Garguille, *c.* 1630. They can be seen also in *Ills. 98* and *100*. An engraving by P. Mariette in the Bibliothèque Nationale (Cabinet des Estampes), Paris.

100 Composite painting by an unknown artist, *c.* 1670, showing comedians of the 1630s with later actors, among them Poisson (*see Ill. 150*), and Molière, first seen with his company in Paris in 1658. The setting resembles Serlio's Comic Scene (*see Ill. 53*). The chandeliers and footlights seen here are shown on an English stage in *Ill. 89*. Comédie-Française, Paris.

101–2 Engravings by Gravelot from an edition of the plays of Pierre Corneille (1606–84) published in 1764. *Le Cid* (*Ill. 101*), was first produced at the Théâtre du Marais early in 1637, and is generally held to have inaugurated the great age of French classical drama. Both *Le Cid* and *Le Menteur* (*Ill. 102*) were based on Spanish originals.

103 A setting by Giacomo Torelli (1608–78) for Corneille's *Andromède*, produced at the Petit-Bourbon in 1649, and written to display the machinery and effects brought from Italy by Torelli. This design shows Perseus descending from the heavens on a winged horse to do battle with the sea-monster who is preparing to devour Andromeda (seen chained to the rocks on the stage left). Osterreichishe Nationalbibliothek, Vienna.

104 Mlle Champmeslé, leading lady of the Comédie-Française on its formation in 1680, where she played opposite Baron (*see Ill. 148*). She had previously been at the Hôtel de Bourgogne with her husband, and was the first to play many famous parts,

including Racine's *Phèdre* and *Bérénice* (*see Ill. 106*).

105–6 Engravings from an edition of the plays of Jean Racine (1639–99) published in 1676. *Ill. 105* is from *Les Plaideurs* (III, 3), first performed in 1668. *Ill. 106* is from *Bérénice*, probably the last scene, in which the lovers part because Titus, being now Emperor of Rome, cannot marry a Jewess.

107 Clowns fighting, an engraving from G. Lambranzi's *Deliciae Theatrales*, 1716 (*see also Ill. 69*). The side wings set at an angle to the stage and the arched windows appear to be painted on the backcloth.

108 Molière in Corneille's *La Mort de Pompée*, 1659, by Paul Mignard. The play was first produced in 1643 at the Théâtre du Marais. Although Molière was not considered good in tragedy, he had a great admiration for Corneille's works, and it was in *Nicomède* (first produced in 1651) that he first appeared in Paris in 1658 before Louis XIV. It was, however, his acting in his own farce, *Le Docteur amoureux* (now lost), that finally won the audience's approval. Comédie-Française, Paris.

109 Molière's *Le Malade Imaginaire*, Versailles, 1674, in an engraving by Le Pautre. This play was first produced at the Palais-Royal in February 1673, with Molière as the hypochondriac Argan. He died a few hours after appearing in the part for the fourth time. This posthumous production was seen at Versailles on the third day of the festivities held there in July.

110 Armande Béjart (1642–1700), wife of Molière, in the title-role of *Psyché*. The dresses worn by Armande in this lavish and very expensive production are itemized in an inventory made after Molière's death, and as this engraving by P. Brizzard is from an edition

of Molière's works published in 1682, it may well show her wearing one of them.

111 A scene from Molière's *Les Femmes Savantes,* an engraving from the edition of Molière's work noted above (*Ill. 110*). The set is interesting as having, behind the curtain, a recess which is reminiscent of the 'inner stage' of the Spanish and Elizabethan stage.

112 An engraving by William Dolle from the 1673 edition of *The Empress of Morocco,* a heroic drama by Elkanah Settle (1648–1724) (the Doeg of Dryden's *Absalom and Achitophel*), and the first English play to be published with scenic illustrations. It probably shows Betterton (*see Ill. 114*) and Mrs Barry.

113 Nell Gwynne (1650–87), studio of Sir Peter Lely. National Portrait Gallery, London.

114 The Closet Scene from *Hamlet* (III, 4), an engraving from Nicholas Rowe's edition of 1709. At the back are the two large portraits of the elder Hamlet and Claudius to which Hamlet refers, often replaced now by miniatures hung round the necks of Hamlet and Gertrude respectively (*see Ill. 127*). The lighting is interesting – candelabra attached to the wing by means of a batten behind.

115 Detail from a satirical print of 1731 showing John Rich (*c.* 1692–1761) as Harlequin with the Doctor and Piero, the anglicized forms of Arlecchino, Il Dottore and Pedrolino. These *commedia dell'arte* masks came into England with the 'Italian Night Scenes' imported by John Weaver (1673–1760), from which Rich developed the harlequinades that led to the development of the later English pantomime. The satire is aimed at the vogue for such ephemeral amusements and *The Beggar's Opera* by John Gay, produced in 1728 with such success that

it made 'Gay rich and Rich gay'. Rich's Harlequin suit is very much like that shown in *Ill. 65.* British Museum Print Room.

116 Colley Cibber (1671–1757) as Lord Foppington in *The Relapse; or, Virtue in Danger* by Sir John Vanbrugh (1664–1726). This was first produced at Drury Lane in 1696, and in 1777 was rewritten by Sheridan as *A Trip to Scarborough.* Cibber is now chiefly remembered for his *Apology,* 1740, which contains some admirable descriptions of Restoration acting. An engraving by J. Simon after Grisoni's portrait.

117 The interior of the Regency Theatre, London, as it was in 1817, an engraving from Robert Wilkinson's *Theatrum Illustrata,* 1825. After a chequered career and many changes of name the theatre was taken over by the Bancrofts (*see Ill. 210*) and became famous as the Prince of Wales's.

118 The exterior of the Tankard Street Theatre, Ipswich, an engraving from Wilkinson's *Theatrum Illustrata,* 1825. Here David Garrick (*see Ill. 119*) made his first professional appearance in 1741 under the name of Lyddal, playing Aboan in *Oroonoko,* by Thomas Southerne (1660–1746), first performed at Drury Lane in 1695.

119 David Garrick (1717–97) and his wife Eva Maria Viegel (1724–1822), a portrait by William Hogarth. Reproduced by gracious permission of Her Majesty the Queen.

120 A 'cut-out' scene by Philip James de Loutherbourg (1740–1812). Having studied in Paris and Italy, he made important reforms at Drury Lane in lighting effects and scenery, and by putting lights behind the proscenium arch helped to confine the actors within the 'picture-frame' to the already attenuated forestage. Victoria and Albert Museum, London.

121 Peg Woffington (*c.* 1714–60) as Mistress Ford in *The Merry Wives of Windsor,* after a portrait by E. Haytley, 1751. Excellent in comedy, though not in tragedy, she became the rage of London when in 1740 she appeared as Sir Harry Wildair in *The Constant Couple* by George Farquhar (1678–1707). British Museum.

122 Kitty Clive (*née* Catherine Raftor, 1711–85), as Isabella in *The Old Debauchees,* by Henry Fielding (1707–54), first produced at Drury Lane in 1732; an engraving of 1750, when the play may have been revived. She was at her best in low comedy and burlesque.

123 Charles Macklin (*c.* 1700–97) as Shylock, in an engraving by Nutter after Boyne. He first played the part on 14 February 1741, making the character dignified and tragic instead of comic.

124 A scene from *She Stoops to Conquer* by Oliver Goldsmith (1730–74). Engraving by W. Humphrey after a painting by Parkinson.

125 The Screen Scene from *The School for Scandal,* by Richard Brinsley Sheridan (1751–1816), an engraving of 1778. The first production took place at Drury Lane on 8 May 1777. Characteristic of the period are the painted backcloth and wings, the large forestage, and the boxes directly rising from it (*see also Ill. 117*).

126 Anglers outside Sadler's Wells Theatre, 1796, a drawing by George Cruikshank. Victoria and Albert Museum, London.

127 William Henry West Betty (1791–1874), a child prodigy known as Master Betty or 'The Young Roscius', who at the age of thirteen astonished London audiences with his acting in the great tragic roles of Shakespeare, here seen as Hamlet. Betty, who was also much admired as Young Norval in *Douglas* by the Rev. John

Home (1722–1808), had a spectacular career for a few years, but passed the rest of his long life in obscurity.

128 James Quin in the title-role of *Coriolanus* by James Thomson (1700–48), Covent Garden, January 1749, with Peg Woffington and George Anne Bellamy (*c*. 1727–88). This shows the final and somewhat eccentric development of the seventeenth-century Roman kilt, and the anachronistic costumes of the women, wearing the Elizabethan head-dress usually associated with Mary Queen of Scots. Burney Collection, British Museum Print Room.

129 A German Fool (*Narr*), end of the fifteenth century, an engraving by Crispinus Passaeus from George Wither's *Emblems*, 1635. His costume is reminiscent of that of the medieval fool (*see Ill. 26*), and persisted for a long time, Shakespeare's Touchstone, for instance, being very often dressed in a similar hooded head-dress with bells. Bodleian Library, Oxford (Douce Portfolio 142, f. 66, no. 68). Courtesy the Curators of the Bodleian Library.

130–1 An open-air stage, woodcuts from a 1574 edition of *Kinderzucht* by Johann Rasser.

132 A woodcut from the title-page of *Der Teufel lässt keinen Landsknecht mehr in die Hölle fahren* by Hans Sachs, probably produced in the Marthakirche, Nuremberg. The devil's costume resembles that of Mephistopheles in Marlowe's *Doctor Faustus* (*see Ill. 84*). The title of the play is a pun, *Hölle* meaning hell and the hot space behind the large porcelain stove up which the devil is climbing.

133 The mastersinger Hans Sachs, whose dramatic activity began about 1518, an engraving by Jost Amman.

134 A seventeenth-century German stage, title-page engraving

from *Teutsche Schaubühne*, 1655, by I. Clauss.

135 John Goodwin as Hanswurst, or, as the German title of the picture has it: '*Der kurtzweillige Hanswurst aus Engelland Johann Guttwen*'. British Museum Print Room (1933, 10, 14, 415).

136 *Pietas Victrix*, by Nicolaus Avancinus (1612–86), one of nine illustrations from an edition published in 1659, the year in which the play was staged in Vienna with all the latest scenery and mechanical devices imported from Italy. Plays of this kind were common in Jesuit schools all over Europe, and served to train the pupils in declamation, singing and movement as well as in Latin, the language in which they were written, while the use of Italian scenery spread from such productions to the Court and so to the public theatres everywhere.

137 Johann Christoph Gottsched and his wife, a portrait by an unknown artist. The modern German theatre is usually considered to have evolved from the collaboration of Gottsched and Carolina Neuber (*Ill. 138*). Of Gottsched's own plays *Der sterbende Cato* (1732), based partly on the *Cato* (1713) of Joseph Addison (1672–1719), was the most successful, in spite of his efforts to costume it in correct Roman style, an innovation too far in advance of the time.

138 Carolina Neuber as Elizabeth I in Thomas Corneille's *Essex*, an engraving after von Hausmann.

139 Actors preparing for a *Haupt- und Staatsaktion* in Nuremberg, *c*. 1730; an engraving by P. Decker. It is interesting to compare the costume of the plumed and kilted hero with that of Quin in *Coriolanus* (*see Ill. 128*). It is not known what play the actors are about to perform,

but it represents the type of popular drama against which Gottsched and Carolina Neuber reacted by producing austere translations of French neoclassical plays of the seventeenth century.

140 Friedrich Schröder as Falstaff, 1780, an engraving by Pippo. Schröder was the leading actor of the German stage from *c*. 1771 to his retirement in 1798. In his first production of *Hamlet* he played the Ghost to Brockmann's Hamlet (*see Ill. 142*), and after playing Laertes and the Gravedigger in subsequent productions he finally appeared in the title-role.

141 Johann Wolfgang Goethe, a portrait by Georg Oswald, 1799.

142 Johann Brockmann (1745–1812) as Hamlet in a production in Berlin in 1778, by the company of Karl Döbbelin (1727–93). After an engraving by Daniel Chodowiecky. Döbbelin, who started his acting career in the company of Carolina Neuber (*see Ill. 138*), played the Ghost in this production, and his daughter Caroline was the Ophelia.

143 The interior of the first Burgtheater in Vienna, from an engraving in the Vienna State Museum. It stood until 1888. After its demolition a new Burgtheater was built on the Franzensring, and rebuilt after severe damage in the Second World War.

144 Goethe (*see Ill. 141*) as Orestes with Corona Schroeter as Iphigenia, 1779, in Goethe's *Iphigenie auf Tauris*, a painting by G. M. Kraus.

145 The Court Theatre at Weimar during the directorship of Goethe (*see Ill. 141*), watercolour.

146 Friedrich von Schiller, a portrait by Anton Graff.

147 Act V, scene 12 of *Die Verschwörung des Fiesko zu Genua* by Schiller, at the Court Theatre, Weimar, in *c*. 1810.

The play deals with the conspiracy of Fiesko against the ruling family of Genoa, during which he accidentally kills his young wife, Leonore. The conspirators, in tragic cloaks and plumed hats, surround the despairing Fiesko and the expiring Leonore. On the stage left are two conspirators watching the tragedy in an attitude which strongly resembles the usual nineteenth-century pose of Hamlet and Horatio watching the funeral of Ophelia. Theatermuseum, Munich.

148 Michel Baron, a portrait by Rigaud. Trained by Molière, on whose death he joined the rival company at the Hôtel de Bourgogne, where he played the young heroes of Racine. He became the leading man of the Comédie-Française on its formation by Louis XIV in 1680. Perpignan Museum.

149 Giuseppe Biancolelli, known as Dominique, a portrait by an unknown artist of the seventeenth-century French school. Museum of La Scala, Milan.

150 Raymond Poisson as Crispin, an engraving by G. Edelinck after a painting by Netscher. The part of Crispin is first found in L'Ecolier de Salamanque (1654) by Paul Scarron (1610–60) (see also Ill. 90), but it was Poisson who made it popular, introducing it into several of his own plays. After his death it was played by his son and grandson, and then passed to Préville (Ill. 162). Kongelige Bibliotek, Copenhagen.

151 Actors of the Comédie-Italienne, Paris, a painting by Nicolas Lancret. The central figure is Scapin, who plays a large part in the comedies of Molière, and grouped round him are Silvie, Mezzetin, Gille, Harlequin, Columbine and Il Dottore. Louvre, Paris.

152 The Italian actors banished from Paris in 1697 on the orders of Louis XIV, an engraving by L. Jacob after Watteau. Col-

umbine (centre) is the daughter of Dominique (Ill. 149). It was not until 1716 that an Italian company returned to Paris, under the leadership of Luigi Riccoboni (c. 1675–1753), known as Lelio. British Museum Print Room.

153 A group of French actors, c. 1720, a detail from a painting by Watteau. The hero wears the usual plumed hat and panniered skirt. The scenery is severely classical with a painted backcloth, and probably represents the courtyard of a palace, forming a permanent set for the entire play. Metropolitan Museum of Art, New York.

154 Actors at the Foire Saint-Laurent, c. 1720. They probably represent (from stage right to left) the confidante, the hero, the heroine, and the villain, in a romantic comedy. An engraving from Foire Saint-Laurent, A. Heulhard, 1878.

155 Theatre at the Foire Saint-Laurent, 1721, destroyed 1761. This painting shows Arlequin and his companions on the balcony which, unlike that in Ill. 154, is raised well above the crowd, parading before appearing in a farce based probably on a commedia dell'arte scenario. Musée Carnavalet, Paris.

156 A scene from Sémiramis by Voltaire (1694–1778) at the Comédie-Française in 1748. Drawing by G. de Saint-Aubin. The setting for this play was designed by the Slotdz brothers, and is reminiscent of that shown in Ill. 153. Private Collection.

157 Adrienne Lecouvreur in Corneille's La Mort de Pompée. From Costumes et Annales des Théâtres de Paris, vol. IV, 1788–9.

158 Henri-Louis Lekain, portrait by S.-B. Lenoir. Comédie-Française, Paris.

159 The 'apotheosis' of Voltaire on 30 March 1778, at the Comédie-Française, an engraving after Moreau le Jeune. It is interesting to compare this theatre with Drury Lane during

The School for Scandal, produced a year earlier (see Ill. 125).

160 A scene from L'Orphelin de la Chine, produced in 1777, from an illustrated edition of Voltaire's plays published in 1883–5.

161 A scene from Le Barbier de Séville (1775) by Pierre-Augustin Caron de Beaumarchais (1732–99). Contemporary pen-and-ink sketch. Collection Rondel, Bibliothèque de l'Arsenal, Paris.

162 The actor Préville as Mezzetin, a portrait by Van Loo. Comédie-Française, Paris.

163 A scene from Beaumarchais's Le Mariage de Figaro (1784) in an engraving attributed to Moreau le Jeune.

164 A stage-set in diagonal perspective by Jean-Nicolas Servandony (Giovanni Niccolò Servandoni). Pen drawing. Albertina, Vienna.

165 A stage-set by Louis-René Boquet (fl. 1760–82). Probably intended for a ballet, it is in marked contrast to the solidity and severity of the work of such designers as Servandony (Ill. 164). Bibliothèque de l'Opera, Paris.

166 The eighteenth-century Dock Street Theatre in Charleston, South Carolina, the second to be built on the site. It was one of the earliest theatres in the American colonies. On stage is a setting of houses in perspective which seems to derive indirectly from Serlio's Comic Scene (see Ill. 53), and over the proscenium arch are the Royal Arms of England. Theatre Collection, Harvard University.

167 The Screen Scene from Sheridan's The School for Scandal, probably at the Park Theatre, New York, c. 1802. Painting by William Dunlap. Theatre Collection, Harvard University.

168 The Chestnut Street Theatre, Philadelphia, Pa., built in 1793 on the plans of the Theatre Royal at Bath. It was burnt down in 1856.

169 Helena Modjeska, formerly Modrzejewska. She made her last appearance at the Metropolitan Opera House, New York, in 1905.
170 François-Joseph Talma, the pupil of Molé (*Ill. 161*), and later acclaimed as the successor of Lekain (*Ill. 158*). A portrait in the Comédie-Française, Paris.
171 The Comédie-Française, 1808. This theatre had opened in 1790 as the Variétes-Amusantes, designed by Victor Louis (1731–1802) who made use of new materials and techniques, with wrought-iron framing replacing all timber in the roof. After some internal reconstruction, which included the installation of the large stage shown here, it reopened in 1799 as the Comédie-Française. Archives of the Comédie-Française, Paris.
172 Mrs Siddons, a sketch by George Romney. She was the leading actress of London from 1782 to her retirement in 1812, and appeared many times at Covent Garden and Drury Lane under the management of her brother John Philip Kemble. Ashmolean Museum, Oxford.
173 John Philip Kemble, a portrait by Sir Thomas Lawrence. Kemble was manager of Covent Garden during the 'Old Prices' riots, which resulted from the increase in the price of seats after rebuilding due to the fire of 1808. Guildhall Art Gallery, London.
174 Drury Lane Theatre, from Ackermann's *Microcosm of London*, 1808. The theatre was destroyed by fire in 1809 and rebuilt, re-opening in 1912.
175 A setting for any historical play, by William Capon, 1808. By permission of the Governors of the Royal Shakespeare Theatre, Stratford-upon-Avon.
176 George Frederick Cooke as Richard III, the part which he played on his first appearance at Covent Garden in 1800, probably in Colley Cibber's

version. British Museum Print Room.
177 James Robinson Planché's costume design for a production of *King John* by Charles Kemble, 1824.
178 Edmund Kean as Othello, a lithograph after a painting by Lambert. Theatre Museum, London.
179 A setting for Charles Kean's production of *Richard II*, 1857. The costumes in conformity with the vogue for historical accuracy introduced by Planché (*see Ill. 177*), were based on the illuminations in a manuscript of 1319, but the scenery seems to derive more from de Loutherbourg's 'cut-outs' (*see Ill. 120*) than from Capon's careful archaeology (*see Ill. 175*). Victoria and Albert Museum, London.
180 A design by the Duke of Saxe-Meiningen for *Der Prinz von Homburg*, by Heinrich von Kleist, first performed ten years after Kleist's death. It has only comparatively recently been recognized as a masterpiece. Theatersammlung der Universität, Hamburg.
181 Ferdinand Raimund in his own play *Das Mädchen aus der Feenwelt, oder der Bauer als Millionär* (1826). Lithograph after a drawing by M. von Schwind.
182 A scene from *Der Traum ein Leben*, by Franz Grillparzer (1791–1872), based on *La vida es sueño*, by Calderón. This had scenery in a quasi-Oriental manner by Antonio de Pian (1784–1851) and costumes designed by Philipp von Stubenrauch (1784–1848). Engraving from the Theatre Collection of the Osterreichische Nationalbibliothek, Vienna.
183 The auditorium of the Comédie-Française during the first night of *Hernani* by Victor Hugo (1802–85), a painting by Albert Besnard. Victor Hugo Museum, Paris.
184 A scene from *Der böse Geist*

Lumpazivagabundus oder das liederliche Kleeblatt by Johann Nestroy (1802–62), at the Theater an der Wien in 1833. Engraving from the Theatermuseum, Munich.
185 Charles Kemble and Harriet Smithson (1800–54) as Romeo and Juliet at the Odéon, Paris, 1827. Lithograph from *Souvenirs du Théâtre Anglais à Paris*, 1827. R. Eddison Collection.
186 Antoine-Louis-Prosper Lemaître (Frédérick), at Pierrefitte with Honoré de Balzac and Théophile Gautier (1811–72), a watercolour by Gautier painted in 1840 while the three friends were collaborating on a play entitled *Mercadet*. Private Collection.
187 Rachel at Covent Garden, 1841, detail of a watercolour by Lami. Enthoven Collection, Victoria and Albert Museum, London.
188 Joseph Grimaldi (1778–1837) as the Clown in *Harlequin Padmanada, or The Golden Fish*, a pantomime, probably by Charles Farley, produced at Covent Garden at Christmas 1811. Enthoven Collection, Victoria and Albert Museum, London.
189 Charles Fechter as Hamlet at the Princess's Theatre, London, 1861. Enthoven Collection, Victoria and Albert Museum, London.
190 William Macready in the title-role of *Werner* by Lord Byron, a painting by Daniel Maclise. Enthoven Collection, Victoria and Albert Museum, London.
191 Samuel Phelps as Cardinal Wolsey in Shakespeare's *Henry VIII*, a painting by Johnston Forbes-Robertson. By kind permission of the Garrick Club, London.
192 Mme Vestris and Charles Mathews the Younger in a scene from *The Conquering Game*, by William Bernard, *Duncombe's British Theatre*, vol. 35, c. 1865.

193 Mme Vestris and her husband in *Mr and Mrs Mathews at Home*. This was a series of vignettes in which they both played several parts, in the style of the solo performance given by the elder Charles Mathews (1776–1835). Enthoven Collection, Victoria and Albert Museum, London.

194 Edwin Booth as Richelieu, in London in 1861. Booth was seen in London again between 1880 and 1882, where he appeared at the Lyceum with Irving. Enthoven Collection, Victoria and Albert Museum, London.

195 Charlotte Cushman as Romeo, 1855. From *The Illustrated London News*, 1855.

196 The first production of Dion Boucicault's *The Corsican Brothers* (an adaptation of *Les Frères Corses* by Dumas *père*) in 1852. Enthoven Collection, Victoria and Albert Museum, London.

197 Edwin Forrest as Spartacus in *The Gladiator*, by Robert M. Bird (1806–54), produced in New York in 1831. This shows the London production of 1836. Enthoven Collection, Victoria and Albert Museum, London.

198 A scene from *The Octoroon; or, Life in Louisiana*, by Dion Boucicault. Enthoven Collection, Victoria and Albert Museum, London.

199 Mrs John Drew as Mrs Malaprop in Sheridan's *The Rivals*. Theatre Collection, Harvard University.

200 Joseph Jefferson the Third as Rip Van Winkle. Theatre Collection, Harvard University.

201 Charlotte Crabtree (Lotta) as Little Nell in a dramatization by John Brougham (1810–80) of Dickens' *Old Curiosity Shop* (1867), in which she also played 'The Marchioness'. Theatre Collection, Harvard University.

202 John Drew and Ada Rehan in *The Railroad of Love*, adapted by Augustin Daly from a German play, *Goldfische*, and first produced at Daly's Theatre, New York, in 1887, and at the Gaiety in London in the same year. Theatre Collection, Harvard University.

203 Fred Terry in *Henry of Navarre*, by William Devereux.

204 Kate and Ellen Bateman in *The Young Couple*, 1851; an engraving by H. Singleton. Enthoven Collection, Victoria and Albert Museum, London.

205 Henry Irving in *The Bells* by Leopold Lewis. *The Bells* was several times revived, and in 1968 was produced with Marius Goring as Mathias. Enthoven Collection, Victoria and Albert Museum, London.

206 John Martin-Harvey as Sidney Carton in *The Only Way*, 1899, the part in which he was constantly forced by an adoring public to re-appear though he was also excellent in Shakespearean and other roles. Enthoven Collection, Victoria and Albert Museum, London.

207 Irving (*see Ill. 205*) and Ellen Terry as Iachimo and Imogen in *Cymbeline*, 1896. In her *Story of My Life* (1908) Ellen Terry says a great deal about her preparations for playing this part, and it also occasioned some interesting letters to her from Shaw, reprinted in their *Correspondence* (1949). Enthoven Collection, Victoria and Albert Museum, London.

208 Johnston Forbes-Robertson as Hamlet, at the Lyceum, London, 1897.

209 A scene from *The Ticket-of-Leave Man* by Tom Taylor, based on a French tale, and first produced at the Olympic, London, 1863. Enthoven Collection, Victoria and Albert Museum, London.

210 Squire Bancroft and Marie Wilton in *Society* by Tom Robertson (1829–71) at the Prince of Wales's Theatre, 1865. This theatre, formerly the Regency (*see Ill. 117*), had fallen into disrepair, and was nicknamed 'The Dust Hole'. Renovated and redecorated, it became one of the most popular and successful theatres in London. The Bancrofts remained there until 1880, when they moved to the Haymarket. The site is now occupied by the Scala Theatre. Enthoven Collection, Victoria and Albert Museum, London.

211 George Alexander and Allan Aynesworth in Oscar Wilde's *The Importance of Being Earnest*, 1895. Enthoven Collection, Victoria and Albert Museum, London.

212 Sarah Bernhardt and Mrs Patrick Campbell as Pelléas and Mélisande in the play of that name by Maurice Maeterlinck (1862–1949). In this 1904 production Mrs Patrick Campbell, who had played the part in English in 1898, played in French. Enthoven Collection, Victoria and Albert Museum, London.

213 Eleonora Duse in an Italian version of *Die Heimat*, by Hermann Sudermann (1857–1928). Enthoven Collection, Victoria and Albert Museum, London.

214 Marie Lloyd. Enthoven Collection, Victoria and Albert Museum, London.

215 George Robey. Unlike most music-hall comedians, he essayed the legitimate stage, appearing with success as Menelaus in *Helen* in 1932 and as Falstaff in *Henry IV, Part I*, in 1935. Enthoven Collection, Victoria and Albert Museum, London.

216 A private reading of *Les Avariés* by its author, Eugène Brieux, in 1901. The play, like Ibsen's *Ghosts*, dealt with the problem of venereal disease in modern society, and was banned for over a year. As *Damaged Goods*, it was publicly performed in London in 1917. Enthoven Collection, Victoria and Albert Museum, London.

217 A scene from *Little Eyolf* by Henrik Ibsen, 1896. The trans-

lation was by William Archer. Elizabeth Robins, who played Asta, for many years held all the stage rights in Ibsen's plays in their English translations, and was instrumental in arranging their first productions in London. Enthoven Collection, Victoria and Albert Museum, London.

218 Richard Mansfield in *The Devil's Disciple* by George Bernard Shaw (1856–1950). Mansfield was famous in romantic roles, but was sympathetic to the 'new drama', playing Peer Gynt for the first time in English in 1906, and Bluntschli in *Arms and the Man* (the first of Shaw's plays to be seen in the United States) in 1894. Theatre Collection, New York Public Library.

219 Sybil Thorndike as Saint Joan. The première of Shaw's play was given in New York at the Garrick Theatre under the auspices of the Theatre Guild in 1923. Enthoven Collection, Victoria and Albert Museum, London.

220 William Poel's production of *Hamlet*, 1900. He had already produced the play, using the text of the First Quarto (which was also used here) in 1881 at the St George's Hall.

221 The Moscow Art Theatre's production of *The Lower Depths* by Maxim Gorky, 1902.

222 A scene from Shaw's *Androcles and the Lion*. The costumes and scenery were by Albert Rutherston. Enthoven Collection, Victoria and Albert Museum, London.

223 Chekhov (1860–1904) reading *The Seagull* to the company of the Moscow Art Theatre. This play, the first of Chekhov's to be done in English, was first produced in 1896 at the Alexandrinsky Theatre in St Petersburg (now the Pushkin in Leningrad) but was a failure. It needed the youth and vitality of the Moscow Art Theatre to bring it to life.

224 Ernesto Rossi as Hamlet, in a version by Rosconia. Rossi himself translated *Julius Caesar* into Italian, and was the first Italian actor to

play *Othello*. Enthoven Collection, Victoria and Albert Museum, London.

225 A scene from *Six Characters in Search of an Author* by Luigi Pirandello (1867–1936). Enthoven Collection, Victoria and Albert Museum, London.

226 A set for *Macbeth* (I. 3) by Edward Gordon Craig, for a production in New York in 1928. Reproduced by courtesy of the Trustees of the E. Gordon Craig Estate.

227 A set by Adolphe Appia for Ibsen's *Little Eyolf*. From the original in the Appia Archives, Swiss Theatre Collection, Bern, reproduced by permission of the Curator, Dr Edmond Stadler.

228 The set for Act II of Ibsen's *Kongsemnerne (The Crown Pretenders)*, by Gordon Craig, for a production of the play in 1926, directed by Johannes Poulsen, at the Danish Royal Theatre in Copenhagen. It was Craig's last direct contact with the living theatre. Reproduced by courtesy of the Trustees of the E. Gordon Craig Estate.

229 A scene from a Japanese *Nōh* play, *The Lady Aoi*, London, 1967.

230 A *kyōgen*, or comic interlude, *The Tied Servants*, London, 1967.

231 An eighteenth-century print of a Japanese *kabuki* theatre. British Museum.

232 A modern *kabuki* play, *Kanjincho*, Tokyo, 1960.

233 Mei Lan-Fang in one of his female parts.

234 A scene from a Chinese play.

235 The heroine in a Chinese play.

236 A scene from *Sizwe Bansi is Dead*, by Athol Fugard and the two actors John Kani and Winston Ntshona, working collectively at the Royal Court Theatre, London, in 1973, and again at the same theatre in 1974 and 1977.

237 The setting for O'Neill's *Dynamo* (1929), designed by Lee Simonson. The set clearly shows the influence of Meyerhold's reforms (*see Ill. 238*), and is based on the interior of the power-house in Stevenson, Conn. Vandamm

Collection, Theatre Collection, New York Public Library.

238 A production of *The Forest*, by A.N. Ostrovsky (1823–86), directed and designed by V.E. Meyerhold.

239 *The Miracle*, by Volmöller, produced at Olympia by Max Reinhardt in 1911. The vast crowds assembled for this production, the relationship between actors and audience, and the general lay-out of the various acting-areas, are all strongly reminiscent of what we know of the productions of the great Miracle plays in the Middle Ages. Enthoven Collection, Victoria and Albert Museum, London.

240 A scene from *Le Chien du Jardinier*, a French version by Georges Neveux of a play by Lope de Vega, a light-hearted comedy of intrigue in which Madeleine Renaud appeared with her husband Jean-Louis Barrault.

241 Louis Jouvet as Molière's *Tartuffe*.

242 *King Lear* at the Shakespeare Memorial Theatre, Stratford-upon-Avon, 1937, designed and produced by Theodore Komisarjevsky (1882–1954), a Russian-born actor and director who made a great reputation in England and eventually settled in the United States. By permission of the Governors of the Royal Shakespeare Theatre, Stratford-upon-Avon.

243 A scene from the *Oresteia* trilogy by Aeschylus, in a powerful translation by Tony Harrison. The actors, who worked collectively, were not named. The five-and-a-half hour-long production at the National Theatre in 1981 was both a popular and a critical success.

244 John Gielgud as Hamlet, 1934. Although Gielgud rose to the top of his profession as a player of Shakespearean parts, he appeared in a number of modern plays, for example Harold Pinter's *No Man's Land* (with Ralph Richardson), seen in London in 1975 and in New York in 1976,

and he also made a name for himself as a director. Costume by Motley (*see Ills.* 245–6).

245–6 Costume designs by Motley for Michael Redgrave as Antony in *Antony and Cleopatra*, and Marius Goring as Richard III. Motley were a young firm of designers consisting of two sisters, Sophie and Margaret Harris, and Elizabeth Montgomery. By permission of the Shakespeare Centre Library, Stratford-upon-Avon.

247 Laurence Olivier in Congreve's *Love for Love*, 1965.

248 A scene from the American production of *Desire Under the Elms*, by Eugene O'Neill, in a set by Robert Edmond Jones (1887–1954). The play was seen in London at the Gate Theatre in 1931. Theatre Collection, Harvard University.

249 Alfred Lunt and Lynn Fontanne in S.N. Behrman's adaptation of *Amphitryon 38*, by Jean Giraudoux. It was given its title because the author reckoned it was the thirty-eighth dramatization of the Alkmena story, first used by Plautus, and later by Molière. Vandamm Collection, Theatre Collection, New York Public Library.

250 The Berliner Ensemble in *Mother Courage and Her Children* by Bertolt Brecht, written in 1938–9 and first performed in Zurich in 1941.

251 Peggy Ashcroft and George Devine in Ibsen's *Hedda Gabler* (1890) at the Lyric Theatre, Hammersmith, in 1954, in an adaptation by Max Faber, directed by Peter Ashmore.

252 Edith Evans in *The Dark is Light Enough*, by Christopher Fry, 1954. Fry's earlier successes in London were *The Lady's Not for Burning* at the Globe in 1949, and *Venus Observed* at the St James's Theatre in 1950.

253 *Ring Round the Moon*, a translation by Christopher Fry of *L'Invitation au Château*, by Jean Anouilh, first produced at the Théâtre de l'Atelier in 1947, with

settings and costumes by André Barsacq.

254 A scene from John Osborne's *Look Back in Anger*, 1956 (New York 1956). The play's director, Tony Richardson, became associate director of the English Stage Company in that year, and went on to make a distinguished career.

255 The final scene from *The Royal Hunt of the Sun*, by Peter Shaffer, London, 1964. The setting was by Michael Annals, and the music by Marc Wilkinson. The play, previously seen on the open stage of the Chichester Festival Theatre, was produced by John Dexter and Desmond O'Donovan.

256 *Waiting for Godot*, the English version of *En attendant Godot*, by Samuel Beckett, Arts Theatre, London, 1955.

257 Peter Brook's *A Midsummer Night's Dream*, first produced at Stratford-upon-Avon in 1970, and seen in London and then on a United States and world tour from 1971. It broke new ground in the approach to Shakespearean production. Brook made no attempt at naturalism, but invented a completely artificial world, in which, for instance, acrobatics were the equivalent of Elizabethan magic, but which was still true to the concept and poetry of the original play.

258 A design by David Hockney for the 1966 London production of *Ubu Roi*, by Alfred Jarry (1873–1907). Translated and directed by Iain Cuthbertson. Jarry's theory of 'pata-physics' – 'the science of imaginary solutions' – is the basis of the Theatre of the Absurd. By kind permission of the Kasmin Gallery.

259 A scene with Adam and Eve from *The Nativity*. In 1980 *The Nativity* joined *The Passion* (first performed in 1977), and in 1985 both were joined by *Doomsday*, as a trilogy compiled from three medieval English Mystery plays, adapted by Tony Harrison, Bill Bryden (the play's director) and the Company. The design was by

William Dudley, the music by John Tams and the Home Service Band. The type of performance is an example of a trend towards peripatetic staging and the removal of the divide between actors and audience.

260 *Nicholas Nickleby*, adapted from Charles Dickens' novel by David Edgar, performed in London in 1980 and 1981, and in New York in 1981. The inventive design by John Napier and Dermot Hayes made use of elaborate catwalks, ramps and, in some scenes, scrapwood props. The production ran for eight-and-a-half hours, playing in two parts.

261 A set by the Czech scene-designer Josef Svoboda for a production of Sophocles' *Oedipus Rex* at the Prague National Theatre in 1963. The steps, which had movable sections that could be raised to form rostrums, provided a perfect setting for the chorus and principal actors.

262 Interior of the Chichester Festival Theatre, with the first thrust stage to be built in Britain.

263 Interior of the Royal Exchange Theatre, Manchester.

264 A scene from *Who's Afraid of Virginia Woolf?* by Edward Albee, London 1962.

265 A scene in a Chicago junk-shop from David Mamet's *American Buffalo* (the title refers to the nickel coin). The play provides strong dramatic roles for the three actors. It received an Obie Award in 1976, and NYDCC Award when it reached Broadway, later in the same year. It was first seen in Britain at the National Theatre, London, in 1978.

266 A scene from *A Soldier's Play* by Charles Fuller, with Geoffrey Ewing and Steven A. Jones of the new-York-based Negro Ensemble Company, founded in 1967. The play, about a Black military unit in the South, received many awards, including Obie Awards and the Pulitzer Prize in 1982. It was taken to the Edinburgh Festival by the Company in 1984.

267 Glenda Jackson, excellent in roles demanding intelligence combined with emotion and a vigorous realism, in O'Neill's *Strange Interlude* (1928), revived at The Duke of York's Theatre, London, in 1984.

268 *Jumpers* by Tom Stoppard, first performed in 1972 with Diana Rigg (seen with some of the gymnasts) and Michael Hordern in the principal roles. The design was by Patrick Robertson and Rosemary Vercoe.

269 A scene from *My Fair Lady*. In the original New York production, Professor Higgins was played by Rex Harrison and Eliza Doolittle by Julie Andrews, who also appeared in these parts at Drury Lane in 1958. The production in both cases was by Moss Hart. Apollo Theatre.

270 *A Chorus Line*, opening in New York in 1975 and seen in London in 1976. It was conceived, choreographed and directed by Michael Bennett using tape-recorded conversations with the dancers as the basis of the script. It represented a breakthrough in being a hugely successful 'concept' musical, with its origins in staging rather than in a narrative plot. The music, by Marvin Hamlisch, was virtually continuous. Martha Swope.

271 Akira Shigeyama and Yasushi Maruishi of the NOHO Theatre Group of Kyoto, Japan, star in Jonas Salz's 1987 *Theatre I*. Jonah Salz.

272 Peter Brook's *The Mahabharata* had an international cast of actors at the Festival d'Avignon in 1985. Agence du Presse Bernard, Paris.

273 Ariane Mnouchkine's 1990 production of *Les Atrides* for the Théâtre du Soleil opened to wide acclaim in France, England, Canada and the United States. Agence du Presse Bernard, Paris.

274 Deborah Warner directed *Titus Andronicus* for the Royal Shakespeare Company in 1987. From left to right: Donald Sumpter as Marcus, Jeremy Gilley as Young Lucius, Brian Cox as Titus and Sonia Ritter as Lavinia, seen here at the Swan Theatre in Stratford-upon-Avon. Joe Cocks Studio Collection, Shakespeare Centre Library.

275 Fiona Shaw played the central role in *Machinal* for the National Theatre in London in 1993. Ian MacNeil designed a heavy-metal set for Stephen Daldry's hard-hitting interpretation of Sophie Treadwell's 1928 play. Ivan Kyncl.

276 Yuri Lyubimov's Russian-language production of *Hamlet* for the Taganka Theatre in Moscow. In 1989 the director mounted a production of the same play for the Leicester Haymarket Theatre in Britain. Alexander Sternin.

277 Mikhail Bulgakov's *The Master and Margarita*, as interpreted for the Moscow stage by the Taganka Theatre under Yuri Lyubimov's direction. Alexander Sternin.

278 The Wooster Group's *House Lights* featured Kate Valk and Roy Faudree in their 1997 production. Mark Gearhart, Courtesy the Wooster Group.

279 Robert Wilson's 1976 *Einstein on the Beach*; the music was written by Philip Glass.

280 Caryl Churchill's *Top Girls*, directed by Max Stafford Clark, opened at the Royal Court Theatre in London in 1982. Shown here are Lindsay Duncan, Carole Hayman and Gwen Taylor. Catherine Ashmore.

281 Anthony Hopkins played René Gallimard in *M. Butterfly* in London in 1989.

282 The National Theatre production of *Angels in America* was directed by Declan Donnellan and designed by Nick Ormerod. *Perestroika* (Part 2) starred Nancy Crane as the Angel and Stephen Dillane as Prior Walter, shown here at the small Cottesloe Theatre in 1993.

283 Karen Finley performed her original work *The American Chestnut* in 1997. Ulli Weiss, Courtesy Brooklyn Academy of Music.

284 Anna Deavere Smith performs *Let Me Down Easy* at New York's Second Stage Theatre in 2009. Joan Marcus/ArenaPAL.

285 Master storyteller Mike Daisey attracted international attention when he performed *The Agony and the Ecstasy of Steve Jobs* at the Berkeley Repertory Theatre in 2011. Courtesy kevinberne.com.

286 David Hare's *Stuff Happens* at London's National Theatre, with Nicholas Farrell as Prime Minister Tony Blair; Alex Jennings as President George W. Bush Jr. Robbie Jack/Corbis.

287 (Left to right) Tonye Patano, Jason Bowen and Pascale Armand starred in Lynn Nottage's Pulitzer Prize-winning play *Ruined* at Berkeley Repertory Theatre. Courtesy kevinberne.com.

288 Paul Rattray, Nabil Stuart, Jonathan Holt, Ali Craig, Henry Pettigrew and David Colvin in Gregory Burke's *Black Watch*, directed by John Tiffany for the National Theatre of Scotland. Robbie Jack/Corbis.

289 Pina Bausch's *Palermo Palermo* was seen at the Brooklyn Academy of Music in New York in 1991 as part of the Next Wave Festival. © Dona McAdams.

290 Richard Bean's *One Man, Two Guvnors* was an adaptation of Carlo Goldoni's *A Servant of Two Masters*, directed by Nicholas Hytner at the National Theatre in London in 2011. Robbie Jack/Corbis.

291 Helen Mirren as Phèdre in Ted Hughes' version of Jean Racine's play, directed by Nicholas Hytner at London's National Theatre. Robbie Jack/Corbis.

292 Eric Ruf and Françoise Gillard played Stanley and Stella Kowalski in the Comédie-Française's Tennessee Williams adaption, *Un Tramway Nommé Desir*, in 2011, directed by Lee Breuer. Raphael Gaillarde/Gamma-Rapho via Getty Images.

293 *The Lion King*, Broadway company, Orpheum Theatre, MN. Joan Marcus/ArenaPAL.

Select Bibliography

General
Antonin Artaud, *The Theatre and its Double*, trans. Mary C. Richards, New York 1958; Martin Banham, ed., *The Cambridge Guide to Theatre*, Cambridge, 1995; Eric Bentley, ed., *The Theory of the Modern Stage*, London 1968; Augusto Boal, *Theatre of the Oppressed*, London, 1979; Gerald Bordman, ed., *The Oxford Companion to the American Theatre*, Oxford and New York 1984; James R. Brandon, ed., *The Cambridge Guide to Asian Theatre*, Cambridge 1997; Enoch Brater, ed., *Feminine Focus: The New Women Playwrights*, Oxford and New York 1989; Oscar G. Brockett and Franklin J. Hilary, *History of the Theatre*, 11th edn, London, 1968; Peter Brook, *The Empty Space*, New York 1969; Sue-Ellen Case, *Feminism and Theatre*, London and New York 1988; Marvin Carlson, *Performance: A Critical Introduction*, 2nd edn, London 2003; S. W. Cheney, *The Theatre: Three Thousand Years of Drama, Acting and Stagecraft*, New York 1959; Barrett H. Clark, ed., *European Theories of the Drama*, rev. by Henry Popkin, New York 1965; Keir Elam, *The Semiotics of Theatre and Drama*, 2nd edn, London 2002; Martin Esslin, ed., *Illustrated Encyclopaedia of World Theatre*, London 1977; John Gassner, *Masters of the Drama*, New York 1954; John Gassner and Edwin Quinn, ed., *Reader's Encyclopaedia of World Drama*, New York 1969, London 1975; RoseLee Goldberg, *Performance Art: From Futurism to the Present*, 3rd edn, London, 2011; Jerzy Grotowski, *Towards a Poor Theatre*, New York 1968; Phyllis Hartnoll and Peter Found, eds, *The Concise Oxford Companion to the Theatre*, 2nd edn, Oxford 1992; Phyllis Hartnoll, *The Oxford Companion to the Theatre*, 4th edn, Oxford 1983; rpt with corrections 1993; Stanley Hochman, ed., *Encyclopaedia of World Drama*, 2nd edn, 5 vols, New York 1984; Jonathan Kalb, *Great Lengths: Seven Works of Marathon Theater*, Ann Arbor, Ann Arbor, MI 2011; Myron Matlaw, *Modern World Drama: An Encyclopedia*, New York 1972; Siegfried Melchinger, ed., *Concise Encyclopaedia of Modern Drama*, New York 1966; A. M. Nagler, *A Source Book of Theatrical History*, New York 1952; Allardyce Nicoll, *The Development of the Theatre*, 5th edn, London 1976; Allardyce Nicoll, *World Drama from Aeschylus to Anouilh*, 2nd edn, London 1976; Janelle G. Reinelt and Joseph R. Roach, eds, *Critical Theory and Performance*, 2nd edn, Ann Arbor, MI 2006; John Russell Brown, ed., *The Oxford Illustrated History of the Theatre*, Oxford 1995; Andrew Sofer, *The Stage Life of Props*, Ann Arbor, MI 2003; W. B. Worthen, *The Idea of the Actor*, Princeton, 1984.

World Theatre
African Theatre. Martin Banham, ed., *A History of Theatre in Africa*, Cambridge 2004; Martin Banham, James Gibbs and Femi Osofisan, eds, *African Theatre: Playwrights and Politics*, Oxford, Indiana and Johannesburg 2001; Michael Etherton, *The Development of African Drama*, London 1982; David Kerr, ed., *African Theatre: Southern Africa*, Trenton, NJ 2004; Anthony Graham-White, *The Drama of Black Africa*, New York 1974
American Theatre. C. W. E. Bigsby, *A Critical Introduction to Twentieth-Century American Drama*, 3 vols, Cambridge 1982–85; Daniel Blum and John Willis, *A Pictorial History of the American Theatre 1860–1976*, 4th edn, New York 1978; Stephen J. Bottoms, *Playing Underground: A Critical History of the 1960s Off-Off Broadway Movement*, Ann Arbor, MI 2004; Deborah R. Geis, *Postmodern Theatric(k)s: Monologue in Contemporary American Drama*, Ann Arbor, MI 1993; Samuel Hay, *African American Theatre: An Historical and Critical Analysis*, Cambridge 1994; Mary C. Henderson, *Theater in America*, New York 1986; Errol G. Hill and James V. Hatch, *A History of African American Theatre*, Cambridge 2003; Bruce A. McConachie, *Melodramatic Formations: American Theatre and Society 1820–1870*, Iowa City 1992; Theodore Shank, *American Alternative Theatre*, London 1982; Don B. Wilmeth, ed., with Tice L. Miller, *Cambridge Guide to American Theatre*, Cambridge and New York 1996.

British Theatre. Richard W. Bevis, *English Drama: Restoration and Eighteenth Century, 1660–1789*, London 1988; Michael R. Booth, *Theatre in the Victorian Age*, Cambridge 1991; Ruby Cohn, *Retreats from Realism in Recent English Drama*, Cambridge 1991; R. David, *Shakespeare in the Theatre* [1971–76], Cambridge 1978; Stephen Greenblatt, *Shakespearean Negotiations*, Berkeley 1989; Peter Holland, *The Ornament of Action: Text and Performance in Restoration Comedy*, Cambridge 1979; Christopher Innes, *Modern British Drama, 1890–1990*, Cambridge and New York 1992; Jan Kott, *Shakespeare Our Contemporary*, trans. Boleslow Taborski, London 1964; Richard Leacock, *The Development of the English Playhouse*, London 1973; Carol Rutter et al., *Clamorous Voices: Shakespeare's Women Today*, London 1988; John Russell Taylor, *Anger and After*, London 1962; rev. ed. 1969; Charles Shattuck, *Shakespeare on the American Stage*, Washington 1976; Simon Trussler, *The Cambridge Illustrated History of the British Theatre*, Cambridge 1994; Stanley Wells, *Shakespeare, an Illustrated Dictionary*, Oxford 1981.
Chinese Theatre. Colin Mackerras, *Chinese Drama: A Historical Survey*, Beijing 1990; Adolphe C. Scott, *The Classical Theatre of China*, London 1957; Adolphe C. Scott, *An Introduction to the Chinese Theatre*, New York 1959.
French Theatre. Peter Arnott, *An Introduction to the French Theatre*, London 1977; Ruby Cohn, *From 'Desire' to 'Godot': Pocket Theater of Postwar Paris*, Berkeley 1987; F. W. J. Hemmings, *Theatre and State in France, 1760–1905*, Cambridge 1994; Harold Hobson, *The French Theatre of Today*, London and New York 1953; Edward Baron Turk, *French Theater Today: The View from New York, Paris, and Avignon*, Iowa City 2011.
German Theatre. F. J. Lamport, *German Classical Drama: Theatre, Humanity and Nation 1750–1870*, Cambridge 1992; Michael Patterson, *The First German Theatre*, London 1990; Simon Williams and Maik Hamburger, eds, *A History of German Theatre*, Cambridge 2011.
Greek and Roman Theatre. Peter Arnott, *An Introduction to the Greek Theatre*, London and New York 1959; W. Beare, *The Roman Stage*, 3rd edn, London 1978; Margarete Bieber, *History of the Greek and Roman Theater*, Princeton 1961; G. E. Duckworth, *The*

Nature of Roman Comedy, Princeton 1952; Marianne McDonald and J. Michael Walton, eds, *The Cambridge Companion to Greek and Roman Theatre*, Cambridge 2007; O. P. Taplin, *Greek Tragedy in Action*, Berkeley and London 1978; David Wiles, *The Masks of Menander*, Cambridge 1991; John J. Winkler and Froma I. Zeitlin, eds, *Nothing to Do with Dionysos?*, Princeton 1990. **Indian Theatre.** B. Gargi, *Theatre in India*, New York 1962; Jagdish C. Mathur, *Drama in Rural India*, New York 1964; Farley P. Richmond, Darius L. Swann, and Phillip B. Zarrilli, eds, *Indian Theatre: Traditions of Performance*, Honolulu 1990; H. W. Wells, *The Classical Drama of India*, New York 1963. **Irish Theatre.** Enoch Brater, *The Essential Samuel Beckett*, London and New York, 2003; Christopher Fitz-Simon, *The Irish Theatre*, London and New York 1983; Mary Trotter, *Modern Irish Theatre*, Cambridge 2008; Katharine Worth, *The Irish Drama of Europe from Yeats to Beckett*, London 1978. **Israeli Theatre.** Glenda Abramson, *Drama and Ideology in Modern Israel*, Cambridge 1998; Linda Ben-Zvi, ed., *Theater in Israel*, Ann Arbor, MI 1996. **Italian Theatre.** Christopher Cairns, ed., *The Commedia dell'Arte from the Renaissance to Dario Fo*, Lewiston, NY 1989; Joseph Farrell and Paolo Puppa, eds, *A History of Italian Theatre*, Cambridge 2006; Kathleen M. Lea, *Italian Popular Comedy (Commedia dell'arte)*, 2 vols, Oxford 1963. **Japanese Theatre.** E. Ernst, *The Kabuki Theatre*, London 1956; T. Immoos, *Japanese Theatre*, trans. Hugh Young, London 1977; Benito Ortolani, *The Japanese Theatre: From Shamanistic Ritual to Contemporary Pluralism*, Princeton 1995; Arthur Waley, *The Nō Plays of Japan*, London 1950. **Latin American Theatre.** Eliado Cortes and Mirta Barrea-Marlys, *Encyclopedia of Latin American Theater*, Westport, CT 2003; Ana Elena Puga, *Memory, Allegory and Testimony in South American Theater*, London 2012. Adam Versenyi, *Theatre in Latin America: Religion, Politics and Culture from Cortés to the 1980s*, Cambridge 2009. **Russian Theatre.** Nikolai A. Gorchakov, *The Theatre in Soviet Russia*, London and New York 1957; Robert Leach and Victor Borovsky, *A History of Russian Theatre*, Cambridge 2006; Herbert Marshall, *The Pictorial History*

of the Russian Theatre, New York 1977; Konstantin Rudnitsky, *Russian and Soviet Theatre*, London 1988; Marc Slonim, *Russian Theater from the Empire to the Soviets*, Cleveland 1961, London 1963; Anatoly Smeliansky, *The Russian Theatre after Stalin*, trans. Patrick Miles, Cambridge 1999; B. V. Vareke, *A History of the Russian Theatre*, New York 1951; Nick Worrall, *The Moscow Art Theatre*, London 1996. **Scandinavian Theatre.** F. L. and L. L. Marker, *A History of Scandinavian Theatre*, Cambridge 2006. **Spanish Theatre.** Melveena McKendrick, *Theatre in Spain 1490–1700*, Cambridge 1989; Ronald E. Surtz, *The Birth of a Theater: Dramatic Convention in the Spanish Theater from Juan del Encina to Lope de Vega*, Princeton 1979.

Technical Studies

Acting. Stella Adler, *The Technique of Acting*, Toronto 1988; Jean Benedetti, *Stanislavski and the Actor*, London 1998; Philip Auslander, *From Acting to Performance*, London 1997; Cicely Berry, *The Actor and his Text*, London 1973; Joseph Chaikin, *The Presence of the Actor*, New York 1972; Toby Cole and H. K. Chinoy, *Actors on Acting: An Anthology*, New York 1949, London 1952; Rosamond Gilder, *Enter the Actress: The First Women in the Theatre*, London 1931, New York 1960; Robert Gordon, *The Purpose of Playing: Modern Acting Theories in Perspective*, Ann Arbor, MI 2006; Uta Hagen, *Respect for Acting*, New York 1973; John Hodgson and Ernest Richards, *Improvisation*, London 1966; Hollis Huston, *The Actor's Instrument: Body, Theory, Stage*, Ann Arbor, MI 1992; Patrice Pavis, *Languages of the Stage*, New York 1982; Joseph R. Roach, *The Player's Passion: Studies in the Science of Acting*, Ann Arbor, MI 1993; Patsy Rodenberg, *The Right to Speak: Working with the Voice*, London 1991; K. S. Stanislavsky, *An Actor Prepares*, London 1926; K. S. Stanislavsky, *Building on Character*, London 1950; G. B. Wilson, *A History of American Acting*, Indiana 1966. **Costume, Scenery and Set Design.** Arnold Aronson, *American Set Design*, New York 1985; Lucy Barton, *Historic Costume for the Stage*, London and Boston 1949; Oscar G. Brockett, Margaret A. Mitchell and Linda Hardberger, *Making the Scene: A History of Stage Design and Technology in Europe*

and the United States, San Antonio, TX 2010; Jane Collins and Andrew Nisbet, *Theatre and Performance Design: A Reader in Scenography*, London 2010; G. C. Izenan, *Theater Design*, New York 1977; Rosemary Ingham and Liz Covey, *The Costume Technician's Handbook*, 3rd edn, London 2003; Stephen Joseph, *Scene Painting and Design*, London 1964; Jo Mielziner, *Designing for the Theatre*, New York 1965; Lynn Pecktal, *Costume Design: Techniques of Modern Masters*, New York 1999; Sybil Rosenfeld, *A Short History of Scene Design in Great Britain*, Oxford 1973; Lee Simonson, *The Stage is Set*, New York 1963; Delbert Unruh, *The Designs of Ming Cho Lee*, Syracuse, NY 2006; D. Welker, *Theatrical Set Design: The Basic Techniques*, 2nd edn, Boston 1979. **Direction and Staging.** Hendrik Baker, *Stage Management and Theatre-Craft*, 3rd edn, London 1977; Anne Bogart, *A Director Prepares*, London 2001; David Bradby and David Williams, *Directors' Theatre*, Basingstoke 1988; Edward Braun, *The Director and the Stage*, London 1982; Bertolt Brecht, *Brecht on Theatre*, ed. John Willett, London 1964; Conrad Carter, etc., *The Producing and Staging of Plays*, New York 1963; Toby Cole and Helen Krich Chinoy, eds, *Directors on Directing*, New York 1963; Bert Gruver, *The Stage-Manager's Handbook*, New York 1961; David Whitton, *Stage Directors in Modern France*, Manchester 1987. **Lighting.** Frederick Bentham, *The Art of Stage Lighting*, 2nd edn, London 1976; G. M. Bergman, etc., *Lighting in the Theatre*, ed. J. Garnet Miller, London and New York 1981; Max Keller, *Light Fantastic: The Art and Design of Stage Lighting*, 3rd edn, Munich and New York 2010; Stanley McCandless, *A Syllabus of Stage Lighting*, 11th edn, New York 1964; Richard Pilbrow, *Stage Lighting*, rev. edn, London and New York 2000; Francis Reid, *The Stage Lighting Handbook*, London 2002; Steven Louis Shelley, *A Practical Guide to Stage Lighting*, 2nd edn, Boston 2009.

Index

Photographic Acknowledgments

H. Acton, 233; American School of Classical Studies, Athens, 10; Bildarchiv der Österreichischen National-bibliothek, Vienna, 103, 109, 136, 138, 139, 140, 142, 143, 181; Brompton Studio, 126, 127, 185, 188, 193, 194, 196, 197, 198, 204, 205, 206, 207, 209, 211, 212, 213, 214, 215, 216, 217, 222, 224; Francis Bruguiere, 248; Photo Bulloz, 60, 104, 108, 148, 155, 158, 162, 170, 183, 186; Central Press Agency, 229, 230; Lucca Chmel, 35; Nobby Clark, 243, 265, 281; Joe Cocks Studio, 257; Donald Cooper, 267, 268; Courtauld Institute of Art, 88; Kevin Cummins, 263; Chris Davies, 260; Zoe Dominic, 247; G. Farnell, 1, 17; Daniel Frasnay, 240; Friedman-Abeles, 264; Photographic Giraudon, 8, 28, 33, 36, 65, 66, 67, 100, 151; Yvonne Gregory, 244; John Haynes, 236, 282; André Held, 23; Photo Hirmer, 5, 6; Dr D. Kalvodová, Prague, 233, 234; Lenare, 225; Lipnitzki, 241; Angus McBean, 251, 252, 255; Babette Mangolte, 279; Mansell Collection, 15, 16, 25, 51; Mas, 92, 93; Nationale Forschungs-und Gedenkstätten in Weimar, 144, 145, 146; Bertram Park, 219; M. Rigal, 171; Royal Institute of British Architects, 261; Houston Rogers, 253, 254, 256; Scala, 29; H. Schmidt-Glassner, 50; Edwin Smith, 24; Society for Cultural Relations with the USSR, 221, 223, 238; Theater-museum, Munich, 147, 250; Alex 'Tug' Wilson, 266; G. B. Wood, 34; Zumbühl Bros., 41.